Lecture Notes in Computer Science   9576

Commenced Publication in 1973
Founding and Former Series Editors:
Gerhard Goos, Juris Hartmanis, and Jan van Leeuwen

More information about this series at http://www.springer.com/series/7407

Jiang Xie · Zhangxin Chen
Craig C. Douglas · Wu Zhang
Yan Chen (Eds.)

High Performance Computing and Applications

Third International Conference, HPCA 2015
Shanghai, China, July 26–30, 2015
Revised Selected Papers

 Springer

Editors
Jiang Xie
School of Computer Engineering
Shanghai University
Shanghai
China

Wu Zhang
School of Computer Engineering
Shanghai University
Shanghai
China

Zhangxin Chen
Chemical and Petroleum Engineering
University of Calgary
Calgary, AB
Canada

Yan Chen
Mathematics and Informatics
South China Agricultural University
Guangzhou
China

Craig C. Douglas
Mathematics Department
University of Wyoming
Laramie, WY
USA

ISSN 0302-9743   ISSN 1611-3349 (electronic)
Lecture Notes in Computer Science
ISBN 978-3-319-32556-9   ISBN 978-3-319-32557-6 (eBook)
DOI 10.1007/978-3-319-32557-6

Library of Congress Control Number: 2016946294

LNCS Sublibrary: SL1 – Theoretical Computer Science and General Issues

Printed on acid-free paper

This Springer imprint is published by Springer Nature
The registered company is Springer International Publishing AG Switzerland

Preface

The Third International Conference on High-Performance Computing and Applications (HPCA 2015) formed part of a series of successful events that started in 2004. It was held in Shanghai, a beautiful, active, and modern city in China, during July 26–30, 2015. This series serves as a forum to present current work by researchers and software developers from around the world as well as to highlight activities in the high-performance computing area. It aims to bring together research scientists, application pioneers, and software developers to discuss problems and solutions and to identify new issues in this area. The third conference emphasized the development and study of novel approaches for high-performance computing, the design and analysis of high-performance numerical algorithms, and their scientific, engineering, and industrial applications. It offered the conference participants a great opportunity to exchange the latest research results, heighten international collaborations, and discuss future research ideas on high-performance computing and applications. High-performance computing and applications are still a hot research topic. The proceedings of the Second International Conference on High-Performance Computing and Applications (HPCA 2009) have been downloaded on-line over 70,000 times.

In addition to 26 invited presentations, the third conference received over 100 submissions from over ten countries and regions worldwide, about 50 of which were accepted for presentation at HPCA 2015. The proceedings contain some of the invited presentations and the contributed submissions, and cover such research areas of interest as numerical algorithms and solutions, high-performance and grid computing, novel approaches to high-performance computing, massive data storage and processing, hardware acceleration, and their wide applications.

The third conference was co-organized by the School of Computer Engineering and Science and High-Performance Computing Center, Shanghai University, and co-sponsored by Shanghai Jiao Tong University, Xi'an Jiao Tong University, and the University of Calgary. The conference organizers would like to thank Springer for publishing the conference proceedings as a volume in the series of *Lecture Notes in Computer Sciences*.

February 2015

Jiang Xie
Zhangxin Chen
Craig C. Douglas
Wu Zhang
Yan Chen

Organization

The Third International Conference on High-Performance Computing and Applications (HPCA 2015)

Shanghai University, Shanghai, China
July 26–30, 2015

Conference Co-chairs

Zhangxing Chen	University of Calgary, Canada
Wu Zhang	Shang University, China

Program Co-chairs

Craig C. Douglas	University of Wyoming, USA
Jiang Xie	Shang University, China

International Scientific Committee

Guoliang Chen (Chair)	University of Science and Technology, China
Mary F. Wheeler (Co-chair)	University of Texas at Austin, USA
Yaosong Chen	Beijing University, China
Junzhi Cui	Institute of Computational Mathematics, China
Jack Dongarra	University of Tennessee, USA
Roland Glowinski	University of Houston, USA
Yike Guo	Imperial College of London, UK
Sanli Li	Tsinghua University and Shanghai University, China
Tatsien Li	Fudan University, China
Qun Lin	Institute of Computational Mathematics, China

Organizing Committee Chairs

Wenhao Zhu (Chair)	Shanghai University, China
Song Dai	Shanghai University, China
Zhiguo Lu	Shanghai University, China
Wenxin Yao	Shanghai University, China

Contents

Evidences that Software Based on Non-overlapping Discretization Is Most Efficient for Applying Highly Parallelized Supercomputers to Solving Partial Differential Equations

Ismael Herrera-Revilla[✉] and Iván Contreras

Instituto de Geofísica Universidad Nacional Autónoma de México, UNAM,
Ciudad de México, Mexico
iherrerarevilla@gmail.com

Abstract. One of the main problems for applying the highly parallelized supercomputers available today to computational physico-mathematical modeling of science and engineering is to develop software capable of effectively solving in parallel partial differential equations or systems of such equations. For this purpose much work on domain decomposition methods has been done. Recently, I. Herrera introduced a new 'non-overlapping discretization method' that for the application of domain decomposition methods has many advantages over standard methods of discretization. Based on theoretical grounds, some of these advantages have been indicated in previous publications. This paper, however, is devoted to present numerical evidences of such advantages and some of the outstanding parallelization-efficiencies that are feasible when domain decomposition methods are applied to the discrete system derived using non-overlapping discretization methods.

Keywords: Discretization-methods, Highly-parallelized super-computers · 100 %-parallel algorithms · Parallel-solution of pdes · Parallel software for elasticity · High performance computing · DDM

1 Introduction

Partial differential equations (PDEs) and systems of such equations are very important in science and engineering since their basic models are constituted by such equations [1]. Due to this fact progress in many fields of engineering and science heavily depends on the effective application of advanced computational tools to the solution of PDEs [2].

For this purpose much work on *domain decomposition methods* has been done [3–10]. In general, after a PDE has been discretized the effective application of parallel computing reduces to efficiently treating the matrix-equation that the discretization method yields. Recently, I. Herrera [11–17] introduced a new *'non-overlapping discretization method'* that for the application of *domain decomposition methods* has many advantages over standard methods of discretization. Methods of this class have the *conspicuous* feature that each node of the *fine-mesh* belongs to one and only one

© Springer International Publishing Switzerland 2016
J. Xie et al. (Eds.): HPCA 2015, LNCS 9576, pp. 1–16, 2016.
DOI: 10.1007/978-3-319-32557-6_1

subdomain of the domain decomposition. Based on theoretical grounds, some of these advantages have been indicated in previous publications. This paper, however, is devoted to present numerical evidences of such advantages and some of the outstanding parallelization-efficiencies that are feasible when domain decomposition methods are applied to the discrete system derived using *non-overlapping discretization methods*.

Non-overlapping discretization methods have a wide range of applicability; in part, this stems from their axiomatic formulation. They are applicable to symmetric matrices - independently of whether or not they are (positive) definite- as well as to non-symmetric matrices. A general procedure developed in this line of research [11] permits transforming standard discretizations -defined on overlapping systems of nodes-, independently of the problems that originated them, into *non-overlapping discretizations*. Such a procedure is applicable to symmetric and non-symmetric matrices, as well as positive-definite or non-positive-definite ones. Because of all this, *non-overlapping discretizations* -and the concomitant *DVS-algorithms*- have arisen high expectations as a means for harnessing highly parallelized supercomputers to the task of solving the partial differential equations of science and engineering, but up to recently no software based on *non-overlapping discretizations* was available on which such expectations could be tested.

Recently, software based on *non-overlapping discretizations* has been carefully coded and applied using highly parallelized supercomputers [13] and tests for the DVS version of BDDC was carried out yielding parallelization-efficiencies close to 100 %. Such results constitute important evidences, which confirm that software based on *non-overlapping discretizations* is most efficient for applying highly parallelized super-computers to resolve boundary-value problems of partial differential equations. Up to now only the case of symmetric and positive-definite matrices has been fully developed; however, the *non-overlapping discretization method* is also applicable to symmetric and non-symmetric matrices and the results so far obtained indicate that its development is a very worthwhile endeavor ahead.

This paper is devoted to present a summary of recent numerical experiments that verify the high parallelization efficiencies theoretically predicted. In particular, to avoid repetitions here the method is not explained in detail, but extensive background material on the *DVS* methodology is given in the references [11–17].

2   Non-overlapping Discretizations and DVS-Algorithms

In summary, this methodology consists of

  I. A general method for transforming standard *overlapping discretizations* into *non-overlapping* ones;
 II. Procedures to accelerate convergence:
       a. Restrictions and
       b. Preconditioning;
III. Definition of four DVS-algorithms; and
 IV. Developing critical routes to construct highly efficient parallelization codes.

As said before, for the application of *DDMs* the *non-overlapping discretization methods* have many advantages over standard methods of discretization, because the matrix-equations they yield are better suited to be treated in parallel. The concomitant algorithms so obtained are known as *DVS-algorithms*. They are four; the construction of two of them is similar to *BDDC* and *FETI-DP*, albeit an essential difference is that the starting matrix-equation is obtained by application of a *non-overlapping discretization*. As for the other two, to our knowledge they are fully independent of previous developments reported in the literature. The DVS-algorithms also benefit of many algebraic properties that have been systematically established in previous work of this line of research [11–17].

3   Transforming a Discretization into a Non-overlapping One

In this Section, the general procedure for transforming a standard discretization method into a *non-overlapping* one is outlined. Consider the partial differential equation, or system of such equations:

$$\mathcal{L}u = f_{\Omega} \qquad (1.1)$$

subjected to certain boundary conditions. Then, a mesh (*'the fine-mesh'*) is introduced and a standard (overlapping) method is applied. In this manner *'the original discretization'* is obtained:

$$\underline{M}\underline{U} = \underline{F} \qquad (1.2)$$

Thereafter, a domain-decomposition (or, *coarse-mesh*) is introduced. Generally, when this is done some of the nodes of the *fine-mesh* are shared by more than one subdomain. The procedure for transforming such an *overlapping* system of nodes into a *non-overlapping* one is summarized in Figs. 1a–d to 4. The *non-overlapping* nodes of Fig. 1d is the system that is used thereafter in the sequel and are referred to as *derived-nodes*. Furthermore, the symbol X is used for the total set of *derived-nodes*, and the functions defined on X are the *derived-vectors*. The general procedure for transforming the original overlapping-discretization into the *non-overlapping* one, consists essentially in defining an equivalent problem in the *space of derived-vectors (DVS)*. The reader is referred to [11–13] for details.

The non-overlapping decomposition of X is given by the family of subsets $X^{\alpha} \equiv \{X^{\alpha} | \alpha = 1, \ldots, E\}$, which for each $\alpha = 1, \ldots, E$, is constituted by the *derived-nodes* that belong to $\bar{\Omega}_{\alpha}$ and are defined by

$$X^{\alpha} \equiv \left\{ (p, \alpha) | p \in \bar{\Omega}_{\alpha} \right\} \qquad (1.3)$$

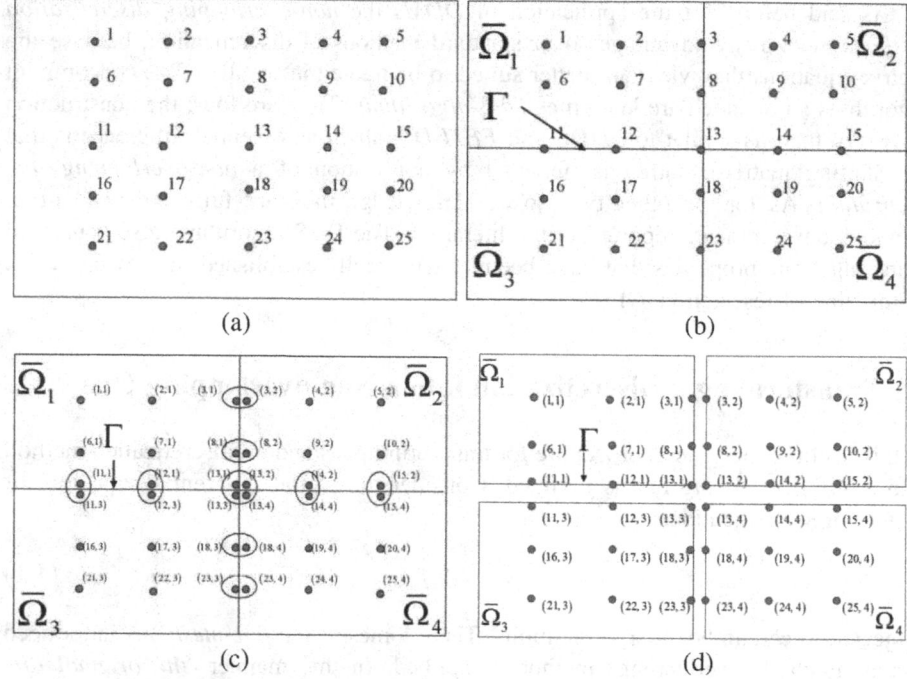

Fig. 1. Transformation of the nodes into a non-overlapping system

Clearly,

$$X = \bigcup_{\alpha=1}^{E} X^{\alpha} \; and \; X^{\alpha} \cap X^{\beta} = \emptyset, when \; \alpha \neq \beta \tag{1.4}$$

Given an *original-node* $p \in \widehat{X}$, the set of *'heirs of p'* is defined to be:

$$Z(p) \equiv \{(p, \alpha) | (p, \alpha) \in X\} \tag{1.5}$$

The multiplicity $m(p)$ of $p \in \widehat{X}$, is the cardinality of $Z(p)$; i.e., the number of heirs that p has. Additional notation and definitions are given in the Appendix, which may be complemented by those of the list of References.

4   The "Derived Vector-Space (DVS)"

Any function, real-valued or vector-valued, defined on the whole set $\widehat{X}$ of *original-nodes* is an *original-vector* and $\widehat{W}$ stands for the vector-space constituted by such vectors. Similarly, any function, real-valued or vector-valued, defined on the whole set

X of *derived-nodes* is a *derived-vector* and W stands for the vector-space constituted by such vectors. The value of a *derived-vector* at a node (p, α) is written as $\underline{u}(p, \alpha)$. When the value itself is a vector, $\underline{u}(p, \alpha, i)$ denotes the $i - th$ component of such a vector, which is a real-number.

Assume $\Lambda \subset X$ is any subset of *derived-nodes*. Then, the notation $W(\Lambda)$ is used to represent the vector subspace of W, whose elements vanish at every *derived-node* that does not belong to Λ. Corresponding to each *local subset of derived-nodes* X^{α}, $\alpha = 1, \ldots$, or E, there is a *'local subspace of derived-vectors'*, defined by $W^{\alpha} \equiv W(X^{\alpha}) \subset W$. The space W is the direct sum of the family of subspaces $\{W^1, \ldots, W^E\}$; i.e.,

$$W = W^1 \oplus \ldots \oplus W^E \tag{1.6}$$

This is an important property, because it implies that every $\underline{u} \in W$ can be written uniquely as

$$\underline{u} = \underline{u}^1 + \ldots + \underline{u}^E, with \underline{u}^{\alpha} \in W^{\alpha}, \alpha = 1, \ldots, E \tag{1.7}$$

For every pair of vectors, $\underline{u} \in W$ and $\underline{w} \in W$, the *'Euclidean inner product'* is defined to be

$$\underline{u} \bullet \underline{w} \equiv \sum_{(p,\alpha) \in X} \underline{u}(p, \alpha) \odot \underline{w}(p, \alpha) = \sum_{\alpha=1}^{E} \sum_{p \in \bar{\Omega}_{\alpha}} \underline{u}(p, \alpha) \odot \underline{w}(p, \alpha) \tag{1.8}$$

Here, the symbol $\odot$ stands for the standard inner-product of $\mathbb{R}^n$ - vectors. When $n = 1$, Eq. (1.8) reduces to

$$\underline{u} \bullet \underline{w} = \sum_{(p,\alpha) \in X} u(p, \alpha)w(p, \alpha) = \sum_{\alpha=1}^{E} \sum_{p \in \bar{\Omega}_{\alpha}} u(p, \alpha)w(p, \alpha) \tag{1.9}$$

We observe that the definition of *Euclidean inner product* is independent of the BVP considered, although it depends on the meshes that are introduced; both, the *fine* and *coarse meshes*.

5 Matrix Notations

Linear transformations of the space W into itself, and also of $\widehat{W}$ into itself, are considered in the *non-overlapping discretizations theory*. There is a one-to-one correspondence between such linear transformations and matrices. For matrices such as $\underline{M}$, occurring in Eq. (1.2), which transform $\widehat{W}$ into itself, we use the notation:

$$\underline{M} \equiv (M_{pq}), where\, p, q \in \widehat{X}. \tag{1.10}$$

Matrices such as a matrix $\underline{\underline{A}}$ that will be introduced later, which transforms W into itself, we use the notation:

$$\underline{\underline{A}} \equiv \left(A_{(p,\alpha)(q,\beta)} \right), where (p, \alpha), (q, \beta) \in \mathrm{X} \tag{1.11}$$

6 Immersion of the Original-Vector Space

Some *derived-vectors* will be said to be *continuous*. A *derived-vector* $\underline{u}$ is *continuous* when for every p, $\underline{u}(p, \alpha)$ is independent of α. The subset of *continuous* vectors, $W_{12} \subset W$, constitutes a linear subspace of W.

Furthermore, there is a one-to-one mapping (see [11]) called the *natural immersion*, $R : \widehat{W} \rightarrow W$, of $\widehat{W}$ into W, and defined by the condition that, for every $\underline{u} \in \widehat{W}$, one has

$$\left(R\underline{\widehat{u}} \right)(p, \alpha) = \underline{\widehat{u}}(p), \forall (p, \alpha) \in \mathrm{X} \tag{1.12}$$

In addition, $R\,\widehat{W} = W_{12}$. Therefore, $R : \widehat{W} \rightarrow W$, when restricted to W_{12} has the an inverse $R^{-1} : W_{12} \rightarrow \widehat{W}$. Essentially what is done in the *DVS-method* is to formulate an equivalent problem in W_{12} and then apply $R^{-1} : W_{12} \rightarrow \widehat{W}$ to obtain the solution in the *original-space*.

To complete the scheme the orthogonal complement of W_{12} is introduced, so that the relation

$$W = W_{11} \oplus W_{12} \tag{1.13}$$

is fulfilled. Here, W_{11} is the above mentioned orthogonal-complement subspace.

The projections $\underline{\underline{a}}$ and $\underline{\underline{j}}$, on W_{12} and W_{11} respectively, are introduced. Clearly,

$$\underline{\underline{I}} = \underline{\underline{j}} + \underline{\underline{a}} \tag{1.14}$$

since $\underline{\underline{a}}$ and $\underline{\underline{j}}$ are complementary projections.

Using these results it can be seen that every *derived-vector*, $\underline{u} \in W$, can be written in a unique manner as:

$$\underline{u} = \underline{u}_{11} + \underline{u}_{12} \, with \begin{cases} \underline{u}_{11} \equiv \underline{\underline{j}}\underline{u} \in W_{11} \\ \underline{u}_{12} \equiv \underline{\underline{a}}\underline{u} \in W_{12} \end{cases} \tag{1.15}$$

Furthermore,

$$\underline{\underline{j}} = \underline{\underline{I}} - \underline{\underline{a}} \tag{1.16}$$

An explicit expression for $\underline{a}$ is:

$$\underline{a} = \left(a_{(p,\alpha)(q,\beta)}\right) with \; a_{(p,\alpha)(q,\beta)} = \frac{\delta_{pq}\delta_{\alpha\beta}}{m(q)} \tag{1.17}$$

7 The Non-overlapping Discretization with Constrains

In the development of the *non-overlapping discretization* methodology and the *DVS-algorithms* a general procedure for transforming any standard (overlapping) discretization into a non-overlapping one was introduced, which is briefly explained in this Section, for further details see [11–13], where additional references are given.

Although such a procedure has a wide range of applicability, including symmetric and non-symmetric matrices, there is an assumption that the *original-matrix* $\underline{\underline{M}}$ of Eq. (1.2) must fulfill and is here stated. To this end, we define

$$\delta_{pq}^\alpha \equiv \begin{cases} 1, \; if \; p,q \in \bar{\Omega}_\alpha \\ 0, \; otherwise \end{cases}, \alpha = 1, \ldots, E; \; and \tag{1.18}$$

together with

$$m(p,q) \equiv \sum_{\alpha=1}^{E} \delta_{pq}^\alpha \tag{1.19}$$

The function $m(p,q)$ is the '*multiplicity of the pair* (p,q)', which can be zero, when the pair p and q do not occur simultaneously in any subdomain-closure. The general procedure for transforming a standard (overlapping) discretization into a non-overlapping one can be applied whenever the *original-matrix* $\underline{\underline{M}} \equiv \left(M_{pq}\right)$ fulfills the following condition:

$$m(p,q) = 0 \Rightarrow M_{pq} = 0 \tag{1.20}$$

The *non-overlapping discretization with constraints* has the form

$$\underline{\underline{a}}\underline{\underline{A}}\underline{u} = \underline{f} \; and \; \underline{\underline{j}}\underline{u} = 0 \tag{1.21}$$

where $\underline{f}$ and $\underline{u}$ are *derived-vectors*. As for $\underline{\underline{a}}$ and $\underline{\underline{j}}$ they are the *projection-matrices* on the subspaces of *continuous-vectors* and *zero-average-vectors*, respectively. The matrix $\underline{\underline{A}}$ is defined by:

$$\underline{\underline{A}} \equiv \underline{\underline{a}}'\underline{\underline{A}}' \tag{1.22}$$

Above, $\underline{\underline{a}}'$ is the projection on the subspace $W' \subset W$, which the DVS-method introduces to accelerate convergence and can be defined by:

$$W' \equiv W(\mathbf{I}) \oplus W(\Delta) \oplus \underline{a}W(\pi) \tag{1.23}$$

The matrix $\underline{\underline{A}}^t$, the *matrix A total* is a block-diagonal matrix that is derived from the original matrix $\underline{\underline{M}}$; each one of its blocks $\underline{\underline{A}}^\alpha$, $\alpha = 1, \ldots, E$, $\underline{\underline{A}}^\alpha : W^\alpha \to W^\alpha$, transforms W^α into itself. Such block-matrices $\underline{\underline{A}}^\alpha$ are similar to restrictions of the original matrix $\underline{\underline{M}}$, but they are already defined in the subspaces W^α of the *derived-vector space*. The full expression of $\underline{\underline{A}}^t$ is:

$$\underline{\underline{A}}^t \equiv \sum_{\alpha=1}^{E} \underline{\underline{A}}^\alpha \tag{1.24}$$

Its detailed expression, in terms of the original matrix $\underline{\underline{M}}$ of Eq. (1.2), is given in [11].

8   The Preconditioned DVS-Algorithms with Constrains

Direct application of Eq. (1.21) is not sufficiently efficient, in spite that a constrained-space formulation has already been incorporated in it. Thus, to enhance parallelization efficiency, in this Section we review the incorporation of the Schur-complement, as well as preconditioning. Finally, the four *DVS-algorithms* obtained in this manner will be listed and briefly explained.

In general, the right-hand member of Eq. (1.21) is written as: $\underline{f} - \underline{f}_\Delta + \underline{f}_\Pi$. When $\underline{f}_\Pi = 0$, the *DVS-algorithms* are easier to write and, furthermore, the transformation of cases when $\underline{f}_\Pi \neq 0$ into others in which $\underline{f}_\Pi = 0$ is straightforward. Thus, in what follows the formulas will be written under the assumption that $\underline{f}_\Pi = 0$. Then, the basic *Schur-complement formulation* is:

$$\underline{\underline{a}}\underline{\underline{S}}\underline{u}_\Delta = \underline{f}_\Delta \text{ and } \underline{\underline{j}}\underline{u}_\Delta = 0 \tag{1.25}$$

complemented by

$$\underline{u}_\Pi = -\left(\underline{\underline{A}}_{\Pi\Pi}\right)^{\sim 1} \underline{\underline{A}}_{\Pi\Delta}\underline{u}_\Delta \tag{1.26}$$

Here, in general, in the DVS approach, the *Schur-complement* is defined by:

$$\underline{\underline{S}} \equiv \underline{\underline{A}}_{\Delta\Delta} - \underline{\underline{A}}_{\Delta\Pi} \left(\underline{\underline{A}}_{\Pi\Pi}\right)^{\sim 1} \underline{\underline{A}}_{\Pi\Delta} \tag{1.27}$$

We recall that this *Schur-complement* definition already incorporates constraints.

Four *preconditioned DVS-algorithms with constraints* have been obtained [11–13]; two of them can be derived by applying BDDC and FETI-DP using for that purpose a *non-overlapping discretization*, while other two are derived following a fully independent path [11]. One feature that characterizes each one of these algorithms is the *sought-information*; in this context, the *sought-information* is a piece of information - the most computationally-expensive to obtain- such that once it has been obtained the *complementary information* (i.e., remaining information required to get the full solution of the problem)- is easy and non-computationally-costly to gather (see [11] for additional details).

8.1 The DVS-BDDC Algorithm

This algorithm follows by application of $\underline{\underline{aS}}^{-1}$ as a *preconditioner* to the *Schur-complement formulation* of Eq. (1.25). In this algorithm the *sought information* is $\underline{u}_\Delta$, and the algorithm that we get for it is:

$$\underline{\underline{aS}}^{-1}\underline{\underline{aS}}\,\underline{u}_\Delta = \underline{\underline{aS}}^{-1}\underline{f}_\Delta \ \text{ and } \ \underline{\underline{ju}}_\Delta = 0 \tag{1.28}$$

while the *complementary information* fulfills Eq. (1.26), which for completeness here we repeat:

$$\underline{u}_\Pi = -\left(\underline{\underline{A}}_{\Pi\Pi}\right)^{\sim 1}\underline{\underline{A}}_{\Pi\Delta}\underline{u}_\Delta \tag{1.29}$$

8.2 The DVS-PRIMAL Algorithm

We set $\underline{v}_\Delta \equiv -\underline{\underline{S}}^{\sim 1}\underline{\underline{jS}}\,\underline{u}_\Delta$ and the algorithm consists in searching for a function $\underline{v}_\Delta \in W_\Delta$, which fulfills

$$\underline{\underline{S}}^{-1}\underline{\underline{jSj}}\,\underline{v}_\Delta = \underline{\underline{S}}^{-1}\underline{\underline{jSjS}}^{-1}\underline{f}_\Delta \ \text{ and } \ \underline{\underline{aS}}\,\underline{v}_\Delta = 0 \tag{1.30}$$

Once $\underline{v}_\Delta \in W(\Delta)$ has been obtained, then

$$\underline{u}_\Delta = \underline{\underline{a}}\left(\underline{\underline{S}}^{-1}\underline{f}_\Delta - \underline{v}_\Delta\right) \tag{1.31}$$

8.3 The DVS-FETI-DP Algorithm

In this case the *sought information* is $\underline{\lambda} \equiv -\underline{\underline{jS}}\,\underline{u}_\Delta$, which is denoted by $\underline{\lambda}$. Thus, the algorithm is: "Given $\underline{f}_\Delta \in \underline{\underline{a}}W_\Delta$, find $\underline{\lambda} \in W_\Delta$ such that

$$\underline{\underline{jSjS}}^{\sim 1}\underline{\lambda} = \underline{\underline{jSjS}}^{\sim 1}\underline{f}_\Delta \ \text{ and } \ \underline{\underline{a}}\underline{\lambda} = 0 \tag{1.32"}$$

Once $\underline{\lambda} \in W_\Delta$ has been obtained, $\underline{u}_\Delta \in \underline{a} W_\Delta$ is given by:

$$\underline{u}_\Delta = \underline{a}\underline{\underline{S}}^{\sim 1}\left(\underline{f}_{-\Delta} + \underline{\lambda}\right) \tag{1.33}$$

8.4   The DVS-Dual Algorithm

The *sought information* is $\underline{\underline{S}}\underline{u}_\Delta$, which is denoted by $\underline{\mu}$. Then, we seek for $\underline{\mu} \in W(\Delta)$ such that

$$\underline{\underline{SaS}}^{-1}\underline{a}\underline{\mu} = \underline{\underline{SaS}}^{-1}\underline{f}_{-\Delta} \ \text{and} \ \underline{j}\underline{\underline{S}}^{-1}\underline{\mu} = 0 \tag{1.34}$$

Once $\underline{\mu} \in W(\Delta)$ has been obtained, $\underline{u}_\Delta \in W(\Delta)$ is given by:

$$\underline{u}_\Delta = \underline{a}\underline{\underline{S}}^{-1}\underline{\mu} \tag{1.35}$$

Remark 1. In these algorithms the matrices to be iterated are: $\underline{a}\underline{\underline{S}}^{-1}\underline{a}\underline{\underline{S}}$, $\underline{\underline{S}}^{-1}\underline{j}\underline{\underline{S}}\underline{j}$, $\underline{j}\underline{\underline{S}}\underline{j}\underline{\underline{S}}^{-1}$ and $\underline{\underline{SaS}}^{-1}\underline{a}$, respectively, and it should be observed that the action of each one of them on any *derived-vector* yields a vector that fulfills the restriction corresponding to each one of the Eqs. (1.28), (1.30), (1.32)and (1.34), respectively. This property is necessary for any iterative algorithm.

Remark 2. The application of the projection-operator $\underline{a}$ at the end, in Eqs. (1.31), (1.33) and (1.35), would be unnecessary if the algorithms of Eqs. (1.30), (1.32) and (1.34), for the the vectors $\underline{v}_\Delta$, $\underline{\lambda}$ and $\underline{\mu}$ would yield exact results; however, their results are only approximate and therefore the application of $\underline{a}$, which furthermore is very cheap, significantly improves the precision.

9   Elementary Pieces of DVS-Software and Critical Coding Routes

The DVS-algorithms are domain-decomposition algorithms. As most of this kind they are iterative algorithms and can be implemented with recourse to Conjugate Gradient Method (CGM), when the matrix is definite and symmetric, or some other iterative procedure such as GMRES, when that is not the case. At each iteration step, depending on the *DVS-algorithm* that is applied, one has to compute the action on a *derived-vector* of one of the following matrices: $\underline{a}\underline{\underline{S}}^{\sim 1}\underline{a}\underline{\underline{S}}$, $\underline{j}\underline{\underline{S}}\underline{j}\underline{\underline{S}}^{\sim 1}$, $\underline{\underline{S}}^{\sim 1}\underline{j}\underline{\underline{S}}\underline{j}$ or $\underline{\underline{SaS}}^{\sim 1}\underline{a}$. In turn, such matrices are different permutations of $\underline{\underline{S}}$, $\underline{\underline{S}}^{\sim 1}$, $\underline{a}$ and $\underline{j}$. Thus, a code for implementing any of the DVS-algorithms can be easily developed when codes for carrying out the action of each one of such matrices are available.

In the absence of constraints the matrices $\underline{\underline{S}}$ and $\underline{\underline{S}}^{\sim 1}$ are block-diagonal and, for its implantation in parallel, each block can be allocated to a different processor. However, when constraints are introduced they are weakly coupled. Such a coupling occurs only when the matrix $\underline{\underline{a}}$ is applied; the application j is equivalent to an application of $\underline{\underline{a}}$, since $j\underline{u} \equiv \underline{u} - \underline{\underline{a}}\underline{u}$. Because of these facts it has been possible to develop optimized routes of general applicability for its parallel implementation that are coded independently in each one of the processors of the parallel hardware. These properties have permitted us to obtain the outstanding parallelization-efficiencies that are reported in the Section on numerical results (see Table 1).

10 Application to Elasticity Problems

As an illustration of the methods described in previous Sections, in this one the *non-overlapping discretization method* will be applied to a system of linear partial differential equations; namely, the system that governs the equilibrium of isotropic elastic solids, whose detailed treatment was explained in the Ph.D. thesis of Iván Contreras [17].

In particular, the following boundary-value problem will be treated:

$$(\lambda + \mu)\nabla\nabla \bullet \underline{u} + \mu\Delta\underline{u} = \underline{f}_{\Omega} \tag{1.36}$$

Subjected to the *Dirichlet* boundary conditions:

$$\underline{u} = 0, \text{ on } \partial\Omega \tag{1.37}$$

Other boundary conditions can also be accommodated.

The software that we have developed treats in parallel the discrete system of linear equations that is obtained when the *standard discretization method* used to obtain the *original discretization* of the Dirichlet BVP defined by Eqs. (1.36) and (1.37) is the finite element method (FEM). In particular, it was obtained applying the well-known variational principle:

$$\int_{\Omega} \{(\lambda + \mu)(\nabla \bullet \underline{u})(\nabla \bullet \underline{w}) + \mu\nabla\underline{u} : \nabla\underline{w}\}dx = \int_{\Omega} \underline{f}_{\Omega} \bullet \underline{w}dx \tag{1.38}$$

In particular, linear functions were used.

Such system of equations can be written as

$$\underline{\underline{M}}\underline{U} = \underline{F} \tag{1.39}$$

Here, it is understood that the vectors $\underline{U}$ and $\underline{F}$, are functions defined on the whole set of *original-nodes* of the mesh used in the FEM discretization, whose values at each node are $3 - D$ vectors. They can be written as $\underline{U} \equiv \left(\underline{U}_p\right) \equiv (U_{pi})$ and $\underline{F} \equiv \left(\underline{F}_p\right) \equiv (F_{pi})$. As for the matrix $\underline{\underline{M}}$, the notation

$$\underline{\underline{M}} \equiv \left(\underline{\underline{M}}_{pq}\right) \equiv \left(M_{piqj}\right) \tag{1.40}$$

is adopted. Above, the range of p and q is the whole set of *original-nodes*, while i and j may take any of the values $1, 2, 3$.

11 Numerical Results

In the numerical experiments that were carried out to test the *DVS-software*, the boundary-value problem for static elasticity introduced in Sect. 10 was treated. Only the DVS-BDDC algorithm was tested. The elastic material was assumed to be homogeneous; so, the Lamé parameters were

Table 1. Numerical Results

Number of Subdomains. = Number of processors	DoF.	Nodes by Subdomain	Primal Nodes	Processing Time in seconds	Parallel efficiency $\left(\frac{p_{min}}{p_{max}} \bullet s\right) \times 100$	Speed up $s = \frac{T(p_{min})}{T(p_{max})}$	Norm of error $\|\underline{e}\|_\infty$
8	22,244,625	941,192	583	14,959	1	1	0.0263
27	21,904,152	274,625	2,312	5,882	75 %	2.543	0.018
64	22,244,625	117,649	5,211	2,676	70 %	5.59	0.029
125	21,904,152	59,319	9,184	1,212	79 %	12.342	0.011
216	22,936,119	35,937	14,525	703	79 %	21.280	0.010
343	22,244,625	21,952	20,628	406	86 %	36.845	0.010
512	23,641,797	13,824	27,391	242	97 %	61.814	0.011
729	23,287,176	10,648	36,800	183	90 %	81.74	0.010
1000	23,641,797	8,000	46,899	136	88 %	109.992	0.009
1331	22,936,119	5,832	57,100	96	94 %	155.823	0.010
1728	20,903,613	4,096	66,671	89	78 %	168.078	0.009
2197	21,904,152	3,375	80,352	64	85 %	233.734	0.008
2744	22,244,625	2,744	94,471	51	86 %	293.313	0.009

assumed to be constant and their values were taken to be

$$\lambda = \frac{Ev}{(1+v)(1-2v)} = 29.6412 \times 10^9 \, \frac{N}{m^2}$$
$$\mu = \frac{E}{2(1+v)} = 27.3611 \times 10^9 \, \frac{N}{m^2} \tag{1.41}$$

These values correspond to a class of cast iron whose *Young modulus*, E, and *Poison ratio*, v, are (for further details about such a material see, http://en.wikipedia.org/wiki/Poisson's_ratio):

$$E = 68.95 \times 10^9 \, \frac{N}{m^2} \ and \ v = 0.26 \tag{1.42}$$

The domain $\Omega \subset R^3$ that the homogeneous-isotropic linearly-elastic solid considered occupies is a unitary cube. The boundary-value problem considered is a *Dirichlet problem*, with homogeneous boundary conditions, whose exact solution is:

$$\underline{u} = (\sin \pi x \sin \pi y \sin \pi z, \ \sin \pi x \sin \pi y \sin \pi z, \ \sin \pi x \sin \pi y \sin \pi z) \tag{1.43}$$

The *fine-mesh* that was introduced consisted of $(193)^3 = 7,189,057$ cubes, which yielded $(194)^3 = 7,301,384$ *original-nodes*.

The *coarse-mesh* consisted of a family of subdomains $\{\Omega_1, \ldots, \Omega_E\}$, whose interfaces constitute the *internal-boundary* Γ. The number E of subdomains was varied taking successively the values 8, 27, 64, 125, 216, 343 and 512 and so on up to 2,744. The total number of *derived-nodes* and corresponding number of *degrees-of-freedom* are around 7.5×10^6 and 22.5×10^6, respectively. The constraints that were imposed consisted of continuity at *primal-nodes*; in every one of the numerical experiments all the nodes located at edges and vertices of the *coarse mesh* were taken as *primal-nodes*. In this manner, the total number of *primal-nodes* varied from a minimum of 583 to a maximum of 94,471. Thereby, it should be mentioned that these conditions granted that at each one of the numerical experiments the matrix $\underline{\underline{A}}$ was positive definite and possessed a well-defined inverse.

All the codes were developed in C ++ and MPI was used. The computations were performed at the Mitzli Supercomputer of the National Autonomous University of Mexico (UNAM), operated by the DGTIC. All calculations were carried out in a 314 node cluster with 8 processors per node. The cluster consists 2.6 GHz Intel Xeon Sandy Bridge E5-2670 processors with 48 GB of RAM.

As it was exhibited in the analysis of the operations, the transmission of information between different processors exclusively occurs when the *average-operators* $\underline{a}$ and $\underline{a}'$ are applied. In a first version of the software reported in the present paper such exchange of information was carried out through a *master-processor*, which is time expensive. However, the efficiency of the software (as a parallelization tool) improved very much when the participation of the *master-processor* in the communication and exchange of information process was avoided. In its new version, the *master-processor* was eliminated altogether. A Table 1, above, summarizes the numerical results.

It should be noticed that the *computational efficiency* is very high, reaching a maximum value of 96.6 %. Furthermore, the efficiency increases as the number of processors increases, a commendable feature for software that intends to be top as a tool for programming the largest supercomputers available at present.

12 Conclusions

The *non-overlapping discretization method* originally introduced by I. Herrera is new procedure for discretizing partial differential equations, or systems of such equations. For the application of highly parallelized hardware to the resulting discrete-problem the *non-overlapping discretization method* has many advantages over standard methods of discretization.

Based on theoretical grounds, in previous publications some of these advantages had been indicated. However, for the first time experimental evidences of such outstanding parallelization-efficiencies are exhibited in this paper. There are *DVS-algorithms* concomitant to the *non-overlapping discretization method*. Here, one of them – the *DVS-BDDC* algorithm- was used to carry out such numerical experiments.

These results constitute a confirmation that the *non-overlapping discretization method* and its concomitant *DVS-algorithms* are very effective tools for harnessing parallelized supercomputers to the task of solving the partial differential equations of science and engineering:

1. Using them very high parallelization effectiveness, close to 100 %, is feasible;
2. The range of its applicability is very wide since there is a general procedure for transforming *standard discretizations* into *non-overlapping discretizations* independently of the problems that originated them;
3. Up to now only the case of symmetric and positive-definite matrices has been fully developed;
4. However, the *non-overlapping discretization method* is also applicable to symmetric and non-symmetric matrices and the results so far obtained indicate that its development is a worthwhile endeavor ahead.

This paper has been mainly devoted to present experimental evidences of the effectiveness of the methodology, but extensive references to the background material have been included.

Acknowlegement. We thank DGTIC-UNAM for the significant support we received to perform the computational experiments presented in Table 1.

Appendix

Here some of the notation used is recalled. The non-overlapping domain-decomposition is $\{\Omega_1, \ldots, \Omega_E\}$. The symbol X is used for the total set of *derived-nodes*. The labels p, q, etc. are reserved for denoting the *original-nodes* whose range is the set $\{1, \ldots, N\}$ of natural-numbers, while the labels α, β, etc. are reserved for the subdomains of the *coarse-mesh*, whose range is the set $\{1, \ldots, E\}$. *Derived-nodes* are identified by pairs: (p, α), p being the *original-node* it derives from and α the subdomain it belongs to. The non-overlapping decomposition of the total set of *derived-nodes* is given by the family of subsets $X^\alpha \equiv \{X^\alpha | \alpha = 1, \ldots, E\}$, which for each $\alpha = 1, \ldots, E$, is constituted by the *derived-nodes* that belong to $\bar{\Omega}_\alpha$; i.e., they are defined by

$$X^\alpha \equiv \{(p,\alpha)|p \in \bar{\Omega}_\alpha\} \tag{1.44}$$

and satisfy:

$$X = \bigcup_{\alpha=1}^{E} X^\alpha \ and \ X^\alpha \cap X^\beta = \emptyset, when \ \alpha \neq \beta \tag{1.45}$$

Given any *original-node* $p \in \widehat{X}$, the set of *heirs of p* is defined to be

$$Z(p) \equiv \{(p,\alpha)|(p,\alpha) \in X\} \tag{1.46}$$

The multiplicity $m(p)$ of $p \in \widehat{X}$, is the number of *heirs of p*.

In DVS developments *derived-nodes* are classified into *interior, interphase, primal* and *dual nodes*. A *derived-node* is: *interior*, when its multiplicity is one and it is *interphase*, otherwise. In the *DVS-methodology* some *interphase-nodes* are chosen to be *primal* and, when they are not *primal*, they are said to be *dual-nodes*. The symbols used are:

(i)   I is the set of *interior-nodes*;
(ii) Γ is the set of *interphase-nodes*;
(iii) π is the set of *primal-nodes*; and
(iv) Δ is the set of *dual-nodes*.

These subsets of *derived-nodes* fulfill the following identities:

$$X = I \cup \Gamma = I \cup \pi \cup \Delta = \Pi \cup \Delta = \Sigma \cup \pi \tag{1.47}$$

and

$$\emptyset = I \cap \Gamma = I \cap \pi = \pi \cap \Delta = \Pi \cap \Delta = \Sigma \cap \pi \tag{1.48}$$

Two more subsets of *derived-nodes* are significant in *non-overlapping discretization methods*: the classes of *extended-primal* and *extended-dual derived-nodes* that are denoted by Π and Σ respectively, and are defined by

$$\Pi \equiv I \cup \pi \ and \ \Sigma \equiv I \cup \Delta \tag{1.49}$$

References

1. Herrera, I., Pinder, G.F.: Mathematical Modelling in Science and Engineering: An axiomatic approach. Wiley, Hoboken (2012)
2. President's Information Technology Advisoty Committee: Pitac. Computational Science: Ensuring America's Competitiveness. Report to the President June 2005. 104 p. www.nitrd. gow/pitac

3. DDM Organization, Proceedings of 23 International Conferences on Domain Decomposition Methods 1988–2015. www.ddm.org
4. Dohrmann, C.R.: A preconditioner for substructuring based on constrained energy minimization. SIAM J. Sci. Comput. **25**(1), 246–258 (2003)
5. Mandel, J., Dohrmann, C.R.: Convergence of a balancing domain decomposition by constraints and energy minimization. Numer. Linear Algebra Appl. **10**(7), 639–659 (2003)
6. Mandel, J., Dohrmann, C.R., Tezaur, R.: An algebraic theory for primal and dual substructuring methods by constraints. Appl. Numer. Math. **54**, 167–193 (2005)
7. Farhat, Ch., Roux, F.: A method of finite element tearing and interconnecting and its parallel solution algorithm. Internat. J. Numer. Methods Engrg. **32**, 1205–1227 (1991)
8. Mandel, J., Tezaur, R.: Convergence of a substructuring method with Lagrange multipliers. Numer. Math. **73**(4), 473–487 (1996)
9. Farhat, C., Lessoinne, M., LeTallec, P., Pierson, K., Rixen, D.: FETI-DP a dual-primal unified FETI method, Part I: A faster alternative to the two-level FETI method. Int. J. Numer. Methods Engrg. **50**, 1523–1544 (2001)
10. Farhat, C., Lessoinne, M., Pierson, K.: A scalable dual-primal domain decomposition method. Numer. Linear Algebra Appl. **7**, 687–714 (2000)
11. Herrera, I., de la Cruz, L.M., Rosas-Medina, A.: Non-Overlapping Discretization Methods for Partial, Differential Equations. Numer. Meth. Part D E **30**, 1427–1454 (2014). doi:10.1002/num21852. (Open source)
12. Herrera, I., Rosas-Medina, A.: The derived-vector space framework and four general purposes massively parallel DDM algorithms. EABE (Engineering Analysis with Boundary Elements) **37**, 646–657 (2013)
13. Herrera, I., Contreras, I.: An innovative tool for effectively applying highly parallelized hardware to problems of elasticity. Geofísica Int. **55**(1), 363–386 (2016)
14. Herrera, I.: Theory of differential equations in discontinuous piecewise-defined-functions. Numer. Meth. Part D E **23**(3), 597–639 (2007). DOI10.1002NO.20182
15. Herrera, I., Yates, R.A.: The multipliers-free domain decomposition methods. Numer. Meth. Part D. E. **26**, 874–905 (2010). doi:10.1002/num.20462
16. Herrera, I., Yates, R.A.: The multipliers-free dual primal domain decomposition methods for nonsymmetrical matrices numer. Meth. Part D. E. **27**(5), 1262–1289 (2011). doi:10.1002/Num.20581
17. Contreras, I.: Parallel Processing of PDEs. Ph.D. thesis, Advisor Herrera I. UNAM (2016)

Large-Scale Reservoir Simulations on IBM Blue Gene/Q

Hui Liu, Kun Wang, and Zhangxin Chen[(✉)]

University of Calgary, 2500 University Dr NW, Calgary, AB T2N 1N4, Canada
{hui.j.liu,wang30,zhachen}@ucalgary.ca

abstract
Abstract. This paper presents our work on simulation of large-scale reservoir models on IBM Blue Gene/Q and studying the scalability of our parallel reservoir simulators. An in-house black oil simulator has been implemented. It uses MPI for communication and is capable of simulating reservoir models with hundreds of millions of grid cells. Benchmarks show that our parallel simulators are thousands of times faster than sequential simulators that are designed for workstations and personal computers, and these simulators have excellent scalability.

Keywords: Large-scale reservoir · Simulation · Blue Gene/Q · Parallel computing

1 Introduction

Nowadays, large-scale reservoir simulations are becoming more and more popular in the oil and gas industry in order to simulate complex geological models. However, when a model is large enough, a simulator may take days or even weeks to finish one run using regular workstations and personal computers. This problem can also be observed in black oil, compositional and thermal simulations. Efficient computational methods and fast reservoir simulators should be investigated.

Reservoir simulations have been studied for decades and various models and methods have been developed. Coats studied black oil, compositional and thermal models, and he also investigated numerical methods, linear solver, preconditioner, grid effects and stability issues in his publications [1–3,8,11,17]. Kaarstad et al. [6] implemented a parallel two-dimensional two-phase oil-water simulator, which could solve problems with millions of grid cells. Rutledge et al. [4] implemented a compositional simulator for parallel computers using the IMPES (implicit pressure-explicit saturation) method. Shiralkar et al. [5] developed a portable parallel production qualified simulator, which could run on a variety of parallel systems. Killough et al. [7] studied locally refined grids in their parallel simulator. Dogru et al. [9] developed a parallel black oil simulator, which was highly efficient and was capable of simulating models with up to one billion cells. Zhang et al. developed a scalable general-purpose platform to support adaptive finite element

© Springer International Publishing Switzerland 2016
J. Xie et al. (Eds.): HPCA 2015, LNCS 9576, pp. 17–30, 2016.
DOI: 10.1007/978-3-319-32557-6_2

and adaptive finite volume methods, which was also applied to reservoir simulations using Discontineous Galerkin method [10,12,23]. For many reservoir simulations, most of the running time is spent on the solution of linear systems. We know that the most important is to develop efficient preconditioners. Many preconditioners have been proposed, such as constrained pressure residual (CPR) methods [13,14], multi-stage methods [15], multiple level preconditioners [22] and fast auxiliary space preconditioners (FASP) [16,18]. Chen et al. studied parallel reservoir simulations and developed a family of CPR-like preconditioners for black oil simulations and compositional simulations, including CPR-FP, CPR-FPF and CPR-FFPF methods [20].

A black oil simulator has been developed based on our in-house parallel platform. The black oil model has three mass conservation equations for three components (water, gas and oil). The system is fully coupled nonlinear system, which is solved by inexact Newton-Raphson methods, and structured grids and finite difference methods are applied. The performance of the black oil simulator is studied on IBM Blue Gene/Q system using large-scale reservoir models for standard black oil model and two-phase oil-water model. Numerical experiments show that our simulator is scalable and it is capable of simulating models with hundreds of millions of grid cells.

2   Reservoir Simulation Models

The black oil model and its simplified model, two-phase oil-water model, are briefly introduced here.

2.1   Black Oil Model

The black oil model has three phases (water, oil and gas), and three components. The model assumes that there is no mass transfer between water phase and the other two phases, and gas component can exist in gas and oil phases. Oil component is also assumed that it can exist in oil phase only. The reservoir is isothermal and no energy change is considered.

The Darcy's law is applied for black oil model, which establishes a relationship between volumetric flow rates of three components and their pressure changes in a reservoir, which is described as:

$$Q = -\frac{\kappa A \Delta p}{\mu L},$$
(1)

where κ is the absolute permeability of rock, A is a cross-section area, Δp is the pressure difference, μ is viscosity of fluid, and L is the length of a porous medium. In three-dimensional space, the differential form of Darcy's law is:

$$q = \frac{Q}{A} = -\frac{\kappa}{\mu}\nabla p.$$
(2)

By combining Darcy's law, black oil model has the following mass conservation equations for each component:

$$\begin{cases} \dfrac{\partial}{\partial t}(\phi s_o \rho_o^o) & = \nabla \cdot (\dfrac{KK_{ro}}{\mu_o}\rho_o^o \nabla \Phi_o) + q_o, \\[2mm] \dfrac{\partial}{\partial t}(\phi s_w \rho_w) & = \nabla \cdot (\dfrac{KK_{rw}}{\mu_w}\rho_w \nabla \Phi_w) + q_w, \\[2mm] \dfrac{\partial(\phi \rho_o^g s_o + \phi \rho_g s_g)}{\partial t} & = \nabla \cdot (\dfrac{KK_{ro}}{\mu_o}\rho_o^g \nabla \Phi_o) + \nabla \cdot (\dfrac{KK_{rg}}{\mu_g}\rho_g \nabla \Phi_g) + q_o^g + q_g, \end{cases}$$

$$(3)$$

where, for phase α ($\alpha = o, w, g$), Φ_α is its potential, ϕ and K are porosity and permeability of a resevoir, and s_α, μ_α, p_α, ρ_α, $K_{r\alpha}$ and q_α are its saturation, phase viscosity, phase pressure, density, relative permeability and production (injection) rate, respectively. ρ_o^o and ρ_o^g are density of the oil component in the oil phase and the density of the solution gas in the oil phase, respectively. They have the following relations:

$$\begin{cases} \Phi_\alpha = p_\alpha + \rho_\alpha g z, \\ S_o + S_w + S_g = 1, \\ p_w = p_o - p_{cow}(S_w), \\ p_g = p_o + p_{cog}(S_g), \end{cases}$$

$$(4)$$

where z is reservoir depth, p_{cow} is capillary pressure between water phase and oil phase, p_α is pressure of phase α, and p_{cog} is capillary between gas phase and oil phase.

The properties of fluids and rock are functions of pressure and saturation. The pressures of water and gas phases are functions of oil phase pressure and saturation; see Eq. (4). The density of water is a function of its pressure:

$$\rho_w = \rho_w(p_w) = \rho_w(p_o, s_w),$$

and the density of the oil phase is a function of its phase pressure and the bubble point pressure:

$$\rho_o^o = \rho_o^o(p_o, p_b),$$

where p_b is bubble point pressure. The bubble point pressure is the pressure at which infinitesimal gas appears. The water viscosity μ_w is assumed to be a constant. The oil phase viscosity is a function of its pressure p_o and the bubble point pressure p_b:

$$\mu_o = \mu_o(p_o, p_b).$$

The relative permeabilities K_{rw}, K_{ro} and K_{rg} are functions of water and gas saturations S_w and S_g:

$$\begin{cases} K_{rw} = K_{rw}(S_w), \\ K_{rg} = K_{rg}(S_g), \\ K_{ro} = K_{ro}(S_w, S_g), \end{cases}$$

where K_{ro} is calculated using the Stone II formula.

For real simulations, the relative permeabilities are given by tables or analytic formulas. Other properties, such as density, viscosity and capillary pressure, have analytic formulas and they can be calculated by table input too. With proper boundary conditions and initial conditions, a close system is given. Here no flow boundary condition is assumed.

2.2   Two-Phase Flow Model

This model is a simplified model of the standard black oil model, which assumes that the reservoir has two phases, oil and water, and they are immiscible. The model is similar to black oil model, which is written as [19]:

$$
\begin{cases}
\dfrac{\partial}{\partial t}(\phi s_o \rho_o) & = \nabla \cdot (\dfrac{K K_{ro}}{\mu_o} \rho_o \nabla \Phi_o) + q_o \\[2mm]
\dfrac{\partial}{\partial t}(\phi s_w \rho_w) & = \nabla \cdot (\dfrac{K K_{rw}}{\mu_w} \rho_w \nabla \Phi_w) + q_w.
\end{cases}
\tag{5}
$$

2.3   Well Modeling

Different well constraints can be set for each active well. One commonly-used method is a sink-source model. For each perforation block m, its well rate (production or injection) $q_{\alpha,m}$ is calculated by:

$$
q_{\alpha,m} = W_i \frac{\rho_\alpha K_{r\alpha}}{\mu_\alpha}(p_h - p_\alpha - \rho_\alpha \wp (z_h - z)),
\tag{6}
$$

where p_h is bottom hole pressure of a well, W_i is its well index, z_h is reference depth of bottom hole pressure, z is depth of the perforated grid block m, and p_α is phase pressure of the perforated grid block, such as oil, gas and water. W_i can be calculated by several different models. In our simulator, a Peaceman model [24] is chosen.

Many operation constraints and their combinations may be applied to each well at different time stages, such as a fixed bottom hole pressure constraint, a fixed oil rate constraint, a fixed water rate constraint, a fixed liquid rate constraint and a fixed gas rate constraint. When the fixed bottom hole pressure condition is applied to some well, its bottom hole pressure, p_h, is known and its well rate $q_{\alpha,m}$ is known if we have phase pressure of the perforated block. The constraint equation for the well is

$$
p_h = c,
\tag{7}
$$

where c is a constant set by the user input. No known exists for this constraint.

When a fixed rate constraint is applied to a well, its bottom hole pressure is an unknown. For the fixed water rate constraint, the equation is

$$
\sum_m q_{w,m} = q_w,
\tag{8}
$$

where q_w is constant. For the fixed oil rate constraint, its equation is

$$\sum_m q_{o,m} = q_o, \tag{9}$$

where q_o is constant and known. A well may be applied different constraints at different time period. A schedule can be set by input, in which users can set operation changes for each well.

2.4   Numerical Methods

In this paper, conservative finite difference schemes are employed to discretize these models. The inexact Newton method is employed to solve the nonlinear equations. The time term is discretized by the backward Euler difference scheme. If we let f^n represent the value of a function f at any time step n, then its derivative at time step $(n+1)$ is approximated by

$$(\frac{\partial f}{\partial t})^{n+1} = \frac{f^{n+1} - f^n}{\Delta t}. \tag{10}$$

The space terms are discretized by cell-centered finite difference method [19]. Here if we assume d is a space direction and A is the area of the corresponding face of a grid cell, the transmissibility term $T_{\alpha,d}$ can be written as:

$$T_{\alpha,d} = \frac{K K_{r\alpha}}{\mu_\alpha} \rho_\alpha \frac{A}{\Delta d}. \tag{11}$$

Inexact Newton Method. The nonlinear system can be represented by

$$F(x) = 0, \tag{12}$$

where x is unknown vector, including oil phase pressure, water saturation and well bottom hole pressure. For black oil model, a gas saturation (or bubble point pressure) is also included. After linearization, a linear system, $Ax = b$, is obtained in each Newton iteration, where A is Jacobian matrix, x is unknown to be determined, and b is right-hand side. The standard Newton method solves the linear system accurately. However, it is computationally expensive and it is not necessary sometimes. In our implementation, the inexact Newton method is applied, whose algorithm is described in Algorithm 1.

The only difference between standard Newton method and inexact Newton method is how to choose θ_l. Usually the parameter, θ_l, for standard Newton method is fixed and small, such as 10^{-5}. The parameter, θ_l, for inexact Newton method is automatically adjusted. Three different choices are listed as follows [23]:

Algorithm 1. The inexact Newton Method

1: Give an initial guess x^0 and stopping criterion ϵ, let $l = 0$, and assemble right-hand side b.
2: **while** $\|b\| \geq \epsilon$ **do**
3:    Assemble the Jacobian matrix A.
4:    Find θ_l and δx such that

$$\|b - A\delta x\| \leq \theta_l \|b\|, \tag{13}$$

5:    Let $l = l + 1$ and $x = x + \delta x$.
6: **end while**
7: x is the solution of the nonlinear system.

$$\theta_l = \begin{cases} \dfrac{\|b^l - r^{l-1}\|}{\|b^{l-1}\|}, \\[2ex] \dfrac{\|b^l\| - \|r^{l-1}\|}{\|b^{l-1}\|}, \\[2ex] \gamma \left(\dfrac{\|b^l\|}{\|b^{l-1}\|} \right)^\beta, \end{cases} \tag{14}$$

where r^l and b^l are residual and right-hand side of l-th iteration, respectively. The residual is defined as,

$$r^l = b^l - A\delta x. \tag{15}$$

Linear Solver. If a proper matrix ordering (numbering of unknowns) is applied, the matrix A derived from each Newton iteration can be written as

$$A = \begin{pmatrix} A_{pp} & A_{ps} & A_{pw} \\ A_{sp} & A_{ss} & A_{sw} \\ A_{wp} & A_{ws} & A_{ww} \end{pmatrix}, \tag{16}$$

where A_{pp} is the matrix corresponding to oil phase pressure unknowns, A_{ss} is the matrix corresponding to other unknowns in each grid cell, such as water saturation, gas saturation and bubble point pressure, and A_{ww} is the matrix coefficients corresponding to well bottom hole pressure unknowns, and other matrices are coupled items.

The matrix A is hard to solve in large-scale reservoir simulations. Many multi-stage preconditioners have been developed to overcome this problem, such as CPR, FASP, CPR-FP and CPR-FPF methods. The key idea is to solve a sub-problem (A_{pp}) using algebraic multi-grid methods (AMG). In this paper, the CPR-FPF method developed by Chen et al. [20] is applied. Matrix decoupling techniques are also employed, such as ABF decoupling and Quasi-IMPES decoupling.

3   Numerical Experiments

An Blue Gene/Q from IBM is employed to run reservoir simulations. The system, Wat2Q, is located in the IBM Thomas J. Watson Research Center. Each node has 32 computer cards (64-bit PowerPC A2 processor), which has 17 cores. One of them is for the operation system and the other 16 cores for computation. The system has 32,768 CPU cores for computation. The performance of each core is really low compared with Intel processors. However, the system has strong network relative to CPU performance, and the system is scalable.

3.1   Oil-Water Model

The SPE10 model is described on a regular Cartesian grid, whose dimensions are $1,200 \times 2,200 \times 170$ (ft) [21]. The model has $60 \times 220 \times 85$ cells (1.122×10^6 cells). It has one injection well and four production wells. The original model is designed for two-phase oil-water model and it has around 2.244 millions of unknowns.

Fig. 1. Permeability in X Direction of the SPE10 benchmark

The model is highly heterogeneous. Its permeability is ranged from $6.65e{-}7$ Darcy to 20 Darcy, and the x-direction permeability, K_x, is shown in Fig. 1. Its porosity shown in Fig. 2, ranges from 0 to 0.5. Data sets for porosity and permeability can be downloaded from SPE10's official website. The relative permeability of water phase is calculated by

$$K_{rw}(s_w) = \frac{(s_w - s_{wc})^2}{(1 - s_{wc} - s_{or})^2},$$ (17)

and the relative permeability of oil phase is calculated by

$$K_{ro}(s_w) = \frac{(1 - s_{or} - s_w)^2}{(1 - s_{wc} - s_{or})^2},$$ (18)

where $s_{wc} = s_{or} = 0.2$. Capillary pressure is ignored.

Fig. 2. Porosity of the SPE10 benchmark

3.2 Numerical Examples

Example 1. The original SPE10 project is simulated. The termination tolerance for inexact Newton method is 10^{-2} and its maximal Newton iterations are 20. The linear solver BiCGSTAB is applied and its maximal inner iterations are 50. The Quasi-IMPES decoupling strategy is used. Simulation period is 2,000 days and maximal time step is 100 days. Summaries of numerical results are shown in Table 1 [20], and its scalability is shown by Fig. 3.

Table 1. Summaries of Example 1

# Procs	# Steps	# Newton	# Solver	# Avg. solver	Time (s)	Avg. time (s)
8	50	298	7189	24.1	27525.6	92.3
16	50	297	7408	24.9	13791.8	46.4
32	51	322	7467	23.1	7044.1	21.8
64	50	294	7609	25.8	3445.8	11.7

Table 1 presents results for time steps, Newton iterations, total linear iterations, average linear iterations per Newton iteration, overall running time and average running time per Newton iteration. From this table, we can see each case has similar time steps and Newton iterations. The linear solver and preconditioner are robust, where each Newton iteration terminate in around 25 linear iterations. The table and Fig. 3 show our simulator has excellent scalability.

Example 2. This example tests a refined SPE10 case, and each grid cell is refined into 27 grid cells. It has around 30 millions of grid cells and around 60 millions of unknowns. The stopping criterion for the inexact Newton method is 1e−3 and its maximal Newton iterations are 20. The BiCGSTAB solver is applied and its

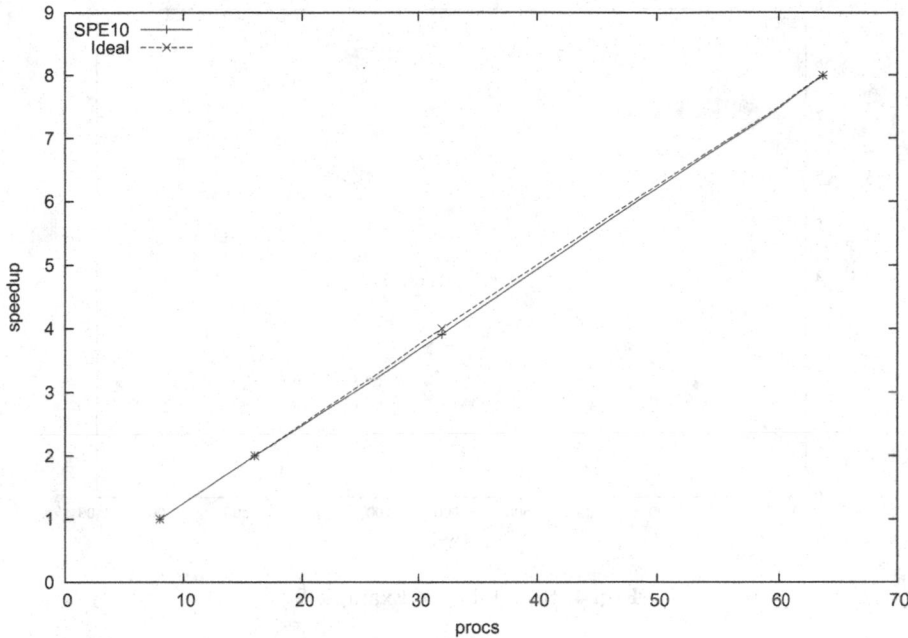

Fig. 3. Scalability of preconditioners, Example 1

maximal iterations are 100. Potential reordering and Quasi-IMPES decoupling strategy are applied. The simulation period is 10 days. Up to 128 computer cards are used. The numerical summaries are shown in Table 2, and its speedup (scalability) is shown in Fig. 4.

Table 2. Numerical summaries of Example 2

# Procs	# Steps	# Newton	# Solver	# Avg. solver	Time (s)	Avg. time (s)
128	40(1)	295	2470	8.3	43591.8	147.7
256	39	269	2386	8.8	20478.4	76.1
512	40	260	2664	10.2	10709.8	41.1
1024	39	259	2665	10.2	5578.7	21.5

The numerical summaries in Table 2 show the inexact Newton method is robust, where around 40 time steps and around 260 N iterations are used for each simulation with different MPI tasks except the case with 128 MPI tasks due to one time step cut that contributes 20 N iterations. The linear solver BiCGSTAB and the preconditioner show good convergence, where the average number of linear iterations for each nonlinear iteration is between 8 and 11. The results

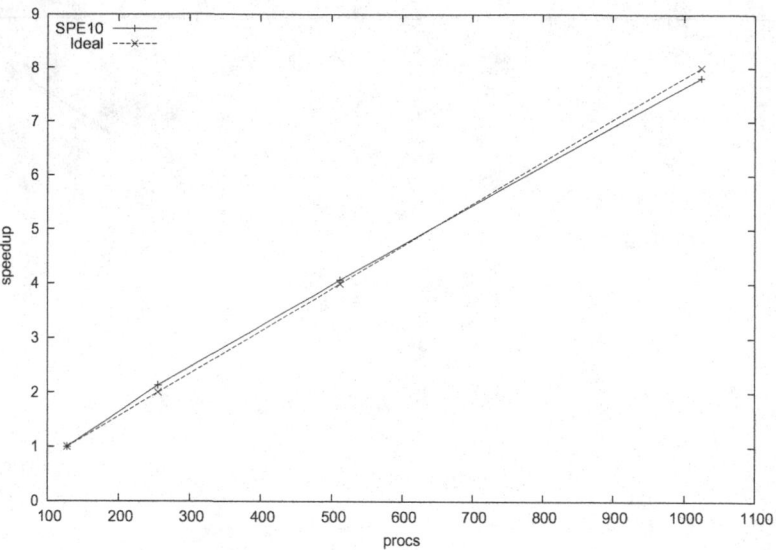

Fig. 4. Scalability of Example 2

mean our linear solver and preconditioner are effective and robust. The overall running time and average time for each Newton iteration show our simulator has excellent scalability, which is almost ideal. The scalability is also demonstrated by Fig. 4.

Example 3. This example also tests a refined SPE10 case, where each grid cell is refined into 125 grid cells. It has around 140 millions of grid cells and around 280 millions of unknowns. The stopping criterion for inexact Newton method is 1e−2 and its maximal Newton iterations are 20. The BiCGSTAB solver is applied and its maximal iterations are 100. The Quasi-IMPES decoupling strategy is applied. The simulation period is 10 days. The numerical summaries are shown in Table 3, and the speedup (scalability) curve is shown in Fig. 5.

Table 3. Numerical summaries of Example 3

# Procs	# Steps	# Newton	# Solver	# Avg. solver	Time (s)	Avg. time (s)
256	57	328	2942	8.9	168619.6	514.0
512	60	328	2236	6.8	72232.4	220.2
1024	62	341	3194	9.3	43206.5	126.7
2048	59	327	3123	9.5	22588.8	69.0

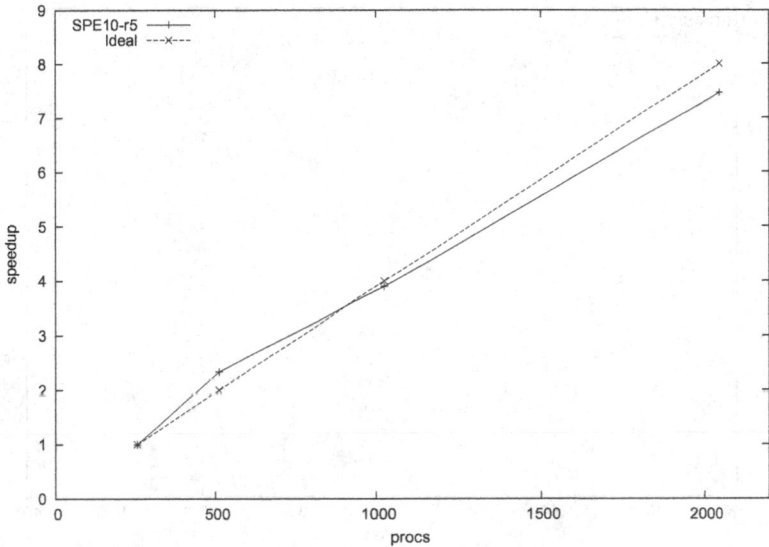

Fig. 5. Scalability of Example 3

This case is difficult. However, results from Table 3 show our nonlinear and linear methods are robust. Each Newton iteration terminate in less than 10 linear iterations. Running time and Fig. 5 show our simulator has good scalability. For the case with 512 MPI tasks, it has super-linear scalability.

Example 4. This case simulates a refined SPE1 model, which has 100 millions of grid cells. The termination tolerance for inexact Newton method is 10^{-2} and maximal Newton iterations is 15. The BICGSTAB linear solver is chosen and its maximal iterations is 20. ABF decoupling strategy is enabled. The simulation period is 10. Summaries of numerical results are shown in Table 4 and scalability curve is shown by Fig. 6.

Table 4. Summaries of Example 4

# Procs	# Steps	# Newton	# Solver	# Avg. solver	Time (s)	Avg. time (s)
512	27 (1)	140	586	4.1	11827.9	84.4
1024	27	129	377	2.9	5328.4	41.3
2048	26	122	362	2.9	2708.5	22.2
4096	27	129	394	3.0	1474.2	11.4

The original SPE1 project is a small one with 300 grid cells ($10 \times 10 \times 3$) and the project is refined to 100 millions of grid cells ($1000 \times 1000 \times 100$).

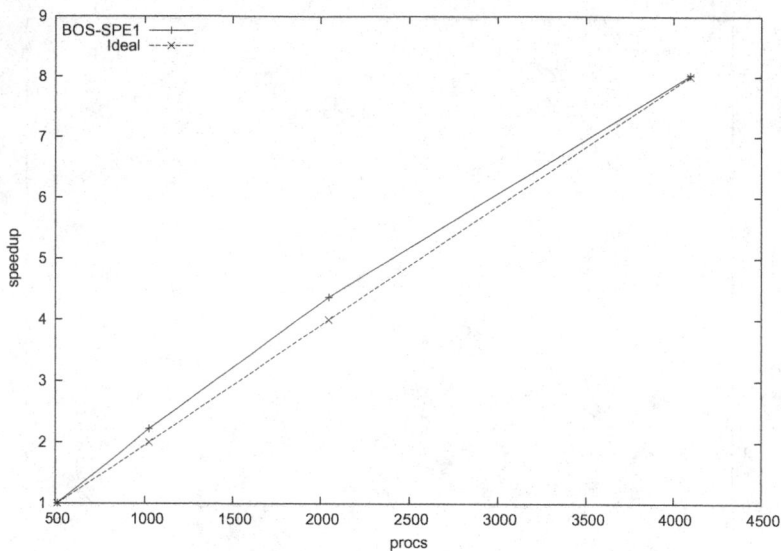

Fig. 6. Scalability (speedup) of Example 4

It has a homogeneous geological model. Table 4 presents numerical summaries for nonlinear method, linear solver and performance. All four simulations use around 27 time steps. The simulation with 512 MPI tasks uses 140 N iterations, which is more than other cases due to one time step cut. The linear solver and preconditioner are robust, which can solve a linear system in a few iterations. Again, running time and Fig. 6 show our simulator has excellent scalability.

4   Conclusion

Parallel reservoir simulations are studied in the paper, which are based on our in-house parallel platform. The platform provides grids, data, linear solvers and pre-conditioners for reservoir simulators. A black oil model is implemented. Numerical experiments show that our simulator has excellent scalability and simulations can be sped up thousands of times faster. The paper also demonstrates that parallel computing techniques are powerful tools for large-scale reservoir simulations and IBM Blue Gene/Q system is scalable.

Acknowledgements. The support of Department of Chemical and Petroleum Engineering, University of Calgary and Reservoir Simulation Group is gratefully acknowledged. The research is partly supported by NSERC/AIEE/Foundation CMG and AITF Chairs.

References

1. Coats, K.: Reservoir simulation. SPE-1987-48-PEH, Society of Petroleum Engineers (1987)
2. Coats, K.: Simulation of steamflooding with distillation and solution gas. SPE-5015-PA, Soc. Petrol. Eng. J., 235–247 (1976)
3. Coats, K.: Reservoir simulation: state of the art. SPE-10020-PA, J. Petrol. Technol. 34(08), 1633–1642 (1982)
4. Rutledge, J., Jones, D., Chen, W., Chung, E.: The use of massively parallel SIMD computer for reservoir simulation. In: SPE-21213, Eleventh SPE Symposium on Reservoir Simulation, Anaheim (1991)
5. Shiralkar, G., Stephenson, R., Joubert, W., Lubeck, O., van Bloemen Waanders, B.: A production quality distributed memory reservoir simulator. In: SPE Reservoir Simulation Symposium (1997)
6. Kaarstad, T., Froyen, J., Bjorstad, P., Espedal, M.: Massively parallel reservoir simulator. SPE-29139, Presented at the 1995 Symposium on Reservoir Simulation, San Antonio, Texas (1995)
7. Killough, J., Camilleri, D., Darlow, B., Foster, J.: Parallel reservoir simulator based on local grid refinement. In: SPE-37978, SPE Reservoir Simulation Symposium, Dallas (1997)
8. Coats, K.: A highly implicit steamflood model. SPE-6105-PA, Soc. Petrol. Eng. J. 18(05), 369–383 (1978)
9. Dogru, A., Fung, L., Middya, U., Al-Shaalan, T., Pita, J.: A next-generation parallel reservoir simulator for giant reservoirs. In: SPE/EAGE Reservoir Characterization & Simulation Conference (2009)
10. Zhang, L.: A parallel algorithm for adaptive local refinement of tetrahedral meshes using bisection. Numer. Math. Theory, Methods Appl. 2, 65–89 (2009)
11. Coats, K.: An equation of state compositional model. SPE-8284-PA, Soc. Petrol. Eng. J. 20(05), 363–376 (1980)
12. Zhang, L., Cui, T., Liu, H.: A set of symmetric quadrature rules on triangles and tetrahedra. J. Comput. Math 27(1), 89–96 (2009)
13. Wallis, J., Kendall, R., Little, T.: Constrained residual acceleration of conjugate residual methods. In: SPE Reservoir Simulation Symposium (1985)
14. Cao, H., Schlumberger, T., Hamdi, A., Wallis, J., Yardumian, H.: Parallel scalable unstructured CPR-type linear solver for reservoir simulation. In: SPE Annual Technical Conference and Exhibition (2005)
15. Al-Shaalan, T., Klie, H., Dogru, A., Wheeler, M.: Studies of robust two stage preconditioners for the solution of fully implicit multiphase flow problems. In: SPE Reservoir Simulation Symposium (2009)
16. Hu, X., Liu, W., Qin, G., Xu, J., Zhang, Z.: Development of a fast auxiliary subspace pre-conditioner for numerical reservoir simulators. In: SPE Reservoir Characterisation and Simulation Conference and Exhibition (2011)
17. Coats, K.: Effects of grid type and difference scheme on pattern steamflood simulation results. SPE-11079-PA, J. Petrol. Technol. 38(05), 557–569 (1986)
18. Feng, C., Shu, S., Xu, J., Zhang, C.: A multi-stage preconditioner for the black oil model and its OpenMP implementation. In: 21st International Conference on Domain Decomposition Methods, France (2012)
19. Chen, Z., Huan, G., Ma, Y.: Computational Methods for Multiphase Flows in Porous Media, vol. 2. SIAM, Philadelphia (2006)

20. Liu, H., Wang, K., Chen, Z.: A family of constrained pressure residual precon-
    ditioners for parallel reservoir simulations. Numer. Linear Algebra Appl. **23**(1),
    120–146 (2016)
21. Christie, M., Blunt, M.: Tenth SPE comparative solution project: a comparison of
    upscaling techniques. SPE Reservoir Eval. Eng. **4**(4), 308–317 (2001)
22. Wang, B., Shuhong, W., Li, Q., Li, X., Li, H., Zhang, C., Jinchao, X.: A multilevel
    preconditioner and its shared memory implementation for new generation reservoir
    simulator. In: SPE-172988-MS, SPE Large Scale Computing and Big Data Chal-
    lenges in Reservoir Simulation Conference and Exhibition, Istanbul, Turkey, 15–17
    September 2014
23. Wang, K., Zhang, L., Chen, Z.: Development of discontinuous Galerkin methods
    and a parallel simulator for reservoir simulation. In: SPE-176168-MS, SPE/IATMI
    Asia Pacific Oil & Gas Conference and Exhibition, Nusa Dua, Bali, Indonesia,
    20–22 October 2015
24. Peaceman, D.: Interpretation of well-block pressures in numerical reservoir simula-
    tion. In: SPE-6893, 52nd Annual Fall Technical Conference and Exhibition, Denver
    (1977)

A TS-PSO Based Artificial Neural Network for Short-Term Load Forecast

Shuihua Wang[1,2], Genlin Ji[1,2], Jiquan Yang[1,2], Xingxing Zhou[1], and Yudong Zhang[1,2(✉)]

[1] School of Computer Science and Technology, Nanjing Normal University, 1 Wenyuan, Nanjing 210023, Jiangsu, China
[2] Jiangsu Key Laboratory of 3D Printing Equipment and Manufacturing, Nanjing 210042, Jiangsu, China

Abstract. (**Aim**) A short-term load forecast is an arduous problem due to the nonlinear characteristics of the load series. (**Method**) The artificial neural network (ANN) was employed. To train the ANN, a novel hybridization of Tabu Search and Particle Swarm Optimization (TS-PSO) methods was introduced. TS-PSO is a novel and powerful global optimization method, which combined the merits of both TS and PSO, and removed the disadvantages of both. (**Results**) Experiments demonstrated that the proposed TS-PSO-ANN is superior to GA-ANN, PSO-ANN, and BFO-ANN with respect to a mean squared error (MSE). (**Conclusion**) The TS-PSO-ANN is effective in a short-term load forecast.

Keywords: Short-term load forecast · Artificial neural network (ANN) · Tabu search · Particle swarm optimization (PSO) · Mean squared error (MSE)

1 Introduction

A short-term load forecast (STLF) is a hot topic. It is used to predict electric loads for a period of minutes, hours, days or weeks. STLF is one of the most important works of power dispatching departments. Improving the forecast performance not only enhances the prediction accuracy, but also provides a reliable basis for the grid operation [1].

Traditionally, research on STLF used classical statistical methods, like ARX models, stochastic time series, and state space models. In recent years, with the rapid development of artificial intelligence (AI), more and more advanced AI methods were applied to STLF problems, such as a genetic algorithm (GA) [2], particle swarm optimization (PSO) [3], an artificial neural network (ANN) [4], fuzzy logic [5], neuro-fuzzy systems [6], and wavelet transform [7].

Among these methods, the use of an artificial neural network (ANN) has received much attention in the last few decades. The advantage of ANN is that it does not need any complicated mathematical formulations or quantitative correlation between outputs and inputs [8]. Normally, ANN is trained by a back-propagation (BP) algorithm or its variants, but BP learning has many limitations [9]; for example, it converges too slowly and the global optimal weights/biases are difficult to obtain.

© Springer International Publishing Switzerland 2016
J. Xie et al. (Eds.): HPCA 2015, LNCS 9576, pp. 31–37, 2016.
DOI: 10.1007/978-3-319-32557-6_3

Scholars tend to use global optimization to train ANN, like a genetic algorithm (GA) [10], particle swarm optimization (PSO) [11–13], Tabu search (TS) [14, 15], and bacterial foraging optimization. In this study, we proposed a novel global optimization method as the hybridization of Tabu search (TS) and Particle Swarm Optimization (PSO).

The structure of the paper is organized as follows: Sect. 2 contains the methodology. Section 3 gives the experiment results and discusses these results. Finally, Sect. 4 concludes with the paper.

2 Methodology

2.1 Feature Selection

Six features are selected with their definitions listed in Table 1. These selected features are coherent with past publication [16].

Table 1. Six features

Feature	Definition
D	Day Type. Here 0 represents Tuesday, Wednesday, Thursday, and Friday. 1 represents Monday and other workdays after holiday. 2 represents Saturday, Sunday, and holidays
$L(t-1)$	The last actual load
$L(t-2)$	The penultimate actual load
$L(t-a)$	The actual load at the same time last day. If the time interval is 1 h, then $a = 24$. If the time interval is 15 m, then $a = 24*60/15 = 96$. If the time interval is 5 m, then $a = 24*60/5 = 288$
T_{min}	The minimum forecast temperature of current day
T_{max}	The maximum forecast temperature of current day

2.2 ANN

In this study, we chose to establish a one-hidden-layer ANN [17], the size of which is set to $6 \times 3 \times 1$. The input layers contain 6 neurons, corresponding to the six features in Sect. 2.1. The number of neurons in hidden layer is set to 3, which is yielded by the information entropy method [18]. The output layer contains only 1 neuron, predicting the value of the load. (See Fig. 1). Note that the transfer functions in the hidden and output layer are set to sigmoid and linear function, respectively.

2.3 TS-PSO

PSO performs good in terms of global search but bad in local search [19, 20], on the other hand, TS perform bad in global search but good in local search [21]. Hence, a novel method was proposed that combines the two algorithm, in the way that the new hybrid TS-PSO performed both global and local search simultaneously in each iteration,

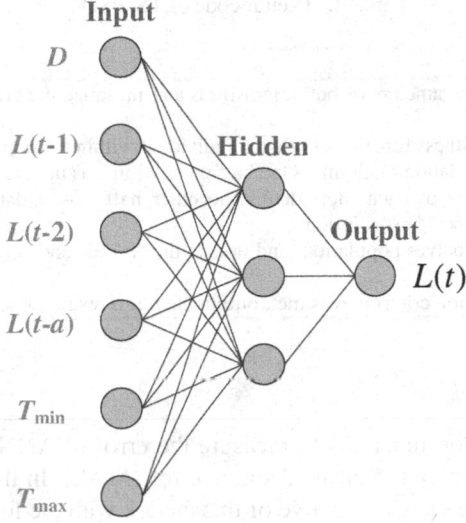

Fig. 1. Structure of the ANN with size of $6 \times 3 \times 1$

and the probability of finding the global optimal increases dramatically as a sequence. This will effectively avoid the optimizer to be trapped into local optima.

The proposed TS-PSO algorithm [22] utilizes the exploitation ability of Tabu search and the exploration ability of particle swarm optimization, and it balances the disadvantage of both TS and PSO [23]. The diagram of TS-PSO is shown in Fig. 2, and the detailed steps are listed in Table 2 below.

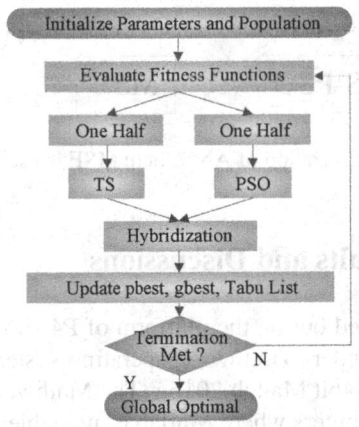

Fig. 2. Diagram of implementing TS-PSO

Table 2. Pseudocode of TS-PSO

Algorithm : TS-PSO
Step 1   Initialize the parameters of both algorithms and initialize the population in a random way.
Step 2   Evaluate the fitness functions f of each individual within the population.
Step 3   Halve the population randomly. One half population was updated by PSO, i.e., update the position and velocity of each individual. The other half was updated by TS, i.e., each individual searches the local best solution.
Step 4   Combine two halves population, and update the "*pbest*" and "*gbest*" particles and the Tabu list (TL).
Step 5   If the termination criterion was met, output the *pbest* result. Otherwise, go to Step 2.

2.4   Training

There are many common functions to measure the error of ANN prediction, such as mean squared error (MSE) and mean absolute error (MAE). In this study, the former was employed to be the search objective of this model, with the form of

$$\text{MSE} = \frac{1}{S} \sum_{i=1}^{S} [u(i) - l(i)]^2 \tag{1}$$

Here u represents the realistic load values that are known, l the output values of the ANN, and S the number of samples. The goal of this task is to minimize the MSE of the network between the realistic values and the prediction values, through TS-PSO (Fig. 3).

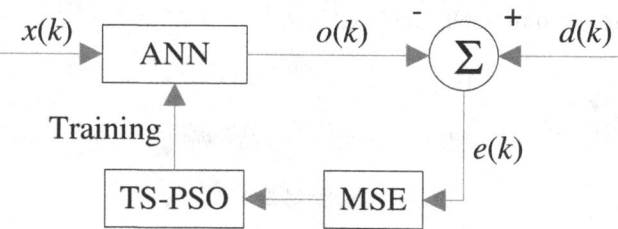

Fig. 3. TS-PSO for optimization of ANN, here MSE is used as the error measure

3   Experiments, Results and Discussions

The experiments were carried out on the platform of P4 IBM with 3.2 GHz processor and 8 GB RAM, running under Windows 7 operating system. The algorithm was in-house developed based on 64bit Matlab 2015a (The Mathworks ©). The programs can be run or tested on any computers where Matlab is available.

3.1 Dataset

The load and weather data was performed on the 09/2008–10/2009 historical load data of New York City (NYC). The interval of the load data is 10 min. The weather data includes the maximum and minimum temperatures of every day. The total days equals to 448, and the number of samples in a day equals to 144. Thus, total instances are 448*144 = 64512.

3.2 Statistical Analysis

Early stop (ES) is employed to prevent overfitting. Without ES, we will obtain the in-sample error estimation, which is unreliable for new instances. To perform ES, We choose 80 % of the whole dataset randomly as the training subset, 10 % the validation subset, and the rest as the test subset (See Table 3). That is, 51610 instances for training, 6451 instances for validation, and the rest 6451 instance for test.

Table 3. Dataset partition

	Training	Validation	Test
No. of instances	51610	6451	6451
Percentage	80 %	10 %	10 %

3.3 Comparison Results

The proposed TS-PSO-ANN was compared with GA-ANN [2], PSO-ANN [3], and BFO-ANN [16]. The maximum epochs are set to 2000. The experiment ran 10 times to avoid randomness. The results are shown in Table 4 w.r.t. different day types.

Table 4. Prediction comparison in terms of MSE

Algorithm	Day Type (0)	Day Type (1)	Day Type (2)
GA-ANN [2]	0.71	0.75	0.84
PSO-ANN [3]	0.65	0.66	**0.71**
BFO-ANN [16]	**0.63**	0.68	0.72
TS-PSO-ANN (Proposed)	**0.63**	**0.64**	**0.71**

We can see for day type of 0, the GA-ANN [2], PSO-ANN [3], BFO-ANN [16], and the proposed TS-PSO-ANN achieve MSE of 0.71, 0.65, 0.63, and 0.63, respectively. For day type of 1, the GA-ANN [2], PSO-ANN [3], BFO-ANN [16], and the proposed TS-PSO-ANN achieve MSE of 0.75, 0.66, 0.68, and 0.64, respectively. For day type of 2, the GA-ANN [2], PSO-ANN [3], BFO-ANN [16], and the proposed TS-PSO-ANN achieve MSE of 0.84, 0.71, 0.72, 0.71, respectively.

Two important facts are derived. First, the errors of TS-PSO-ANN are the least among the four algorithms, which demonstrated that the TS-PSO-ANN is more suitable in this study. Second, the MSEs of Day Type 0 are less than those of Day Type 1, which are less than those of Day Type 2, namely, the weekdays are the easiest to predict, next is workdays after holiday, the holidays are most difficult to predict.

4 Conclusions

A novel TS-PSO-ANN for short-term load forecast was proposed in this work. We demonstrated that the TS-PSO-ANN is better than GA-ANN, PSO-ANN, and BFO-ANN.

The future work mainly focuses on following points: (i) We will apply TS-PSO to other academic and industrial applications; (ii) We will test this proposed method on a larger dataset; (iii) Advanced PSO algorithms [24] and genetic pattern research [25] approach will be tested for short-term load forecast.

Acknowledgements. This paper was supported by NSFC (61273243, 51407095, 61503188), Natural Science Foundation of Jiangsu Province (BK20150982, BK20150983), Jiangsu Key Laboratory of 3D Printing Equipment and Manufacturing (BM2013006), Key Supporting Science and Technology Program (Industry) of Jiangsu Province (BE2012201, BE2013012-2, BE2014009-3), Program of Natural Science Research of Jiangsu Higher Education Institutions (13KJB460011, 14KJB520021), Special Funds for Scientific and Technological Achievement Transformation Project in Jiangsu Province (BA2013058), Nanjing Normal University Research Foundation for Talented Scholars (2013119XGQ0061, 2014119XGQ0080), Education Reform Project in NJNU (18122000090615).

References

1. Zhai, M.Y.: A new method for short-term load forecasting based on fractal interpretation and wavelet analysis. Int. J. Electr. Power Energy Syst. **69**, 241–245 (2015)
2. Moazzami, M., Hooshmand, R.A.: Short-term nodal congestion price forecasting in a large-scale power market using ANN with genetic optimization training. Turk. J. Electr. Eng. Comput. Sci. **20**, 751–768 (2012)
3. Quan, H., Srinivasan, D., Khosravi, A.: Short-term load and wind power forecasting using neural network-based prediction intervals. IEEE Trans. Neural Netw. Learn. Syst. **25**, 303–315 (2014)
4. Zjavka, L.: Short-term power demand forecasting using the differential polynomial neural network. Int. J. Comput. Intell. Syst. **8**, 297–306 (2015)
5. Hong, T., Wang, P.: Fuzzy interaction regression for short term load forecasting. Fuzzy Optim. Decis. Making **13**, 91–103 (2014)
6. Kazemi, S.M.R., Hoseini, M.M.S., Abbasian-Naghneh, S., Rahmati, S.H.A.: An evolutionary-based adaptive neuro-fuzzy inference system for intelligent short-term load forecasting. Int. Trans. Oper. Res. **21**, 311–326 (2014)
7. Chaturvedi, D.K., Sinha, A.P., Malik, O.P.: Short term load forecast using fuzzy logic and wavelet transform integrated generalized neural network. Int. J. Electr. Power Energy Syst. **67**, 230–237 (2015)
8. Wang, S., Ji, G., Phillips, P.: Fruit classification using computer vision and feedforward neural network. J. Food Eng. **143**, 167–177 (2014)

9. Guo, D., Zhang, Y., Xiang, Q., Li, Z.: Improved radio frequency identification indoor localization method via radial basis function neural network. Math. Probl. Eng. **2014**, Article ID 420482 (2014). doi:10.1155/2014/420482

10. Chandwani, V., Agrawal, V., Nagar, R.: Modeling slump of ready mix concrete using genetic algorithms assisted training of Artificial Neural Networks. Expert Syst. Appl. **42**, 885–893 (2015)

11. Zhang, Y., Wu, L.: Crop Classification by forward neural network with adaptive chaotic particle swarm optimization. Sensors **11**, 4721–4743 (2011)

12. Ganguly, S.: Multi-objective planning for reactive power compensation of radial distribution networks with unified power quality conditioner allocation using particle swarm optimization. IEEE Trans. Power Syst. **29**, 1801–1810 (2014)

13. Wang, S., Wu, L.: A novel method for magnetic resonance brain image classification based on adaptive chaotic PSO. Prog. Electromagnet. Res. **109**, 325–343 (2010)

14. Peyghami, M.R., Khanduzi, R.: Novel MLP neural network with hybrid tabu search algorithm. Neural Netw. World **23**, 255–270 (2013)

15. Dengiz, B., Alabas-Uslu, C., Dengiz, O.: A tabu search algorithm for the training of neural networks. J. Oper. Res. Soc. **60**, 282–291 (2009)

16. Zhang, Y., Wu, L., Wang, S.: Bacterial foraging optimization based neural network for short-term load forecasting. J. Comput. Inf. Syst. **6**, 2099–2105 (2010)

17. Chen, Y., Zhang, Y., Yang, J., Cao, Q., Yang, G., Chen, J., Shu, H., Luo, L., Coatrieux, J.-L., Feng, Q.: Curve-like structure extraction using minimal path propagation with back-tracing. IEEE Trans. Image Process. **99**, 1–16 (2015)

18. Yuan, H.C., Xiong, F.L., Huai, X.Y.: A method for estimating the number of hidden neurons in feed-forward neural networks based on information entropy. Comput. Electron. Agric. **40**, 57–64 (2003)

19. Zhang, Y., Wang, S., Phillips, P., Ji, G.: Binary PSO with mutation operator for feature selection using decision tree applied to spam detection. Knowl.-Based Syst. **64**, 22–31 (2014)

20. Wang, S., Zhang, Y., Dong, Z., Du, S., Ji, G., Yan, J., Yang, J., Wang, Q., Feng, C., Phillips, P.: Feed-forward neural network optimized by hybridization of PSO and ABC for abnormal brain detection. Int. J. Imaging Syst. Technol. **25**, 153–164 (2015)

21. Escobar, J.W., Linfati, R., Toth, P., Baldoquin, M.G.: A hybrid Granular Tabu Search algorithm for the Multi-Depot Vehicle Routing Problem. J. Heuristics **20**, 483–509 (2014)

22. Wu, L.: A hybrid TS-PSO optimization algorithm. J. Convergence Inf. Technol. **6**, 169–174 (2011)

23. Wang, J.X., Lu, J.M., Bie, Z.H., You, S.T., Cao, X.Y.: Long-term maintenance scheduling of smart distribution system through a PSO-TS algorithm. J. Appl. Math. 12 (2014)

24. Zhang, Y., Wang, S., Ji, G.: A comprehensive survey on particle swarm optimization algorithm and its applications. Math. Probl. Eng. **2015**, 38 (2015). doi:10.1155/2015/931256

25. Wang, S., Ji, G., Dong, Z.: Genetic pattern search and its application to brain image classification. Math. Probl. Eng. **2013**, 8 (2013). doi:10.1155/2013/580876

An Improved Differential Evolution Algorithm for Solving Absolute Value Equations

Guiying Ning[1(✉)] and Yongquan Zhou[2]

[1] Lushan College of Guangxi University Science and Technology,
Liuzhou 545616, Guangxi, China
guiyingning@126.com
[2] College of Math and Computer Science, Guangxi University for Nationalities,
Nanning 530006, Guangxi, China

Abstract. Absolute value equations $Ax - |x| = b$ are non-differentiable hard problems. Many linear and quadratic programming problems can ultimately be converted into absolute value equation problems so research on solving an absolute value problem has important practical and theoretical significance. An improved adaptive differential evolution algorithm was proposed to solve the absolute value equations in this paper. The algorithm combined global search ability and local search ability, using an adaptive quadratic mutation operation and crossover operation. Numerical results show that the improved algorithm can quickly find the solutions of these equations.

Keywords: Absolute value equations · Differential evolution algorithm · Mutation operation · Crossover operation · Adaptive

1 Introduction

The absolute value equations are

$$Ax - |x| = b \tag{1}$$

where $A \in R^{n \times n}$, $x, b \in R^n$; $|x|$ means taking the absolute value of each component of x. This problem is called an absolute value equation (absolute value equation, AVE). It is an important subclass of the absolute value matrix equations which was proposed by Rohn [1]. It is a typical non-differentiable optimization problem and has important research value. Reference [2] pointed out that an absolute value equation is equivalent to a knapsack feasibility problem; therefore, the absolute value Eq. (1) is an hard problem. Currently the research focuses on two aspects of its theory and algorithms, the main theoretical aspects of existence and uniqueness of the solution of the problem [3, 4]. The algorithms are mainly on how to build an effective solution method and its corresponding convergence analysis [5, 6]. Reference [7] converted the absolute value

Foundation Item: Education Department of Guangxi Zhuang Autonomous Region universities scientific research items (KY2015YB521).

© Springer International Publishing Switzerland 2016
J. Xie et al. (Eds.): HPCA 2015, LNCS 9576, pp. 38–47, 2016.
DOI: 10.1007/978-3-319-32557-6_4

equations into concave optimization problems for solving and found the local optima of (1). Reference [8] converted a knapsack feasibility problem into (1) for solving, obtaining better numerical results. Paper [9] proposed a generalized Newton method to solve absolute value equations. Their algorithm combines the characteristics of a semi-smooth Newton method and a smoothing Newton method, and they studied the convergence of the algorithm. Caccetta [6] gave a smoothing Newton method to solve the absolute value equations; his algorithms replaced the original absolute value function of the absolute value equations with a smooth function, and prove that the smoothing method has quadratic convergence, which are currently the best results of the theoretical study of the absolute value equations. In recent years, Huang and Xiu's research in the absolute value equations also yielded some results [10].

The current research on the absolute value equations involves mainly some traditional algorithms such as the penalty function method, fixed point method, and sub-gradient methods [11, 12]. Most of these methods are only in theory; there is little research on their application. Because general functions require their gradients, which is very difficult, research for some of the non-smooth optimization problems is worth exploring [13].

A swarm intelligence algorithm is a search algorithm that randomly generates an initial point of a feasible region through a series of operations (crossover and mutation selection) and finally converges to the approximate solution of a problem. Because the swarm intelligence algorithm begins from multiple points, it is possible to find a solution of the original problem as many as possible. A differential evolution algorithm (differential evolution Algorithm - DE) is proposed by Stron and Price [14, 15] in 1995 and it is a group difference algorithm based on randomized parallelization. The algorithm can adapt to a variety of nonlinear functions, has a strong parallel computing ability and other characteristics, and is widely used. In this paper, the basic differential evolution algorithm is easier to fall into locally a very excellent missing limit, and an improved differential evolution algorithm is put forward; the main change is the use of adaptive quadratic variation and crossover, simultaneously combining with mutation patterns which have the global search ability and the ability of local search. Numerical simulation results show that the improved algorithm can quickly determine the solution of an absolute value equation as much as possible, and the results are better than those by the existing algorithms.

2 Conversion Problems

Firstly, the presence of the solution of the problem (1) is given:

Theorem 1 [2]: For any b, if all of the singular values of A are more than 1 (or ($||A^{-1}|| < 1$)), then the AVE has a unique solution.

Proof: See literature [2].

Theorem 2 [16]: If $b < 0$ and $||A||_\infty < \frac{r}{2}$, here $\gamma = \min_i |b_i| / \max_i |b_i|$, then the AVE problem has 2^n solutions and the 2^n solutions were calculated by the formula of $x^* = D(AD - I)^{-1}$, here $D = diag(\pm 1, \pm 1, \cdots, \pm 1)$.

Proof: See literature [16].

In this paper, the problem of (1) is transformed into the following optimization problem:

$$\min f(x) = \frac{1}{2}(Ax - |x| - b)^T(Ax - |x| - b) \tag{2}$$

Finding the solution of problem (1) is equivalent to seeking the solution of the problem (2), because $f(x)$ is the non-smooth function, the problem (2) is a non-differentiable optimization problem too. In this paper, the adaptive function of algorithm will be set to (2) above.

3 Improved Adaptive Differential Evolution Algorithms

Differential evolution algorithm is based on real-coded evolutionary algorithm for optimizing the minimum of function, and its overall structure is similar to the genetic algorithm, compared with the basic genetic algorithm, the main difference lies in the mutation, variation is the main operating of the differential evolution algorithm, it uses population difference vector between individuals disturbance on individuals to achieve individual variation, effective use of population distribution characteristics, improving search capabilities, inadequate in terms of variation of genetic algorithm can well avoid; Also in the selection operation, differential evolution algorithm uses a greedy way of one to one out mechanism to select the best [17–19], if the objective function values of the new target individuals are better than old individuals, then the next generation will use a new individual replaced, otherwise the old self is still preserved.

3.1 The Basic Differential Evolution Algorithm Steps

3.1.1 Mutation Operation

In the differential evolution algorithm, the mutation is an important step which produces new individuals, mutation operations are based on the difference vector between individuals, the specific implementation as follow:

$$v_{ij}(t+1) = x_{ij}(t) + F(x_{p1,j}(t) - x_{p2,j}(t)) \tag{3}$$

In which: x_{p1} and x_{p2} are any two selected difference vector, p_1 and p_2 are an integer of $[1, M]$ in each other or the like, F is a factor of the variation, it is usually a real number of $[0,2]$. The main function is to control deviation variable amplification.$i = 1, 2, \cdots, M, j = 1, 2, \cdots, n$.

3.1.2 Crossover Operation

Crossover operation of the differential evolution algorithm is to mix the individuals of after variation with the current individuals. And according to certain rules to select which individuals will enter the next generation. Typically, it uses a crossover probability factor p_c to decide. If the random number $randl_{ij}$ generated by a random does not exceed pre-specified crossover probability p_c, then a new individual v_i into the next generation, otherwise x_i into the next generation, crossover operation is as follows:

$$u_{ij}(t+1) = \begin{cases} v_{ij}(t+1) & randl_{ij} \leq p_c \\ x_{ij}(t) & randl_{ij} > p_c \end{cases} \tag{4}$$

Where p_c is the crossover probability factors, usually taking a real number of $(0, 1]$, $randl_{ij}$ is a random number of $[0, 1]$.

3.1.3 Selection Operation

To decide the vector after crossing whether to become the next generation members, the differential evolution algorithm uses "greedy" search strategy, it will be compared with the current population of the vector X_i. If the target fitness value of U_i is better than the X_i, then choose the vector U_i as the offspring after crossover; otherwise, directly to X_i as offspring. The operation of the selection operation is as follows:

$$X_i(t+1) = \begin{cases} U_i(t+1) & if \quad J(U_i(t+1)) < J(X_i(t)) \\ X_i(t) & otherwise \end{cases} \tag{5}$$

3.2 Adaptive Parameter Settings

For a global optimization algorithm, the impact of control parameters is great, if there is a good variation factor F and crossover factor CR, then solving the results are better. The basic differential evolution algorithm variability factor $F \in [0, 2]$ is a real constant factor, which determines the magnification error vector, F is bigger, stronger global search capability, but slow convergence. Cross factor $CR \in [0, 1]$ is a real number; it controls a vector parameter from the mutation vector randomly selected instead of the original probability vector, CR is larger, faster convergence, but easily trapped in local excellent. Research to date indicates, $F \in [0.4, 1]$ is more effective. $F = 0.5$ is usual a better choice. In order both to maintain good global search capability, but also improve the convergence speed and accuracy. To the non-smooth problems which have several solutions, in this paper, the adaptive mutation and crossover operations to form quadratic mutation and crossover, because quadratic function changes slowly than the linear function change between $[0, 1]$, in the case of the new mutation in this paper, it is more conducive to global search during the early and accurate local search late, the adaptive mutation operator and crossover operator as follows:

Adaptive quadratic mutation operator: $F = 0.8 - \left(\frac{t}{t+T}\right)^2$,

Adaptive quadratic crossover operator: $CR = \left(\frac{t}{T}\right)^2$.

In which t is the current evolution generation, T is the maximum evolution generation, in this setting, mutation operator decreases in $[0.55, 1]$ with the evolution generation increase, crossover operator exponential increases in $(0, 1]$, this setting can guarantee early evolutionary algorithm has strong global search ability, to speed up the convergence late.

3.3   Mutation Operator Settings

For the individual x_i^t of each time t differential evolution algorithm mutates to get its corresponding new individual v_i^{t+1}, common mutation operation are:

DE/rand/1/bin: $v_{ij}(t+1) = x_{ij}(t) + F(x_{p1,j}(t) - x_{p2,j}(t))$

DE/best/1/bin: $v_{ij}(t+1) = x_{best,j}(t) + F(x_{p1,j}(t) - x_{p2,j}(t))$

The former variation is conducive to maintaining population diversity, and thus it has strong global search capability and slow convergence, the latter variation has strong local search ability, high accuracy, fast convergence, but it will speed up the algorithm may be trapped in local excellent. Combined with the characteristics of these two variations, this paper presents a new mutation strategy, the specific operation as follows:

$$v_{ij}(t+1) = \lambda x_{ij}(t) + (1 - \lambda)x_{best,j}(t) + F(x_{p1,j}(t) - x_{p2,j}(t)) \qquad (6)$$

In which $\lambda \in [0,1]$ and $\lambda = \frac{T-t}{T}$, t is the current evolution generation, T is the maximum evolution generation.

In the searching process, λ linear change gradually from one to zero, when $\lambda = 1$, the formula becomes DE/rand/1/bin, when $\lambda = 0$, the formula becomes DE/best/1/bin, In the initial stages of this evolutionary algorithm has strong global search capability, as many find the global optimum, and has strong local search ability at a later stage, to improve the algorithm accuracy and convergence rate, which not only guarantee algorithm has strong global search capability, but also to ensure the convergence speed and accuracy.

In addition, the individual elimination method is used in this paper, after the completion of an evolution, the bubbling method is used to compare the distance between individuals, when the distance of the individuals is less than a given value ε, removing the neighboring individuals and regenerating new individuals into the next generation of evolution in the feasible region, the purpose of doing so is to remove the fitness value similar point, it can find a different solution as possible.

3.4   Improved Adaptive Differential Evolution Algorithm Process

Step 1: Determine the population size N, the biggest evolution generation T, the distance ε between the individual need to meet;

Step 2: Randomly generated initial population;

Step 3: Calculation of population fitness of each individual, to choose the best individual;

Step 4: Running improved adaptive mutation and adaptive crossover;

Step 5: After cross, calculating the fitness of new individuals and running selection operation;

Step 6: Comparing new generation distance between any two individuals, when an individual is less than a given distance ε, regenerating new individuals to replace the current individual;

Step 7: Determine whether the termination condition is reached, and if so, evolution is terminated, this results as the best individual solution output; otherwise transferred step 8;

Step 8: evolution generation $t = t + 1$, go to Step 3.

Improved algorithm flowchart in this article is below:

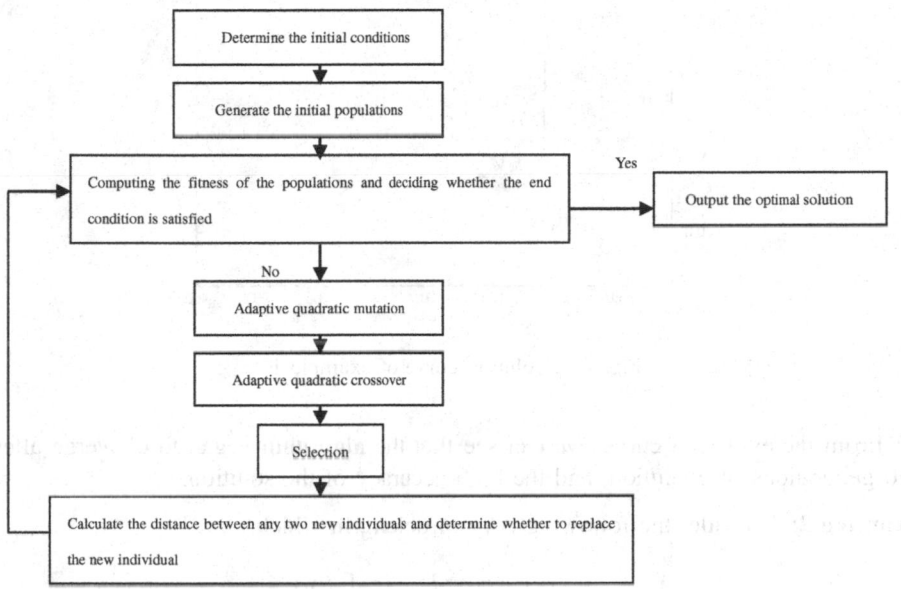

Algorithm Evolution Figure

4 Numerical Experiments

In the algorithm of this paper, population size N is taken as five times of variable, $\varepsilon = 10^{-4}$ is the distance between the individual, running the following example 20, to get the best results, and average evolution graph showing as follows:

Example 1: Consider the following AVE problem, where

$$ A = \begin{bmatrix} 2 & 1 \\ 1 & 3 \end{bmatrix}, \ b = \begin{bmatrix} 2 \\ 3 \end{bmatrix} $$

Since the singular values of the matrix is greater than 1, so the existence of a unique solution of the problem AVE.

This algorithm to obtain the solution is: [1.0000, 1.0002], the real solution is [1, 1]; the following curve figure (Fig. 1) shows the results of the improved algorithm (MDE) in this article run 20 times:

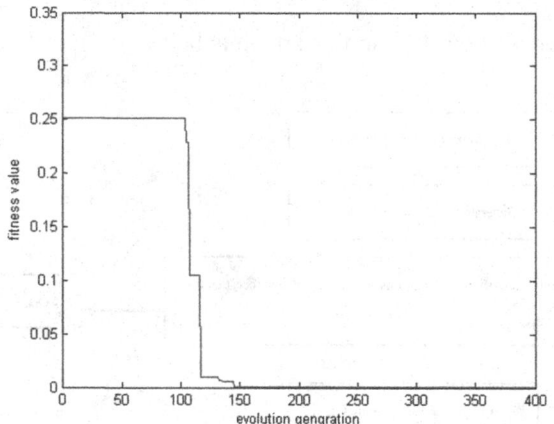

Fig. 1. Evolution curve of example 1

From the evolution curve, we can see that the algorithm began to converge after 150 generations of evolution, and the high accuracy of the solution.

Example 2: Consider the following AVE problem, in which:

$$A = \begin{bmatrix} 0.1 & 0.02 \\ 0.2 & 0.01 \end{bmatrix}, \quad b = \begin{bmatrix} -1 \\ -2 \end{bmatrix}$$

According to the literature [16] concluded, there are $2^2 = 4$ solutions of this problem. And the forms of the solutions are:

$$\begin{bmatrix} + \\ + \end{bmatrix}, \quad \begin{bmatrix} + \\ - \end{bmatrix}, \quad \begin{bmatrix} - \\ + \end{bmatrix}, \quad \begin{bmatrix} - \\ - \end{bmatrix},$$

This algorithm in this paper was run 20 times, all solutions of the algorithm as follows:

$$x^1 = \begin{bmatrix} 1.4283 \\ 1.4279 \end{bmatrix}, \quad x^2 = \begin{bmatrix} -0.7685 \\ -0.7683 \end{bmatrix}, \quad x^3 = \begin{bmatrix} -0.9281 \\ 1.1341 \end{bmatrix}, \quad x^4 = \begin{bmatrix} 1.1343 \\ -0.9281 \end{bmatrix}$$

Algorithms evolution curve and find solutions in Figs. 2 and 3:

This example illustrates the algorithm convergence speed, stability, algorithms evolved about 2000 generations to begin to converge to the optimal solution, and high accuracy solution.

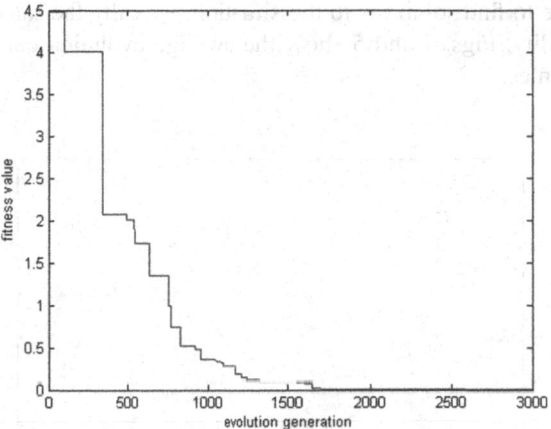

Fig. 2. Evolution curve of example 2

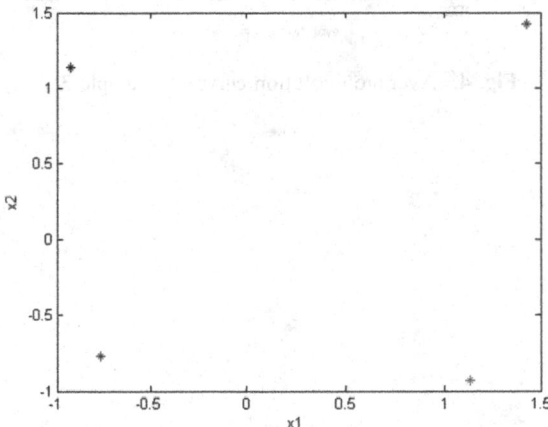

Fig. 3. The algorithm to find the solutions (4)

Example 3: Consider the following AVE problem, in which:

$$A = \begin{bmatrix} 0.01 & 0.02 & 0.03 \\ 0.02 & 0.03 & 0.01 \\ 0.03 & 0.02 & 0.01 \end{bmatrix}, \quad b = \begin{bmatrix} -1 \\ -2 \\ -3 \end{bmatrix}$$

According to the literature [16] concluded, there are $2^3 = 8$ solutions of this problem. This algorithm runs 20 times, found seven solutions, the algorithm is currently appearing up to find solutions to the literature [16] found 6 solutions, and the algorithm in this paper can find 8 solutions, and fast convergence rate. In the run

20 times, each time to find solutions to the situation basically the same, indicating that the algorithm stability, Figs. 4 and 5 show the average evolution curve and situations after running 20 times:

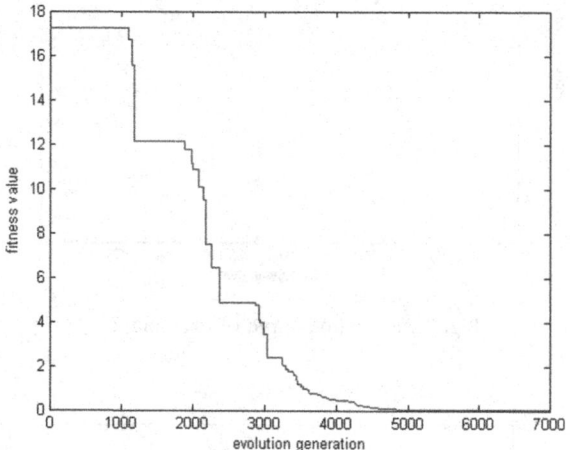

Fig. 4. Average evolution curve of example 3

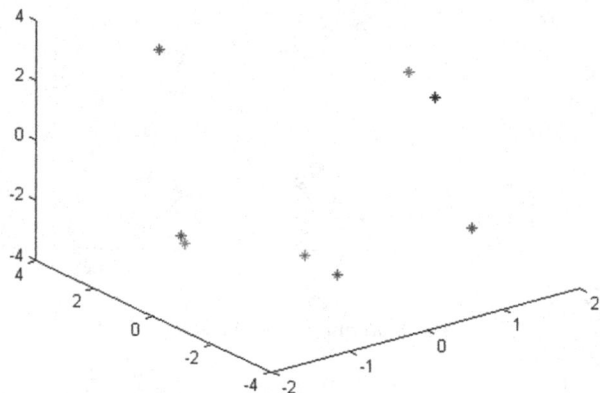

Fig. 5. The algorithm to find the solutions (8)

Through the above typical examples: the existence of multiple solutions can be seen, the improved quadratic crossover and mutation differential evolution algorithm has strong stability, due to a quadratic function changes slowly, high search precision, it can be adequately local search in late and find all the solutions of the problem. Experiments show that the proposed algorithm is an effective method for absolute value equations.

5 Conclusions

According to the basic differential evolution algorithm is easy to fall into a partial very excellent characteristics. An improved adaptive differential evolution algorithm was proposed, it is used to solve non-differentiable hard problem, and numerical results show that the improved algorithm has strong stability, fast convergence, the existence of multiple solutions for the absolute value equations able to find all the solutions of the problem, it is an effective way to solve this kind of problem.

References

1. Rohn, J.: Systems of linear interval equations. J. Linear Algebra Appl. **126**, 39–78 (1989)
2. Mangasarian, O.L., Meyer, R.: R: Absolute value equations. Linear Algebra Appl. **419**(2), 359–367 (2006)
3. Prokopyev, O.: On equivalent reformulations for absolute value equations. Comput. Optim. Appl. **44**(3), 363–372 (2009)
4. Rohn, J.: A residual existence theorem for linear equations. J. Optim. Lett. **4**(2), 287–292 (2010)
5. Wei, Q.: Absolute Value Equations Generalized Newton Algorithm and its Convergence. Beijing Jiao tong University, Beijing (2009)
6. Caccetta, L., Qu, B., Zhou, G.: A globally and quadratic ally convergent method for absolute value equations. Comput. Optim. Appl. **48**(1), 45–58 (2010)
7. Mangasarian, O.L.: Absolute value programming. Comput. Optim. Appl. **36**(1), 43–53 (2006)
8. Mangasarian, O.L.: Knapsack feasibility as an absolute value equation solvable by successive linear programming. Optim. Lett. **3**(2), 161–170 (2009)
9. Zhang, C., Wei, Q.J.: Global and finite convergence of a generalized Newton method for absolute value equations. J. Optim. Theory Appl. **142**(2), 391–403 (2009)
10. Hu, S., Huang, Z.: A note on absolute value equations. J. Optim. Appl. **48**(1), 45–58 (2011)
11. Liu, J.: An Integral decent method for non-smooth optimization. J. Appl. Math. **13**(4), 444–455 (1990)
12. Lin, Y.: Projection Sub gradient method for a Non-smooth Optimization with Constraints. J. Adv. Math. Comput. Math. **12**(3), 270–283 (1990)
13. Ou, Y.: Non-smooth Optimization Algorithm and its progress. Nat. Sci. J. Hainan Univ. **16**(2), 175–177 (1998)
14. Storn, R., Price, K.: Differential evolution—a simple and efficient adaptive scheme for global optimization over continuous spaces. J. Int. Comput. Sci. Inst. **12**(3), 4–7 (1995)
15. Storn, R., Price, K.: Differential evolution—a simple and efficient adaptive scheme for global optimization over continuous spaces. J. Glob. Optim. **11**(4), 341–359 (1997)
16. Yong, L., Liu, S., Tuo, S., et al.: Improved harmony search algorithm for the absolute value equation. J. Nat. Sci. Heilongjiang Univ. **6**(3), 322 (2013)
17. Yang, Q., Liang, C., Xue, Y.: Differential evolution review. J. Pattern Recogn. Artif. Intell. **21**(4), 506–511 (2008)
18. Duan, Y., Gao, Y.: Based on differential evolution particle swarm algorithm. J. Comput. Simul. **26**(6), 212–245 (2009)
19. Yu, Q., Zhao, H.: BP neural network prediction model based on differential evolution algorithm and its application. Comput. Eng. Appl. **44**(14), 246–248 (2008)

Tea Category Classification Based on Feed-Forward Neural Network and Two-Dimensional Wavelet Entropy

Xingxing Zhou[1,2,3], Guangshuai Zhang[3,4], Zhengchao Dong[5], Shuihua Wang[1,6(✉)], and Yudong Zhang[1(✉)]

[1] School of Computer Science and Technology, Nanjing Normal University, 1 Wenyuan, Nanjing 210023, Jiangsu, China
zhangyudong@njnu.edu.cn
[2] Key Laboratory of Statistical Information Technology and Data Mining, State Statistics Bureau, Chengdu 610225, Sichuan, China
[3] Jiangsu Key Laboratory of 3D Printing Equipment and Manufacturing, Nanjing 210042, Jiangsu, China
[4] Key Laboratory of Symbolic Computation and Knowledge Engineering of Ministry of Education, Jilin University, Changchun 130012, Jilin, China
[5] Translational Imaging Division and MRI Unit, New York State Psychiatric Institute, Columbia University, New York, NY 10032, USA
[6] School of Electronic Science and Engineering, Nanjing University, Nanjing 210046, Jiangsu, China
wangshuihua@njnu.edu.cn

Abstract. (**Aim**) Tea plays a significant role because of its high value throughout the world. Computer vision techniques were successfully employed for rapid identification of teas. (**Method**) In our work, we present a computer assisted discrimination system on the basis of two steps: (i) two-dimensional wavelet-entropy for feature extraction; (ii) the feedforward Neural Network (FNN) for classification. Specifically, the wavelet entropy features were fed into a FNN classifier. (**Results**) The 10 runs of 75 images of three categories showed that the average accuracy achieved **90.70 %**. The sensitivities of green, Oolong, and black tea are 92.80 %, 84.60 %, and 96.30 %, respectively. (**Conclusions**) It was easily observed that the proposed classifier can distinguish tea categories with satisfying performances, which was competitive with recent existing systems.

Keywords: Tea classification · Two dimensional wavelet entropy · Feed-forward neural network

1 Introduction

Tea category classification is a main problem in the production and monitoring of tea-leaves [1, 2]. Traditional tea production factories are now facing the problem of converting human classification to computer-aided automatic classification, since it can save the human labor.

However, high volume of tea data obtained by camera will lead to the curse of dimensionality. Traditional method is to extract conventional image features, such as

© Springer International Publishing Switzerland 2016
J. Xie et al. (Eds.): HPCA 2015, LNCS 9576, pp. 48–54, 2016.
DOI: 10.1007/978-3-319-32557-6_5

color histogram [3], edge detection [4], blob detection [5], ridge detection [6], etc. Recently, wavelet entropy was proposed as a novel global image feature descriptor. It calculates the entropy over wavelet coefficients of a given image. Now the two-dimensional wavelet entropy (2D-WE) has obtained satisfying results in many fields such as pathological brain detection [7], cancel cell detection [8], fault diagnosis [9], abnormal MR brain detection [10], etc. In this study, we aimed to apply wavelet entropy in the tea category classification.

Next problem is the classification. At present, there are a large number of classifiers, such as feedforward neural network [11], support vector machine [12], extreme learning machine [13], naive Bayes classifier (NBC) [14], and decision tree [15]. We used FNN in our tea category classification system, since FNN is simple and effective.

The proposed methodology for the tea classification is a combination of 2D-WE and FNN. Both individual technique is proven successful. Next Sect. 2 offers the materials and methodology. Section 3 presents the experiments and results. The concluding remarks are given in final section.

2   Materials and Methodology

2.1   Two-Dimensional Wavelet-Entropy

The proposed two-dimensional wavelet entropy (2D-WE) [16–18] consists of two steps: (i) discrete wavelet transforms, (ii) entropy calculation.

Figure 1 shows the diagram of 2D-WE. Here Fig. 1(a) shows a notion of a tea image, Fig. 1(b) shows its 1-level decomposition with four subbands, Fig. 1(c) shows its 2-level decomposition with seven subbands, and Fig. 1(d) shows the seven-element entropy vector.

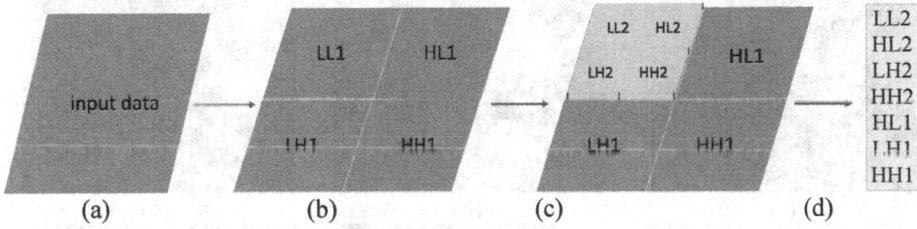

Fig. 1. Diagram of 2D-WE.

2.2   FNN

Suppose there are n input features, the feed-forward neural network (FNN) will initiate a three-layer neural network—input layer, hidden layer, and output layer [19–21]. The weights are assigned to the links of between input and hidden layers, and the links of between hidden and output layers (See Fig. 2). Back propagation (BP) algorithm [22–24] was used as the training algorithm.

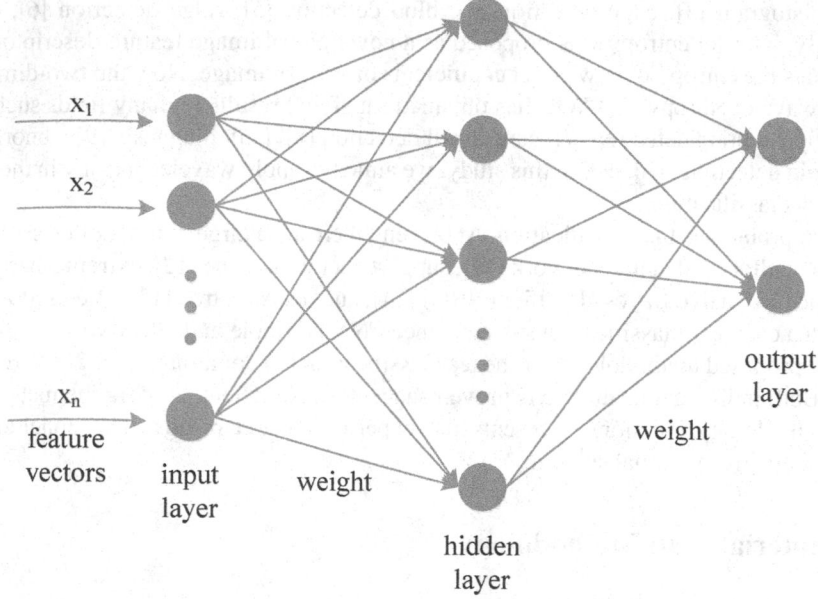

Fig. 2. Diagram of a FNN ($x_1, x_2, ..., x_n$ are input vectors)

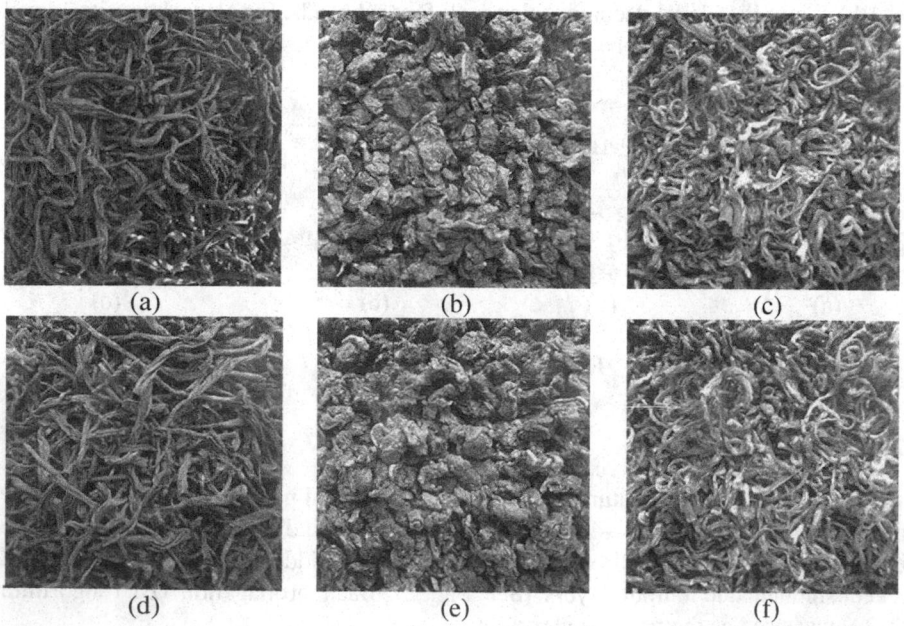

Fig. 3. Examples of three categories of tea: (a & d) black tea, (b & e) Oolong tea, and (c & f) Green tea

2.3 Materials

Our tea dataset consist of 75 images that were captured by a common digital camera. Each category (green, Oolong, and black tea) contains 25 images. The samples of each category are shown in Fig. 3.

3 Experiments, Results, and Discussions

All the programs were developed by ourselves using Matlab2014a. The programs were run on an IBM desktop, which is of 3 GHz Intel Core i3 processor and 4 GB RAM.

3.1 Wavelet Decomposition

In this experiment, we performed 2-level 2D-WE to each tea image. At this step, seven features were extracted. Figure 4(a) shows the original tea image. Figure 4(b) shows the 1-level decomposition result. Figure 4(c) shows the final 2-level 2D-WE result.

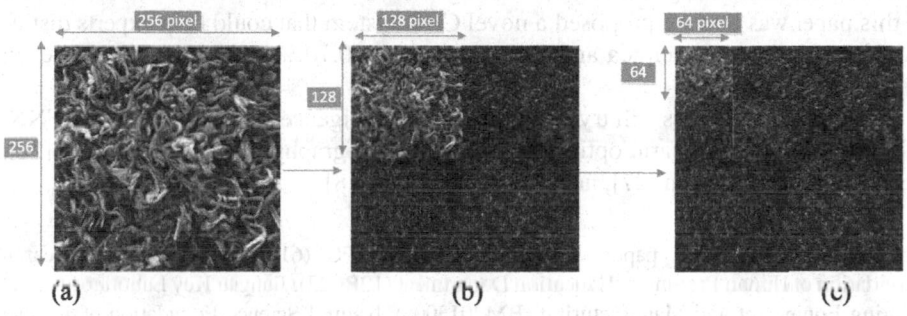

Fig. 4. A 2D-WE of a tea image

3.2 Classification Result

53 images were used for training, 11 images for validation, and the left 11 images for test. We run our method 10 times. Each time, the training, validation, and test sets are divided randomly. We report the average results in following Table 1. In addition, Fig. 5 shows a typical run result.

Table 1. Average Results on 10 independent runs

Method	Sensitivity (Green)	Sensitivity (Oolong)	Sensitivity (Black)	Overall Accuracy
WE + FNN	92.80 %	84.60 %	96.30 %	90.70 %

Figure 5 and Table 1 show that the proposed WE + FNN yielded excellent result on tea image classification. Particularly, the images of Oolong tea are easily misclassified with sensitivity of 84.60 %.

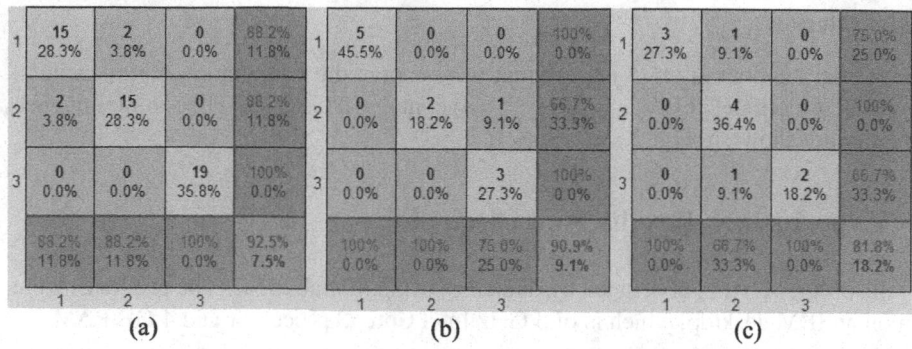

Fig. 5. The result on (a) training, (b) validation, and (c) test of 1 typical run

4   Conclusions

This study proposed a new approach on the basis of 2D-WE and FNN, for the classification of the black tea, green tea and Oolong tea from the image data. The contribution of this paper was that we proposed a novel CAD system that could help experts distinguish the black tea, green tea and Oolong tea with 90.70 % accuracy and only seven features.

The future researches will try to apply swarm intelligence methods to train the FNN. We will test particle swarm optimization [25], biogeography-based optimization [26], hybrid genetic algorithm [27], and firefly algorithm [28].

Acknowledgment. This paper was supported by NSFC (61503188), Science Research Foundation of Hunan Provincial Education Department (12B023), Jiangsu Key Laboratory of 3D Printing Equipment and Manufacturing (BM2013006), Natural Science Foundation of Jiangsu Province (BK20150983), Open Fund of Key Laboratory of Statistical information technology and data mining, State Statistics Bureau, (SDL201608), Open Fund of Key laboratory of symbolic computation and knowledge engineering of ministry of education, Jilin University (93K172016K17), Open Project Program of the State Key Lab of CAD&CG, Zhejiang University (A1616), Ordinary University Graduate Student Scientific Research Innovation Projects of Jiangsu Province (KYLX15_0768).

Conflict of Interest. We have no conflicts of interest to disclose with regard to the subject matter of this paper.

References

1. Choi, S.J., Park, S.Y., Park, J.S., Park, S.K., Jung, M.Y.: Contents and compositions of policosanols in green tea (Camellia sinensis) leaves. Food Chem. **204**, 94–101 (2016)
2. Diniz, P., Barbosa, M.F., Milanez, K., Pistonesi, M.F., de Araujo, M.C.U.: Using UV-V is spectroscopy for simultaneous geographical and varietal classification of tea infusions simulating a home-made tea cup. Food Chem. **192**, 374–379 (2016)

3. Yuvaraj, D., Hariharan, S.: Content-based image retrieval based on integrating region segmentation and colour histogram. Int. Arab J. Inf. Technol. **13**, 203–207 (2016)
4. Shahverdi, R., Tavana, M., Ebrahimnejad, A., Zahedi, K., Omranpour, H.: An improved method for edge detection and image segmentation using fuzzy cellular automata. Cybern. Syst. **47**, 161–179 (2016)
5. Zhou, H.L., Llewellyn, L., Wei, L., Creighton, D., Nahavandi, S.: Marine object detection using background modelling and blob analysis. In: 2015 IEEE International Conference on Systems, Man and Cybernetics, pp. 430–435. IEEE Computer Society, Los Alamitos (2015)
6. Anada, K., Kikuchi, T., Koka, S., Miyadera, Y., Yaku, T.: A method of ridge detection in triangular dissections generated by homogeneous rectangular dissections. In: Lee, R. (ed.) Software Engineering, Artificial Intelligence, Networking and Parallel/Distributed Computing 2015, vol. 612, pp. 131–142. Springer, Heidelberg (2016)
7. Sun, P., Wang, S., Phillips, P., Zhang, Y.: Pathological brain detection based on wavelet entropy and Hu moment invariants. Bio-Med. Mater. Eng. **26**, 1283–1290 (2015)
8. Korkmaz, S.A.: Diagnosis of cervical cancer cell taken from scanning electron and atomic force microscope images of the same patients using discrete wavelet entropy energy and Jensen Shannon, Hellinger, Triangle Measure classifier. Spectrochim. Acta Part A Mol. Biomol. Spectrosc. **160**, 39–49 (2016)
9. Hu, K.T., Liu, Z.G., Lin, S.S.: Wavelet entropy-based traction inverter open switch fault diagnosis in high-speed railways. Entropy **18**, 19 (2016)
10. Zhou, X.X., Zhang, Y.D., Ji, G.L., Yang, J.Q., Dong, Z.C., Wang, S.H., Zhang, G.S., Phillips, P.: Detection of abnormal MR brains based on wavelet entropy and feature selection. IEEJ Trans. Electr. Electron. Eng. **11**, 364–373 (2016)
11. Wang S, Dong Z, Du, S., Ji, G., Yan, J., Yang, J., Wang, Q., Feng, C., Phillips, P.: Feed-forward neural network optimized by hybridization of PSO and ABC for abnormal brain detection. Int. J. Imaging Syst. Technol. **25**, 153–164 (2015)
12. Wang, S., Yang, X., Zhang, Y., Phillips, P., Yang, J., Yuan, T.-F.: Identification of green, Oolong and black teas in China via wavelet packet entropy and fuzzy support vector machine. Entropy **17**, 6663–6682 (2015)
13. Chandar, S.K., Sumathi, M., Sivanadam, S.N.: Forecasting gold prices based on extreme learning machine. Int. J. Comput. Commun. Control **11**, 372–380 (2016)
14. Zhou, X., Wang, S., Xu, W., Ji, G., Phillips, P., Sun, P., Zhang, Y.: Detection of pathological brain in MRI scanning based on wavelet-entropy and Naive Bayes classifier. In: Ortuño, F., Rojas, I. (eds.) IWBBIO 2015, Part I. LNCS, vol. 9043, pp. 201–209. Springer, Heidelberg (2015)
15. Turnbull, O., Lawry, J., Lowenberg, M., Richards, A.: A cloned linguistic decision tree controller for real-time path planning in hostile environments. Fuzzy Sets Syst. **293**, 1–29 (2016)
16. Zhang, Y., Wang, S., Dong, Z., Phillips, P., Ji, G., Yang, J.: Pathological brain detection in magnetic resonance imaging scanning by wavelet entropy and hybridization of biogeography-based optimization and particle swarm optimization. Prog. Electromagnet. Res. **152**, 41–58 (2015)
17. Schumann, A., Kralisch, C., Bar, K.-J.: Spectral decomposition of pupillary unrest using wavelet entropy. In: Annual International Conference of the IEEE Engineering in Medicine and Biology Society. IEEE Engineering in Medicine and Biology Society, pp. 6154–6157 (2015)
18. Langley, P.: Wavelet entropy as a measure of ventricular beat suppression from the electrocardiogram in atrial fibrillation. Entropy **17**, 6397–6411 (2015)

19. Ji, G., Yang, J., Wu, J., Wei, L.: Fruit classification by wavelet-entropy and feedforward neural network trained by fitness-scaled chaotic ABC and biogeography-based optimization. Entropy **17**, 5711–5728 (2015)
20. Lahmiri, S.: Interest rate next-day variation prediction based on hybrid feedforward neural network, particle swarm optimization, and multiresolution techniques. Phys. A **444**, 388–396 (2016)
21. Asadi, R., Asadi, M., Kareem, S.A.: An efficient semisupervised feedforward neural network clustering. AI EDAM-Artif. Intell. Eng. Des. Anal. Manuf. **30**, 1–15 (2016)
22. Zhang, Y., Wu, L.: Stock market prediction of S&P 500 via combination of improved BCO approach and BP neural network. Expert Syst. Appl. **36**, 8849–8854 (2009)
23. Doh, J., Lee, S.U., Lee, J.: Back-propagation neural network-based approximate analysis of true stress-strain behaviors of high-strength metallic material. J. Mech. Sci. Technol. **30**, 1233–1241 (2016)
24. Khan, Y.: Partial discharge pattern analysis using PCA and back-propagation artificial neural network for the estimation of size and position of metallic particle adhering to spacer in GIS. Electr. Eng. **98**, 29–42 (2016)
25. Ji, G.: A comprehensive survey on particle swarm optimization algorithm and its applications. Math. Prob. Eng. **2015**, 38 (2015)
26. Zhang, Y., Phillips, P., Wang, S., Ji, G., Yang, J., Wu, J.: Fruit classification by biogeography-based optimization and feedforward neural network. Expert Syst. **33**(3), 239–253 (2016)
27. Lu, S., Wang, S., Zhang, Y.: A note on the weight of inverse complexity in improved hybrid genetic algorithm. J. Med. Syst. **40**, 1–2 (2016)
28. Zhang, Y., Wu, L., Wang, S.: Solving two-dimensional HP model by firefly algorithm and simplified energy function. Math. Prob. Eng. **13**, 1–9 (2013)

Development of Krylov and AMG Linear Solvers for Large-Scale Sparse Matrices on GPUs

Bo Yang, Hui Liu, and Zhangxin Chen[✉]

Department of Chemical and Petroleum Engineering,
University of Calgary, Calgary, Canada
{yang6,hui.j.liu,zhachen}@ucalgary.ca

Abstract. This paper introduces our work on developing Krylov subspace and AMG solvers on NVIDIA GPUs. As SpMV is a crucial part for these iterative methods, SpMV algorithms for a single GPU and multiple GPUs are implemented. A HEC matrix format and a communication mechanism are established. Also, a set of specific algorithms for solving preconditioned systems in parallel environments are designed, including ILU(k), RAS and parallel triangular solvers. Based on these work, several Krylov solvers and AMG solvers are developed. According to numerical experiments, favorable acceleration performance is obtained from our Krylov solver and AMG solver under various parameter conditions.

Keywords: Krylov subspace · GPU · SpMV · ILU · RAS · GMRES · AMG

1 Introduction

Iterative algorithms have widely applications in kinds of scientific computing fields, such as the reservoir simulation [1]. For large-scale sparse linear systems, Krylov subspace and AMG algorithms are commonly used. Krylov subspace algorithms include the GMRES (Generalized Minimal Residual), CG (Conjugate Gradient) and BiCGSTAB (Biconjugate Gradient Stabilized), etc. These algorithms are available to general matrices [2,3]. Preconditioners are always employed to optimize the performance of an iterative algorithm and many efficient proecondtioners have been developed [4–6,20]. We have developed the Krylov subspace algorithms with ILU preconditioners. Many researchers have devoted their efforts into designing AMG solvers which is specific for symmetric positive definite matrices. Ruge and Stüben designed the RS (Ruge-Stüben) coarsening strategy and developed a classical AMG solver which is the foundation of developing other AMG solvers [7–11]. The parallel coarsening strategy CLJP was proposed by Luby, Jones and Plassmann [12,13]. We have also developed the AMG algorithm with a series of smoothers, coarsening operators and prolongation operators.

GPU (Graphics Processing Unit) computing emerges as an acceleration technique for image displaying. However, it has more and more utility in other scientific computing disciplines. Zhang et al. completed some professional performance

© Springer International Publishing Switzerland 2016
J. Xie et al. (Eds.): HPCA 2015, LNCS 9576, pp. 55–72, 2016.
DOI: 10.1007/978-3-319-32557-6_6

analysis about GPUs [14]. A NVIDIA Tesla K40 which has 2880 CUDA cores and a peak performance of 1.43 TFlops (Base Clocks) in double precision has greater performance than an Intel Core i7-5960X with 8 cores and 16 threads which has a typical peak performance of 385 GFlops [15,16]. A NVIDIA Tesla K40 also has 288 G/sec memory speed which is much faster than the speed 68 GB/s of an Intel Core i7-5960X [15,16]. As GPU has great priority in parallel computing, we have designed and developed our iterative algorithms on GPUs.

SpMV (sparse matrix-vector multiplication) is a core part for iterative algorithms. For a large and sparse matrix, it is necessary to partition it into sub matrices for GPU computation. The METIS partition method is adopted in our algorithms [17]. Because data communication is unavoidable for SpMV implementation on multiple GPUs, we have designed a specific communication mechanism for partition matrices to share vector data among different GPUs. In order to make full use of the characteristic of GPU memory access, we adopted a HEC matrix format which is more friendly to the SpMV algorithm. A NVIDIA GPU platform provides high parallel capability depending on its hundreds of fine CUDA cores. An algorithm must be designed as a parallel algorithm to run on the CUDA cores. RAS (Restricted Additive Schwarz) proposed by Cai et al. is adopted in our algorithms to improve the parallel structure of a preconditioner matrix [18]. Because the ILU preconditioners and AMG smoothers all need to solve triangular systems, we implemented a parallel triangular solver on GPUs [19]. It is based on the level schedule method [2,21]. In this research, we designed a set of numerical experiments to test our algorithms from different aspects. The experiment results and analysis are given in the experiment section.

The layout of this paper is presented as follows: In Sect. 2, the matrix format, SpMV, vector operations, ILU (k), RAS, parallel triangular solver, Krylov subspace algorithms and AMG algorithms are introduced. In Sect. 3, the numerical experiments are presented and analyzed. In Sect. 4, conclusions are given.

2   GPU Computation

2.1   Matrix Format

Several matrix formats are presented in this section. They are ELL, HYB and HEC. The ELL format is provided in ELLPACK [22]. Figure 1 shows the ELL's structure consisting of two parts. We can see the two parts are both regular and have the same dimensions. Regular storage has a high speed for data access. However, it is not wise to store a large-scale sparse matrix in such a format as lots of storage spaces are always wasted. For instance, if there are a large number of nonzero entries in one row, the other rows must maintain the same size of entries most of which are zero. In order to make the limited memory space be used efficiently, N. Bell and M. Garland suggested a hybrid matrix format named HYB (Hybrid of ELL and COO). An original matrix is split into two parts. One part is regular and the remain part is irregular. The COO format is used to store the irregular part. It has three one-dimensional arrays illustrated in Fig. 2. The HYB format has good average performance. In our research, we adopt another hybrid format called HEC which saved the irregular part in a CSR format shown in Fig. 3. It also contains three one-dimensional arrays. Ap is used for storing the start position of each row. Ax and Aj have the same length and used for storing the entry data and column indices, respectively.

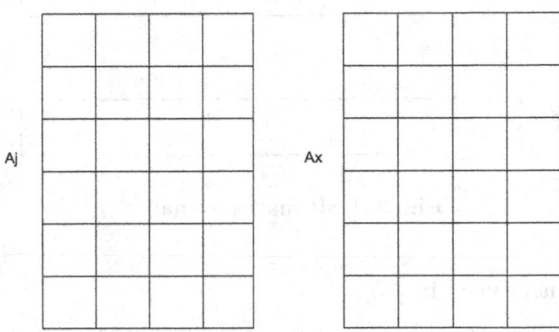

Fig. 1. ELL matrix format

Fig. 2. COO matrix format

According to the mathematic method of SpMV, it is always calculated based on the column vectors. This can be explained by Eq. (1). Thereby, it's better for us to store the entries in the computer column by column. The GPU architecture provides a wrap concept to execute CUDA cores. That means 32 threads are bounded to be executed together. So the stride of the ELL part should be a multiple of 32 to acquire enhanced parallel performance. In our algorithms, we set it as 256 or other multiples. Another problem is how to decide the boundary between the ELL and CSR. We use a recommended value 20 whose theoretical

Fig. 3. CSR matrix format

explanation are introduced in [23].

$$\begin{pmatrix} A_{11} & A_{12} & \cdots & A_{1n} \\ A_{21} & A_{22} & \cdots & A_{2n} \\ \vdots & \vdots & \ddots & \vdots \\ A_{n1} & A_{n2} & \cdots & A_{nn} \end{pmatrix} \begin{pmatrix} x_1 \\ x_2 \\ \vdots \\ x_n \end{pmatrix} = x_1 \begin{pmatrix} A_{11} \\ A_{21} \\ \vdots \\ A_{n1} \end{pmatrix} + x_2 \begin{pmatrix} A_{12} \\ A_{22} \\ \vdots \\ A_{n2} \end{pmatrix} + \cdots + x_n \begin{pmatrix} A_{1n} \\ A_{2n} \\ \vdots \\ A_{nn} \end{pmatrix}$$

$$(1)$$

2.2 SpMV Algorithm

Based on the HEC matrix format, the SpMV algorithm is designed as two parts apparently. As a GPU executes hundreds of CUDA cores simultaneously, a parallel algorithm can be implemented with each CUDA core computing a row. The ELL part has high efficient and is performed firstly. Algorithm 1 gives the SpMV algorithm. This algorithm runs well on a single GPU. However, it is not suitable for multiple GPUs. Multiple GPUs bring stronger parallel computing capability but import extra data communication. We need to partition the original matrix into partition matrices first.

Algorithm 1. Sparse matrix-vector multiplication
1: **for** i = 1: n **do**	▷ ELL
2: Calculate the i-th row of ELL matrix;	▷ one CUDA core
3: **end for**	
4:	
5: **for** i = 1: n **do**	▷ CSR
6: Calculate the i-th row of CSR matrix;	▷ one CUDA core
7: **end for**	

If a matrix has a regular structure. For instance, it is derived from the FDM (Finite Difference Method) or FVM (Finite Volume Method). A sequence partition method can be used. But if it is irregular structure which is often derived

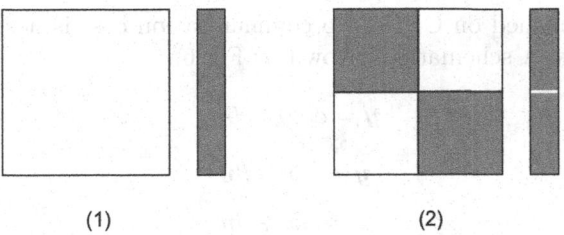

(1)   (2)

Fig. 4. Matrix and vector partition

from the FEM (Finite Element Method) or FVM. A specific partition method should be used. We select a quasi-optimal partition method METIS to complete the matrix partition. During the partition process, the rows of the matrix are switched first and all the nonzero entries are put along the diagonal as close as possible. Then the pivot blocks have most of the nonzero entries and the communication cost between any two partition matrices is reduced; see Fig. 4.

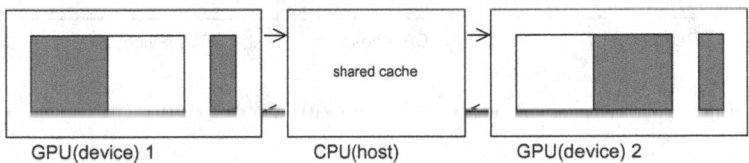

GPU(device) 1   CPU(host)   GPU(device) 2

Fig. 5. Vector communication

The vector is also partitioned into segments. Each pair of a partition matrix and a segment vector is distributed onto a GPU. Although most of the nonzero entries are concentrated at the pivot block, there are still some sparse nonzero entries outside it, for which a segment vector can not provide a corresponding element to complete multiplication. Thus, the necessary communication is unavoidable. We establish a shared cache for communication. The cache is located on the CPU (host). It receives all the communication data from each GPU (device) and then sends the data to needed GPU. As we have used partition method to reduce the communication load, this mechanism is reasonable (Fig. 5).

2.3 Vector Operations

Vector operations are necessary for developing iterative algorithms. They can be categorized into some categories by Eqs. (2)-(6). Some of them are linear combinations of vectors. Some of them are about dot products. As two vectors are operated by one-to-one correspondence of elements, it is easy to design parallel algorithms for them. First, vectors are divided into segments. Then each pair of segments are distributed onto a GPU. All the sub results are sent back to CPU after tasks are finished on GPUs. No communication cost is needed during the vector operations. A schematic is shown by Fig. 6.

$$\boldsymbol{y} = \alpha A\boldsymbol{x} + \beta\boldsymbol{y} \tag{2}$$

$$\boldsymbol{y} = \alpha\boldsymbol{x} + \beta\boldsymbol{y} \tag{3}$$

$$\boldsymbol{z} = \alpha\boldsymbol{x} + \beta\boldsymbol{y} \tag{4}$$

$$a = \langle \boldsymbol{x}, \boldsymbol{y} \rangle \tag{5}$$

$$r = \|\boldsymbol{x}\|_2 = \sqrt{\langle \boldsymbol{x}, \boldsymbol{x} \rangle} \tag{6}$$

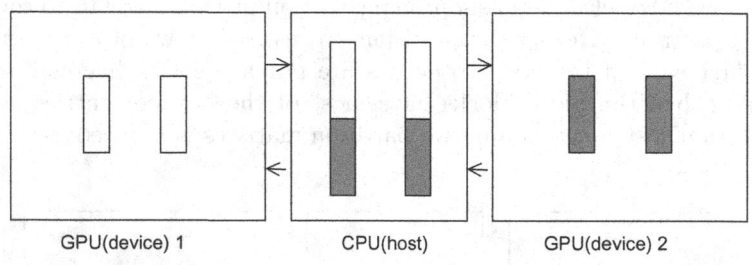

GPU(device) 1   CPU(host)   GPU(device) 2

Fig. 6. Vector operations

2.4 ILU(k)

A preconditioner system is expressed as Eq. (7). M is the preconditioner matrix which is factorized from the original matrix A. The ILU is a commonly used precondtioner. It means M can be factorized into one lower triangular matrix L and an upper triangular matrix U, as shown by Eq. (8). The matrix A and LU are stored in the same memory space in the program implementation. In other words, L is stored in the low triangular part and U is stored in the upper triangular part. A level k can be used to control the factorization process. Only the entry positions meeting the requirement are allowed to have nonzero entries in the result pattern. The requirement condition is described by Eqs. (9) and (10) [2].

$$M\boldsymbol{x} = \boldsymbol{y} \tag{7}$$

where

- M: the preconditioner matrix
- $\boldsymbol{x}$: the unknown vector
- $\boldsymbol{y}$: the right hand side vector

$$M = LU \tag{8}$$

$$L_{ij} = \begin{cases} 0, & (i,j) \in P \\ \infty, & (i,j) \notin P. \end{cases} \tag{9}$$

$$L_{ij} = min\{L_{ij}, L_{ip} + L_{pj} + 1\}. \tag{10}$$

Equation 9 gives an initial level for each entry A_{ij}. P is the nonzero pattern of A. So if A_{ij} is zero, its level L_{ij} is infinite; otherwise, L_{ij} is zero. Equation (9) provides an updated algorithm for levels. This update process are executed at each loop of ILU(k) algorithm and only the satisfactory entry positions have nonzero values in the final factorization pattern. The Algorithm 2 details a complete ILU(k) procedure.

Algorithm 2. ILU(k) factorization

1: For all nonzero entries in nonzero pattern P, define $L_{ij} = 0$
2: **for** $i = 2 : n$ **do**
3:     **for** $p = 1 : i - 1$ & $L_{ip} \leq k$ **do**
4:         $A_{ip} = A_{ip}/A_{pp}$
5:         **for** $j = p + 1 : n$ **do**
6:             $A_{ij} = A_{ij} - A_{ip}A_{pj}$
7:             $L_{ij} = min\{L_{ij}, L_{ip} + L_{pj} + 1\}$
8:         **end for**
9:     **end for**
10:    **if** $L_{ij} > k$ **then**
11:        $A_{ij} = 0$
12:    **end if**
13: **end for**

2.5 Restricted Additive Schwarz

A preconditioner system is always solved at least once in a loop of an iterative algorithm. Its solution speed has great influence on the entire solution process. A GPU platform provides hundreds of CUDA cores to complete a parallel task. If we can improve the parallel structure of a preconditioner matrix, the solution process can be accelerated. Cai et al. proposed a Restricted Additive Schwarz method to optimize the parallel structure for a preconditioner, as illustrated by Fig. 7. The original matrix A is partitioned into some sub matrices first. By the METIS method mentioned above, we got these rectangular matrices whose pivot blocks are dense and other positions are sparse; see Fig. 7-(2). Because the ILU factorization only needs an approximate factorization result from A, we can remove the sparse entries situated outside the pivot blocks. Analyzed from a graph aspect, the entries in the pivot blocks represent vertices and the entries outside them represent edges.

If we remove the edges from the graph by RAS process, the communication among GPUs are ruled out. The remained pivot blocks can be solved in parallel. The improvement of parallel performance leads to an accuracy decrease as we discard some entries. So more iteration times are required to reach a convergence. There is an alternative way named overlap to compensate for the loss of accuracy. As shown by Fig. 7-(3), the overlap technique requires each pivot block to include its some layers of neighbor entries into the block matrices to be computed. Extra entries improve the calculation accuracy and reduce the iteration times. But extra entries also have a negative influence on the parallel performance. Parallelization and convergence like a cake. We cannot eat it and have it. This characteristic is reflected in the numerical experiment section. As a multiple-GPU platform has two levels of parallelization, the situation becomes complex. One level is composed by the GPUs. The other level is the CUDA cores on each GPU. Both levels need a partition and a overlap.

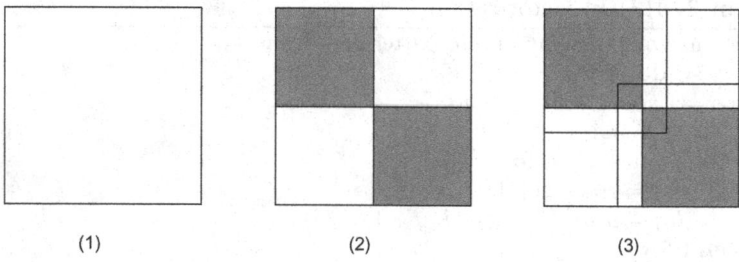

Fig. 7. Restricted Additive Schwarz

2.6   Parallel Triangular Solver

In order to solve L and U on GPUs, we design a parallel triangular solver based on the level schedule method. As an upper triangular system can be easily changed into a lower one, only the lower triangular system is analyzed. The algorithm of a parallel triangular solver is divided into two steps. Each unknown $x(i)$ is assigned a level which is defined by Eq. (11) in the first step [2]. The second step is the solution process. The triangular problem is solved level by level. All the unknowns in the same level are solved simultaneously. The first level is dependence free. So it is solved at the very first. After the unknowns in the first level is obtained, the second level becomes free and can be solved. This procedure proceeded until all the levels are computed and all the unknowns are solved. A complete algorithm of the level schedule method is given by Algorithm 3.

$$l(i) = 1 + \max_j l(j) \quad \text{for all } j \text{ such that } L_{ij} \neq 0, i = 1, 2, \ldots, n, \quad (11)$$

where

- L_{ij}: the (i,j)th entry of L
- $l(i)$: initialized by zeroes
- n: the number of rows

Algorithm 3. Level schedule method for a lower triangular system, $Lx = b$

1: Maximal level is n
2: **for** k = 1 : n **do**
3:     start = level(k);
4:     end = level(k + 1) - 1;
5:     **for** i = start: end **do**
6:         solve the ith row;
7:     **end for**
8: **end for**

2.7 Krylov Iterative Algorithms

By now, we have explained the SpMV, vector operations, precondtioner systems and parallel solution process. All these are components of an iterative algorithm. Krylov subspace algorithms contain a series of iterative Algorithms, such as CG (Biconjugate Gradient), GMRES (Generalized Minimal Residual), BiCGSTAB (Biconjugate Gradient Stabilized), etc. We have implemented all of them. For instance, an implementation analysis of the BiCGSTAB is shown in the Algorithm 4. All the operations on GPUs are commented. Detailed principle of BiCGSTAB and other Krylov subspace algorithms can be found in [2,3].

2.8 AMG Algorithms

If the coefficient matrix of a system to be solved is symmetric positive definite, an AMG solver should be a better choice. An AMG algorithm has a $L + 1$ levels architecture. The grid of the level is finer with a smaller level number. So the level 0 is the finest level but the level L is the coarsest level. Figure 8 shows the level structure of an AMG solver. An AMG algorithm can be designed as V-cycle, W-cycle or F-cycle. Figure 8 is a V-cycle which has the best acceleration effect on a parallel platform. W-cycle has the worst effect. An AMG process has two phases. The first one is called a setup phase in which the coarser grids, the smoothers, the restriction and prolongation operators are all established. The second one is the solution phase in which the multiple-levels system is solved. As a coarser grid has

Algorithm 4. BiCGSTAB algorithm

1:	$r_0 = b - Ax_0$; x_0 is an initial guess vector	▷ SpMV; Vector update
2:	**for** k = 1, 2, ⋯ **do**	
3:	$\rho_{k-1} = (r_0, r)$	▷ Dot product
4:	**if** $\rho_{k-1} = 0$ **then**	
5:	Fails	
6:	**end if**	
7:	**if** $k = 1$ **then**	
8:	$p = r$	
9:	**else**	
10:	$\beta_{k-1} = (\rho_{k-1}/\rho_{k-2})(\alpha_{k-1}/\omega_{k-1})$	
11:	$p = r + \beta_{k-1}(p - \omega_{k-1}v)$	▷ Vector update
12:	**end if**	
13:	Solve p^* from $Mp^* = p$	▷ Preconditioner system
14:	$v = Ap^*$	▷ SpMV
15:	$\alpha_i = \rho_{k-1}/(r_0, v)$	▷ Dot product
16:	$s = r - \alpha_k v$	▷ Vector update
17:	**if** $\|s\|_2$ is satisfied **then**	▷ Dot product
18:	$x = x + \alpha_k p^*$	▷ Vector update
19:	Stop	
20:	**end if**	
21:	Solve s^* from $Ms^* = s$	▷ Preconditioner system
22:	$t = As^*$	▷ SpMV
23:	$\omega_i = (t, s)/\|t\|^2$	▷ Dot product
24:	$x = x + \alpha_k p^* + \omega_k s^*$	▷ Vector update
25:	$r = s - \omega_k t$	▷ Vector update
26:	**if** $\|r\|_2$ is satisfied or $\omega_k = 0$ **then**	▷ Dot product
27:	Stop	
28:	**end if**	
29:	**end for**	

much smaller dimension size compared to its neighbor finer grid, a problem on a coarser grid is easier to be solved. A restriction operation is used for transferring the problem from a finer level to a coarser level. After the problem on the coarser grid is solved, a prolongation operator is used to transfer the solution back to a finer grid. On level l, let A_l be the system matrix, R_l be the restriction operator and P_l be the prolongation operator. S_l is the pre-smoother and T_l is the post-smoother. An example AMG algorithm for V-cycle can be designed as Algorithm 5.

We have developed the AMG solver with a series of smoothers, coarsening operators and prolongation operators. The smoothers include damped Jacobi and weighted Jacobi, etc. The coarsening operator RS and the prolongation operator RSSTD are proposed by Ruge and Stüben [7,8]. The CLJP coarsening operator is proposed by Cleary et al. [12,13].

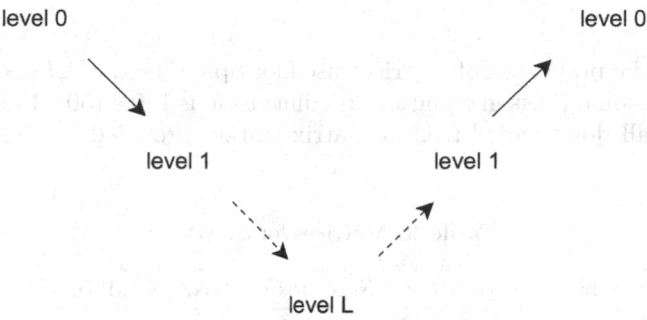

Fig. 8. Structure of AMG solver.

Algorithm 5. AMG V-cycle

Require: $0 \leq l < L$

if $(l < L)$ then
    $\boldsymbol{x}_l = S_l(\boldsymbol{x}_l, A_l, \boldsymbol{b}_l)$ $\triangleright$ Pre-smoothing
    $\boldsymbol{r} = \boldsymbol{b}_l - A_l\boldsymbol{x}_l$
    $\boldsymbol{b}_{l+1} = R_l\boldsymbol{r}$ $\triangleright$ Restriction
    amg_solve$(l + 1)$ $\triangleright$ Recursion
    $\boldsymbol{x}_l = \boldsymbol{x}_l + P_l\boldsymbol{x}_{l+1}$ $\triangleright$ Prolongation
    $\boldsymbol{x}_l - T_l(\boldsymbol{x}_l, A_l, \boldsymbol{b}_l)$ $\triangleright$ Post-smoothing
else
    $\boldsymbol{x}_l = A_l^{-1}\boldsymbol{b}_l$
end if

---

3 Numerical Experiments

A series of numerical experiments are designed to test our algorithms. We use the speedup to measure the parallel acceleration on GPUs. It is calculated by the ratio of the CPU sequential running time to the GPU parallel running time of the same algorithm. The development environment parameters are listed in Table 1.

Table 1. Experiment environment parameters

Parameter	Value
CPU	Intel Xeon X5570
GPU	NVIDIA Tesla C2050/C2070
Operating system	CentOS X86_64
CUDA Toolkit	5.1
GCC	4.4
CPU codes compilation	-O3 option
Float point number precision	Double

3.1 SpMV

Table 2 gives the properties of matrices used for SpMV test. $3D\_Poisson$ is from a three-dimensional Poisson equation. Its dimension is $150 \times 150 \times 150$. The other matrices are all downloaded from a matrix market provided by the University of Florida [24].

Table 2. Matrices for SPMV

Matrix	# of rows	Nonzeros	NNZ/N	Mb(CSR)
ESOC	327, 062	6, 019, 939	18	70
af_shell8	504, 855	9, 042, 005	18	105
tmt_sym	726, 713	2, 903, 837	4	36
ecology2	999, 999	2, 997, 995	3	38
Thermal2	1, 228, 045	4, 904, 179	4	61
Hook_1498	1, 498, 023	30, 436, 237	20	354
G3_circuit	1, 585, 478	4, 623, 152	3	59
kkt_power	2, 063, 494	7, 209, 692	3	90
Memchip	2, 707, 524	13, 343, 948	5	163
3D_Poisson	3, 375, 000	23, 490, 000	7	282
Freescale1	3, 428, 755	17, 052, 626	5	208
Cage15	5, 154, 859	99, 199, 551	19	1155

The speedup of SpMV on a single GPU is collected in Table 3. Three matrix formats are tested for each matrix. We can see that most of the speedup for HEC format are over 10 and the highest speedup can reach 18. The algorithm on GPUs has good parallel acceleration performance. Figure 9 makes a comparison of different matrix formats. The number of nonzero entries per row is written in the brackets after each matrix name. We can see that the HEC format represented by the red curve shows better performance than the other two formats. From the Figure, the matrices with relative larger NNZ/N have a lower speedup.

3.2 BiCGSTAB with ILU(K)

In this experiment, we use the BiCGSTAB algorithm with an ILU(k) preconditioner to test our Krylov algorithms. The testing matrix is from a three-dimensional Poisson equation whose dimension is 3,375,000 ($150 \times 150 \times 150$). It has 23,490,000 nonzero entries and about 7 nonzero entries per row. Table 4 collects the running results. There are six parameter combinations which are numbered in the *Seq No.* column. The *Outer RAS* and *Inner RAS* represent the outer layer partition numbers and inner layer partition numbers based on the RAS technique. The number of GPUs employed is equal to the *Outer RAS*. The outer and inner overlap layers are listed in the *Outer overlap* and *Inner overlap* columns, respectively. These parameters form various parameter combinations.

Table 3. SPMV speedup for different matrix formats

Matrix	ELL	HYB	HEC
ESOC	13.08	13.16	13.16
af_shell8	9.05	10.08	11.20
tmt_sym	16.23	16.27	16.14
ecology2	18.38	18.24	18.11
Thermal2	8.45	8.00	9.25
Hook_1498	5.44	7.35	7.79
G3_circuit	12.84	14.08	11.22
kkt_power	2.49	5.71	6.27
Memchip	4.39	10.53	11.46
3D_Poisson	13.60	13.63	13.63
Freescale1	5.00	9.76	11.25
cage15	6.40	10.00	9.89

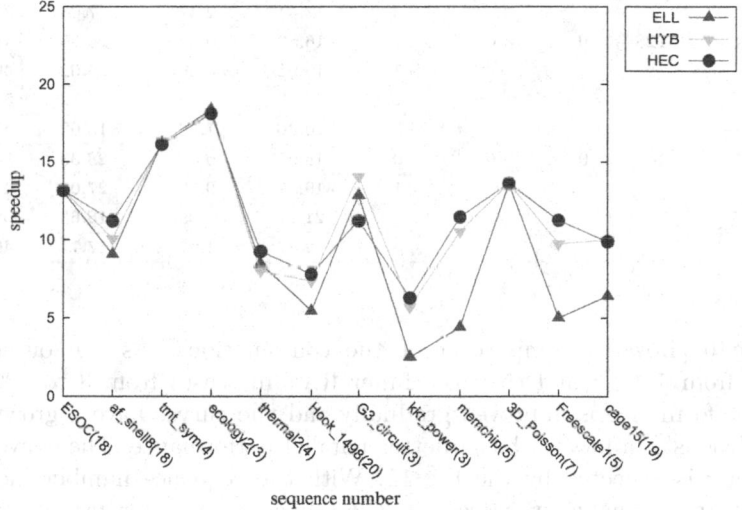

Fig. 9. SpMV speedup curves

As all the data sections have a similar data tendency, we take the first data section as an sample analysis, where the outer RAS, the inner RAS, the ouer overlap and the inner overlap are 1, 8, 0 and 0, respectively. The speedup reaches 8.97 when the k level is set to 0. As k goes up from 0 to 3, the speedup goes down from 8.97 to 4.75 in a general data tendency. That is because more fill-in entries are imported by a higher k. These entries contribute to improve the calculation accuracy. So the iteration is saved and goes down from 45 to 33. However, it goes back to 42 when k is 2. That might is caused by the matrix pattern which has also great influence on the performance.

Table 4. BiCGSTAB with ILU(k) for **3D_Poisson** (RAS)

Seq. No.	Outer RAS	Inner RAS	Outer overlap	Inner overlap	ILU(k) level k	CPU time (second)	GPU time (second)	Speedup	Iteration
1	1	8	0	0	0	16.36	1.82	8.97	45
					1	12.25	1.56	7.86	30
					2	15.75	3.95	3.99	42
					3	16.26	3.42	4.75	33
2	2	8	0	0	0	15.29	1.07	14.30	46
					1	14.64	1.18	12.41	36
					2	18.55	2.66	6.96	43
					3	16.94	2.80	6.05	36
3	3	8	0	0	0	16.57	0.82	20.28	46
					1	14.51	1.07	13.59	39
					2	18.32	2.53	7.25	44
					3	17.85	2.66	6.71	38
4	4	8	0	0	0	17.13	0.62	27.84	44
					1	13.92	0.81	17.14	34
					2	18.15	2.05	8.87	39
					3	17.51	2.47	7.08	38
5	4	128	0	0	0	16.59	0.62	26.96	48
					1	16.91	0.66	25.62	40
					2	20.53	1.50	13.72	51
					3	20.36	1.56	13.02	45
6	4	1024	0	0	0	18.98	0.67	28.33	55
					1	19.37	0.72	27.03	47
					2	21.77	1.39	15.63	58
					3	22.47	1.27	17.74	46

Figure 10 shows a comparison of the combinations. As the outer RAS increases from 1 to 4 and then the inner RAS increases from 8 to 1024, the parallel performance is improved gradually and the curves have a growth tendency. Obviously, a lower k has a better parallel performance. The convergence performance is reflected by the Fig. 11. With the sequence number increases, the parallel performance increases but the convergence performance decreases. Thereby more iteration times are needed to reach a convergence. We can see that high iteration times are needed for $k = 0$ because it has high speedup.

As we mentioned, the overlap technique is used for compensating for the loss of calculation accuracy. Higher overlaps are supposed to use smaller iteration. But the speedup is supposed to decrease as more entries are introduced by the overlap. The results of different overlapping configurations are collected in Table 5.

The combination one has the highest speedup 27.82 and iteration 44. Its acceleration performance is the best but convergence performance is the worst. The combination four has an opposite effect with both the outer overlap and

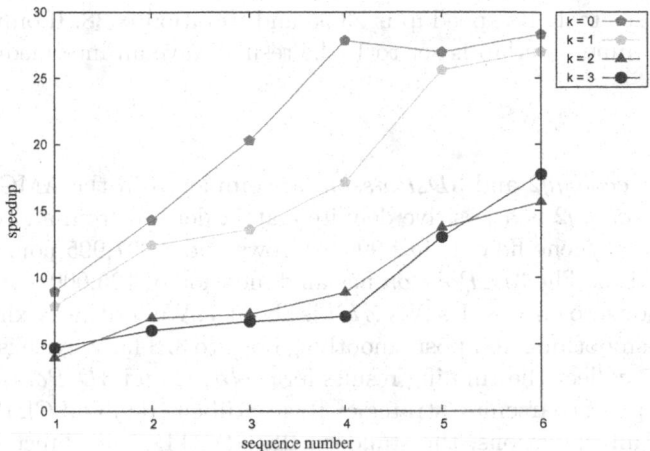

Fig. 10. Speedup for 3D_Poisson

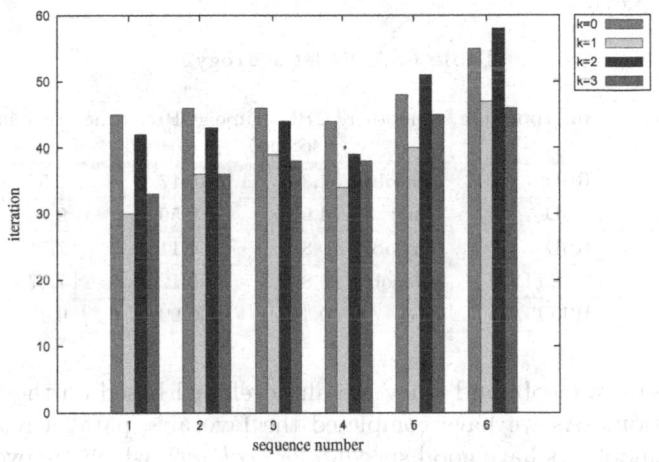

Fig. 11. Iteration for 3D_Poisson

Table 5. BiCGSTAB with ILU(k) for 3D_Poisson (overlap)

Seq. No.	Outer RAS	Inner RAS	Outer overlap	Inner overlap	ILU(k) level k	CPU time (second)	GPU time (second)	Speedup	Iteration
1	4	8	0	0	0	17.07	0.61	27.82	44
2	4	8	1	0	0	15.91	0.70	22.70	43
3	4	8	0	1	0	15.43	0.60	25.78	41
4	4	8	1	1	0	15.04	0.63	23.95	38

inner overlap set to 1. Its speedup is 23.95 and iteration is 38. If only the outer overlap or the inner overlap is set to 1, the results have an intermediate effect.

3.3 AMG

Two matrices, *ecology*2 and 3*D_Poisson*, are employed in the AMG algorithm testing. The *ecology*2 is a positive definite matrix derived from a circuit theory applied to animal/gene flow. It has 999,999 rows and 2,997,995 nonzero entries. The NNZ/N is 3. The 3*D_Poisson* has an dimension of 125,000 ($50 \times 50 \times 50$)) and 860,000 nonzero entries. Its NNZ/N is about 7. We set the maximal level to 8 and the pre-smoothing and post-smoothing both to 3. The V-cycle is employed. Tables 6 and 7 collect the running results for *ecology*2 and 3*D_Poisson*, respectively. Two type of coarsening strategies Ruge-Stüben (RS) and CLJP are used. Two types of interpolations, the standard RS (RSSTD) and direct (RSD), are used. Four types of smoothers are tested. They are the damped Jacobi (dJacobi), weighted Jacobi (wJacobi), Chebyshev polynomial smoothers (Chev) and Gauss-Seidel (GS).

Table 6. AMG for `ecology2`

Seq. No.	Coarsening strategy	Interpolation	Smoother	CPU time (second)	GPU time (second)	Speedup	Iteration
1	CLJP	RSD	dJacobi	1.30	0.17	7.57	3
2	CLJP	RSD	Chev	4.92	0.50	9.78	11
3	RS	RSD	dJacobi	0.82	0.11	7.71	3
4	RS	RSSTD	wJacobi	0.86	0.12	7.07	3
5	RS	RSSTD	GS	0.46	0.99	0.46	1

The dJacobi, wJacobi and Chev are all developed based on the SpMV and vector operations. As we have completed the favorable parallel realization of them, these smoothers have good speedup for *ecology*2, which are over 7. When the CLJP and RSD are used, the speedup reaches to the maximal value 9.78. If we select the GS smoother, the speedup is 0.46 which is very low. That means the running time on a GPU is even longer than that on a CPU. The purpose of acceleration on a GPU fails. Although the GS has the worst parallel performance, it has the best convergence performance and only once iteration is

Table 7. AMG for 3*D_Poisson*

Seq. No.	Coarsening strategy	Interpolation	Smoother	CPU time (second)	GPU time (second)	Speedup	Iteration
1	CLJP	RSD	dJacobi	1.64	0.65	2.54	8
2	CLJP	RSD	Chev	1.86	1.13	1.64	8
3	RS	RSD	dJacobi	0.25	0.05	4.71	7
4	RS	RSSTD	wJacobi	0.46	0.13	3.61	9
5	RS	RSSTD	GS	0.28	4.53	0.06	4

needed. So it is better to develop an AMG algorithm with the GS on a CPU. This also shows there is a contradictory effect between acceleration and convergence performance. Our experiment results show that the dJacobi, wJacobi and Chev are suitable for GPU computation while the GS is suitable for CPU.

The $3D\_Poisson$ has worse acceleration results than the $ecology2$ has; shown by Table 7. Different matrices has different nonzero patterns which have great influence on the computing performance. The algorithm on GPU has an acceleration effect for the smoothers of dJacobi, wJacobi and Chev. The combination three with the RS, RSD, dJacobi has the highest speedup 4.71. However, a very poor speedup 0.06 is obtained for the smoother GS. This result is similar to that of the matrix $ecology2$. The GS is not suitable for GPU computing is proved again.

4   Conclusion

We have developed the Krylov and AMG linear solvers on GPUs. The SpMV algorithm can be accelerated over 10 times faster on a single GPU against a CPU for most large-scale sparse matrices. Our preconditioned Krylov subspace algorithms have favorable speedups on GPUs. When four GPUs are employed and the inner RAS is set to 1024, the BiCGSTAB with ILU(0) can be sped up to 28 times faster. Our AMG solver shows good parallel performance for dJacobi, wJacobi and Chev smoothers. The numerical experiments verify that a contradictory effect exists between the performance of convergence and acceleration in many cases.

Acknowledgments. The support of Department of Chemical and Petroleum Engineering, University of Calgary and Reservoir Simulation Research Group is gratefully acknowledged. The research is partly supported by NSERC/AIEES/Foundation CMG, AITF iCore, IBM Thomas J. Watson Research Center, and the Frank and Sarah Meyer FCMG Collaboration Centre for Visualization and Simulation. The research is also enabled in part by support provided by WestGrid (www.westgrid.ca) and Compute Canada Calcul Canada (www.computecanada.ca).

References

1. Chen, Z.: Reservoir Simulation: Mathematical Techniques in Oil Recovery. CBMS-NSF Regional Conference Series in Applied Mathematics, vol. 77. SIAM, Philadelphia (2007)
2. Saad, Y.: Iterative Methods for Sparse Linear Systems, 2nd edn. SIAM, Philadelphia (2003)
3. Barrett, R., Berry, M., Chan, T.F., Demmel, J., Donato, J., Dongarra, J., Eijkhout, V., Pozo, R., Romine, C., Vorst, H.V.: Templates for the Solution of Linear Systems: Building Blocks for Iterative Methods, 2nd edn. SIAM, Philadelphia (1994)
4. Hu, X., Liu, W., Qin, G., Xu, J., Yan, Y., Zhang, C.: Development of a fast auxiliary subspace pre-conditioner for numerical reservoir simulators. In: SPE Reservoir Characterisation and Simulation Conference and Exhibition, Abu Dhabi, UAE, SPE-148388-MS, pp. 9–11, October 2011

5. Chen, Z., Huan, G., Ma, Y.: Computational Methods for Multiphase Flows in Porous Media. Computational Science and Engineering Series, vol. 2. SIAM, Philadelphia (2006)
6. Liu, H., Wang, K., Chen, Z., Jordan, K.E.: Efficient multi-stage preconditioners for highly heterogeneous reservoir simulations on parallel distributed systems. In: SPE Reservoir Simulation Symposium, Houston, Texas, USA, SPE-173208-MS, pp. 23–25 (2015)
7. Stüben, K.: A review of algebraic multigrid. J. Comput. Appl. Math. **128**(1–2), 281–309 (2001)
8. Ruge, J.W., Stüben, K.: Algebraic multigrid (AMG). In: McCormick, S.F. (ed.) Multigrid Methods, Frontiers in Applied Mathematics, vol. 5. SIAM, Philadelphia (1986)
9. Brandt, A., McCormick, S.F., Ruge, J.: Algebraic multigrid (AMG) for sparse matrix equations. In: Evans, D.J. (ed.) Sparsity and its Applications, pp. 257–284. Cambridge University Press, Cambridge (1984)
10. Wagner, C.: Introduction to algebraic multigrid, course notes of an algebraic multigrid course at the University of Heidelberg in the Wintersemester (1999)
11. Vassilevski, P.S.: Lecture Notes on Multigrid Methods. Center for Applied Scientific Computing, Lawrence Livermore National Laboratory (2010)
12. Falgout, R., Cleary, A., Jones, J., Chow, E., Henson, V., Baldwin, C., Brown, P., Vassilevski, P., Yang, U.M.: Hypre home page (2011). http://acts.nersc.gov/hypre
13. Cleary, A.J., Falgout, R.D., Henson, V.E., Jones, J.E., Manteuffel, T.A., McCormick, S.F., Miranda, G.N., Ruge, J.W.: Robustness and scalability of algebraic multigrid. SIAM J. Sci. Comput. **21**, 1886–1908 (2000)
14. Gao, Y., Iqbal, S., Zhang, P., Qiu, M.: Performance and power analysis of high-density multi-GPGPU architectures.: a preliminary case study. In: 2015 IEEE 17th International Conference on High Performance Computing and Communications (HPCC-ICESS-CSS 2015), New York, USA, 24–26 August (2015)
15. NVIDIA official website. http://www.nvidia.com/object/tesla-servers.html
16. Fujitsu official website. http://techcommunity.ts.fujitsu.com/en/client-computing-devices-2/d/uid-5911b36b-324b-fc23-45fa-2438e4c546f3.html
17. Karypis, G., Kumar, V.: A fast and highly quality multilevel scheme for partitioning irregular graphs. SIAM J. Sci. Comput. **20**(1), 359–392 (1999)
18. Cai, X.-C., Sarkis, M.: A restricted additive schwarz preconditioner for general sparse linear systems. SIAM J. Sci. Comput. **21**, 792–797 (1999)
19. Liu, H., Yu, S., Chen, Z., Hsieh, B., Shao, L.: Sparse matrix-vector multiplication on NVIDIA GPU. Int. J. Numer. Anal. Model. Ser. B **3**(2), 185–191 (2012)
20. Liu, H., Yu, S., Chen, Z., Hsieh, B., Shao, L.: Parallel preconditioners for reservoir simulation on GPU. In: SPE Latin American and Caribbean Petroleum Engineering Conference, Mexico City, Mexico, SPE 152811-PP, pp. 16–18 (2012)
21. Li, R., Saad, Y.: GPU-accelerated preconditioned iterative linear solvers. Technical Report Umsi-2010-112. University of Minnesota, Minneapolis, MN, Minnesota Supercomputer Institute (2010)
22. Grimes, R., Kincaid, D., Young, D.: ITPACK 2.0 user's guide. Technical Report CNA-150, Center for Numerical Analysis, University of Texas, August 1979
23. Bell, N., Garland, M.: Implementing sparse matrix-vector multiplication on throughput-oriented processors. In: Proceedings of Supercomputing, pp. 1–11, November 2009
24. Davis, T.A.: University of Florida Sparse Matrix Collection, NA digest (1994). https://www.cise.ufl.edu/research/sparse/matrices/

A Study on Anonymous Communication Technology in MANET

Weidong Fang[1], Jianping Wang[1], Zhidong Shi[1], Fengrong Li[2], and Lianhai Shan[3(✉)]

[1] Key Laboratory of Specialty Fiber Optics and Optical Access Networks,
Shanghai University, Shanghai 200444, China
[2] Key Laboratory of Wireless Sensor Network and Communication,
Shanghai Institute of Microsystem and Information Technology, Chinese Academy of Sciences,
Shanghai 201899, China
[3] Shanghai Research Center for Wireless Communications, Shanghai Internet of Things Co., Ltd.,
Shanghai 201800, China
shanlianhai@163.com

Abstract. This paper addresses the anonymous communications technology. Multiple hops, self-organization, no fixed facilities and limited computing resources of wireless ad hoc networks (MANET) make it hard to apply high complexity of a traditional network security algorithm. Security mechanisms can better solve the security issues of anonymous communication. This paper mainly studies the existing anonymous technology of traditional networks and MANET, and summarizes its advantages and disadvantages. With this article, readers can have a more thorough understanding of anonymous communication security and research trends in this area.

Keywords: MANET · Security · Anonymous communication · Privacy

1 Introduction

With the development of micro mobile communications, digital electronic technology, especially the widely use of the PDAs, mobile phones, pocket computers and other personal electronic terminals, a Wireless Ad hoc Network (MANET) has gained worldwide attention in recent years, and has great potential for many applications in scenarios such as body area networks, personal area networks, and internets of vehicles [1].

Security is becoming more and more serious while a scope application of MANET is becoming wider. Traditional security protocols do not work well in a MANET since they are not designed to meet its features, including multi-hops, self-organization, no fixed facilities and limited computing resources [2]. The current state-of-art security research focuses mostly on contents security for the MANET information security by introducing new design concepts and creating or improving new algorithms. There have been significant research focuses on encryption and authentication mechanisms, and relatively limited results on communication security. Combining the application scenario and the inherent characteristics of the MANET, we found that the security issues of node privacy and communication privacy can be better solved by light security mechanisms combined with an anonymous technology.

© Springer International Publishing Switzerland 2016
J. Xie et al. (Eds.): HPCA 2015, LNCS 9576, pp. 73–81, 2016.
DOI: 10.1007/978-3-319-32557-6_7

The rest of this paper is organized as follows: in Sect. 2, we show a general overview of the traditional anonymous communication technology. Section 3 presents an existing anonymous mechanism in MANET. An analysis of an anonymous communication technology from anonymity, memory overhead and security is shown in Sect. 4. We conclude this paper in Sect. 5.

2   Related Works

In order to provide a network protected from eavesdropper, anonymous communication of security professionals must be taken to secure communication node identity, location or the relationship. Anonymous protection is generally divided into anonymous sender, receiver anonymity, unrelated sender and receiver according to the hidden object [3]. In this section, we describe the typical traditional anonymous communication technology such as Mix, Onion routing and tor, crowds.

2.1   Mix

Mix [4] was firstly mentioned and explained by Chaum in 1981 to protect the E-mail untraceable, which allow email system to hide communication participants and content of communication by public key encryption technology. The network anonymous system is demonstrated in Fig. 1. Researchers focus on heavy encryption of Mix later. Among them, Golle et al. [5] proposed general re-encryption technology in 2004, which is very effective for privacy protection. Compared to the traditional encryption, general re-encryption does not need to know the public key encryption [6].

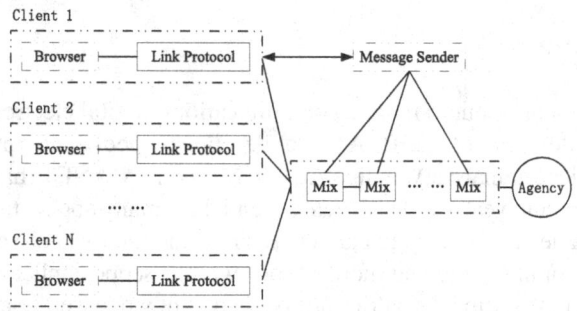

Fig. 1. Anonymous network of mix

2.2   Onion Routing and Tor

Onion routing is a low-latency connection-oriented anonymous communication system, which has almost real-time information transmission provided by onion router [7]. In onion routing, anonymous connections are established through the hierarchical data structure of public-key encryption, called the onion. Proxy mechanism multiple, mixed technology and encryption technology were mainly used in onion routing to realize anonymity of the path and the hiding of key information such as address of both sides. The second generation of onion routing, called Tor, is currently the most successful public anonymous Internet communication system. Tor works in real-time network without the modification of privileges or the kernel. Tor can significantly improve the network performance in terms of anonymity, availability and efficiency by increasing the perfect secret forward, congestion control, the directory server, integrity check, configurable exit policy etc. There are many improvement programs in the onion routing and Tor [8, 9].

2.3 Crowds

Crowds [10] is the anonymity of web transactions to protect the users of the Internet, which is demonstrated in Fig. 2. The sender anonymity is realized based on the thought of group and reroute. Real source of the request can not be identified in the Web server, Crowds has lower communication delay, higher system efficiency, better scalability than Mix. Tao et al. [11] extended the work of Crowds to overcome the drawback of poor anti aggression. In [12], Wu et al. proposed to combine Mix anonymous communication technology and random filling technology.

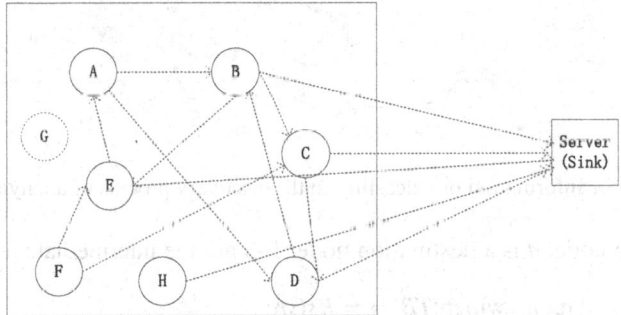

Fig. 2. Anonymous communication system of crowds (A~H represent sensor nodes in group)

In addition to the typical traditional network anonymous technology, there are many other anonymous communication protocol, such as Mixmaster [13], MorphMix [14], Tarzan [15], PipeNet [16], I2P [17] etc.

3 Anonymous Mechanism of Ad Hoc Network

In this section, we explore current secure proposals in ad hoc network that have been developed over the period after 2003. To provide a deeper understanding of current security approaches, we describe the representative anonymous mechanisms such as ANODR, ARM, MASR, etc.

3.1 ANODR

ANODR (Anonymous on Demand Routing) [18] used the trapdoor information broad-casting, pseudonym mechanism and jump encryption technology. Two closely related problems were solved: for routing anonymity, ANODR prevent powerful enemy tracking packet flow tracing to its source and destination. For location privacy, ANODR ensured the opponent not be able to find the true identity of the local transmitter by the trapdoor information.

The advantage of ANODR is the use of TBO (Trapdoor Boomerang Onion) to ensure the node anonymity. A symmetric key encryption was used to reduce the computational burden of the public key cryptography. The trapdoor information broadcasting is shown in Fig. 3. In request phase, the intermediate node X added a random number N_x into onion package when it received $RREQ$, encrypt the results used the random symmetric, and then broadcast the $RREQ$. The trapdoor information contains N_x and K_x, and only know X. In reply phase, the threshold could only be opened correctly by the next-hop node when the destination broadcast $RREP$ and then a layer of the onion envelope was removed.

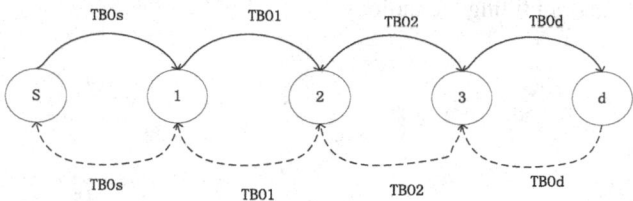

Fig. 3. Trapdoor information broadcasting in the discovery process of anonymous routing

S is a source node, d is a destination node, 1~3 are the intermediate nodes

$$\text{Among which:} TBOs = Ks(src)$$
$$TBO1 = K1(N1, Ks(src))$$
$$TBO2 = K2(N2, K1(N1, Ks(src)))$$
$$TBOd = Kd(Nd, K2(N2, K1(N1, Ks(src))))$$

3.2 ARM

ARM (Anonymous Routing Protocol for Mobile Ad hoc Networks) [19] established the shared secret key and pseudonym mechanism between source and destination. In the request phase, a private key k_{SD} and current identified pseudonym Nym_{SD} can shared between source and destination. First of all, new asymmetric keys $Priv_D/Pub_D$ and a private key k were generated by S. Then, the threshold id_{dest} was generated by S, that could only be opened by node D which had the private information of k_{SD}, among which, $k[Nym_{SD}]$ was used to proof later that $RREP$ was exactly come from the desired node D. S would also generate a random link status of (n_s, k_s) to identify the information of

RREP. In the end, S would use Pub_{SD} to encrypt random link status (n_s, k_s) and broadcast $RREQ: S- \rightarrow M:Nym_{SD}, ttl, Pub_D, id_{dest}, Pub_D(n_s, k_s)$.

The node N_i that receives the *RREQ* packets later will determine whether it is the destination node. Firstly, it will judge whether Nym_{SD} is in the current pseudonym tables of the node N_i, if so, N_i will try to decrypt id_{dest} and judge the consistency of identity, if not, N_i is not the destination node. And then Nym_{SD} will be determined whether it is in its routing table, the *RREQ* packets will be discarded if it is in the table, if not, will be saved in its routing table. *TTL* of packets minus 1, and generate a random link status (n_i, k_i), add these to the received encrypted link status with Pub_D encryption, and broadcast the following *RREQ*. If N_i is the target node, it stores complete *RREQ* in memory and performs the operations like intermediate nodes. The destination node starts preparing reply information after it has forwarded the *RREQ* information once or more, which realizes the purpose of hidden nodes. In the recovery phase of routing, after the decryption of threshold identity id_{dest}, the destination node has the information of k and $Priv_D$. Node D can decrypt the link status contained in the received *RREQ* packet by the use of $Priv_D$.

In the ARM, the destination nodes will execute routing reply after forwarding operation after receiving the routing request packets like the forwarding performs of intermediate nodes to hide their identity information. In routing reply phase, the destination will generate onion structure routing reply packet. The random number filling technology is used in the process of routing requests and routing reply to resist traffic analysis attack, prevent enemy to obtain the hop count of source or destination.

3.3 MASR

Pan and Li proposed a kind of effective and anonymous on-demand anonymous secure routing protocol named MASR [20], which combined the adaptability of the unidirectional links in the DSR, the layer encryption method in the TOR and the global trapdoor method in ANDOR. In the request phase, a source node broadcasted RREQ. The solicitation packet contained the trapdoor information of symmetric key encryption, in which only destination could be decrypted like ANDOR. Jiang and Xing proposed a comprehensive anonymous communication protocol, called ARSC [21]. ASRC combined the symmetric key algorithm, public key encryption algorithms and hash functions, integrated key exchange mechanism of inter-operative authentication. By keeping the visible information dynamic in the RREP and packet, it resisted against global attackers and achieved strong routing anonymity. ASRC adopted the concept of onion routing only in the reply stage, using one-way onion routing more efficient than a two-way onion routing. The passive attack such as packet loss could be found by the hash value examining of the intermediate nodes.

Li and Feng proposed an anonymous routing protocol based on lightweight dynamic pseudonym, called DPAR [22]. In DPAR, the entire network was divided into several grids, and each grid had a base station, information transferred between the grids through a base station. Its security was got by performing a lightweight symmetric key encryption and hash operation, its pseudonym was generated by hash operation and subsequent pseudonym would repeat this operation, and whose dynamic update and synchronization was finished by precise message interaction. MASK [23] used the node pseudonym mechanism and linear pairing to get anonymous authentication. A strict synchronization of pseudonym and key was needed to establish among the adjacent nodes. The target address used plain-text, the receiver anonymity could not be realized. ASR [24] was a unicast routing protocol using shared key, TAG certification, replacement scheme and random number XOR mechanism. ASR could avoid the path tracking and prevent the flow analysis attack.

Recently, Kalai Selvi S put forward an Energy-aware Anonymous Routing Protocol in MANETs (EARP) [25]. EARP could offer anonymity protection to sources, destinations, and routes, through dynamically partitioning the network area into zones and randomly choosing nodes in zones as intermediate Relay Nodes. Liu W and Yu M proposed authenticated anonymous secure routing (AASR) [26] for MANETs in adversarial environments. In this protocol, the route request packets were authenticated by a group signature, to defend against potential active attacks without unveiling the node identities.

4   Analysis of Anonymous Communication Technology

The difference between traditional networks and Ad hoc network is obvious, and the related anonymous technology will be analyzed in the following subsections.

4.1   Traditional Network Analysis of Anonymous Mechanism

Mix implemented the sender anonymous well with high latency characteristics. The general output rules of message took the following three ways: threshold value Mix, the buffer pool Mix, stop forwarding Mix. Nodes needed strong ability of calculation and large storage space to prevent the enemy from tracking the direction of data flow by measuring the size of the packet, and padding must be done to the decrypted information which also increased the cost. The delay of Onion Routing was smaller than Mix, which was the reason why the wireless networks adopt the similar structure of onion routing. The Onion Routing could withstand the flow analysis attack and hacking attack effectively, but resistance ability was very weak for that of disrupting attack. The Onion Routing did not support path rearrangement, and the agent was easy to become the focus of the enemy attack.

For Crowds, it could realize the sender anonymous, but could not achieve the recipient anonymous. Since establishment of the path was random and with no restriction to the length, the network performance would be affected by the frequent encryption when the path was long. The advantages of Crowds have good expansibility because nodes could be the members of the group at any time. Traditional anonymous agreement had its merits, but it still too expensive in terms of computation. These mechanisms were not suitable for MANET and still need further study.

4.2   MANET Analysis of Anonymous Mechanism

Common anonymous technologies for anonymous communication system are packet filling mechanism, encryption mechanism, onion routing, the trapdoor information building, pseudonym mechanism and so on. ANDOR, ARM, MASR were typical wireless anonymous protocols similar to the onion routing. Though using the onion structure, ANDOR, MASK used pseudonym mechanism to hide the real nodes identity. However, some inevitable problems appeared, for example, the pseudonym mechanism generally had the requirements of timely update for pseudonym. If the pseudonym fixed, the effect was consistent without a false name, the pseudonym update synchronization problems was introduced. Many anonymous protocols adopted packet filling mechanism to defend traffic analysis attack.

ANODR broadcast routing request packets, and each forwarding node generates public/private key pairs for each request packets. The efficiency of ANDOR was low due to the use onion structure of TBO. Nodes would try each shared key with other nodes to open TBO, which made the cost large. ASR also had these problems. ANODR could not resist the global attacker effectively if global attacker tracked, compared and sent the same element of the packets.

MASK required more demanding clock to keep synchronization because the nodes should establish strict synchronization pseudonyms. Shared pseudonym list and session key should be preset in the ARM. Each node received routing requests attempted to decrypt the trapdoor or the extra consumption when random number filled the redundant information. For ASRC, a credible authority was needed for generation and release public key. MASR could neither achieve anonymous protection for the global attacker, nor realize the destination anonymity when it combined the relevant technology of DSR, TOR and ANDOR. We assumed that the base station was reliable in DPAR, and the anonymity was achieved under uncaptured conditions. Table 1 summarizes the analysis security performance of typical anonymous protocols.

Table 1.   Anonymous protocol analysis in ad hoc network

Anonymous protocol	Anonymity	Memory overhead etc.	Security
ANDOR	Medium	High	Medium
AASR	High	High	High
ARM	High	Medium	High
ARSC	High	Low	High
ASR	High	High	Medium
EARP	Medium	Low	High
MASR	Medium	Medium	Medium
MASK	Low	Medium	Low
DPAR	Medium	Low	Medium

5   Conclusions

This paper is mainly on the anonymous technology of traditional network and MANET. Through the analysis of the existing anonymity, we compared the typical anonymous protocols to offer help for future study of the anonymity technology in MANETs.

The research of anonymous technology is mainly the continuation of traditional anonymous mechanism, taking insufficient account of the intrinsic characteristics of Ad hoc network, such as mobility, dynamic topology and so on. In addition, these studies lacked the combination of node energy, which would greatly limit the realization of some algorithm. For future work, we will investigate anonymous technology with combination of node energy.

Acknowledgment. This work is partially supported by the National Natural Science Foundation of China (61302113), the Shanghai Natural Science Foundation (13ZR1440800), the Shanghai Rising-Star Program (14QB1404400), Shanghai Key Laboratory of Specialty Fiber Optics and Optical Access Networks (SKLSFO 2014-03), the Science and Technology Innovation Program of Shanghai (14511101303) and Shanghai Sailing Program (15YF1414500, 14YF1408900).

References

1. Yuan, J., Lu, J.F.: The research and application of terminal using in vehicle network. In: Proceeding IEEE ICEIEC, Beijing, China, pp. 305–308 (2013)
2. Sood, M., Kanwar, S.: Clustering in MANET and VANET: a survey. In: Proceeding CSCITA, Mumbai, Maharashtra, India, pp. 375–380 (2014)
3. Chen, X., Makki, K., Yen, K., Pissinou, N.: Sensor network security: a survey. IEEE Commun. Surv. Tut. **11**, 52–73 (2009)
4. Chaum, D.L.: Untraceable electronic mail, return addresses, and digital pseudonyms. Commun. ACM **24**, 84–90 (1981)
5. Golle, P., Jakobsson, M., Juels, A., Syverson, P.F.: Universal re-encryption for mixnets. In: Okamoto, T. (ed.) CT-RSA 2004. LNCS, vol. 2964, pp. 163–178. Springer, Heidelberg (2004)
6. Gomułkiewicz, M., Klonowski, M., Kutyłowski, M.: Onions based on universal re-encryption – anonymous communication immune against repetitive attack. In: Lim, C.H., Yung, M. (eds.) WISA 2004. LNCS, vol. 3325, pp. 400–410. Springer, Heidelberg (2005)
7. Goldschlag, D., Reed, M., Syverson, P.: Onion routing. Commun. ACM **42**, 39–41 (1999)
8. Zhao, F.X., Wang, Y.M., Wang, C.J.: An authenticated scheme of onion routing. Chin. J. Comput. **24**, 463–467 (2001)
9. Li, L.H., Fu, S.F., Su, R.D., Che, X.Q.: Cryptanalysis of a hybrid-structured onion routing scheme. J. Commun. **34**, 88–98 (2013)
10. Reiter, M.K., Rubin, A.D.: Crowds: anonymity for web transactions. ACM Trans. Inf. Syst. Secur. **1**, 66–92 (1998)
11. Tao, T., Bao, R.D., Sun, L.C.: Research on performance of S-crowds anonymous communication protocol. J. Naval Univ. Eng. **20**, 109–112 (2008)
12. Wu, Y.X., Huang, M.H., Wang, H.: An improved anonymous communication system based on crowds. Jiangxi Norm. Univ. (Natural Science) **33**, 88–91 (2008)
13. Möller, U,, Cottrell, L., Palfrader, P., Sassaman, L.: Mixmaster protocol - version 2. Draft (2003). http://www.freehaven.net/anonbib

14. Rennhard, M., Plattner, B.: Introducing MorphMix: peer-to-peer based anonymous internet usage with collusion detection. In: Proceeding WPES, Washington, DC, USA, pp. 91–102 (2002)
15. Freedman, M.J., Morris, R.: Tarzan: a peer-to-peer anonymizing network layer. In: Proceeding ACM CCS, Washington, DC, USA, pp. 193–206 (2002)
16. Dai, W.: PipeNet 1.1. (1996). http://www.eskimo.com/~weidai/pipenet.txt
17. https://geti2p.net
18. Kong, J., Hong, X.: ANODR: anonymous on demand routing with untraceable routes for mobile ad-hoc networks. In: Proceeding ACM MOBIHOC, Annapolis, Maryland, USA, pp. 291–302 (2003)
19. Seys, S., Preneel, B.: ARM: anonymous routing protocol for mobile ad hoc networks. Int. J. Wireless Mob. Comput. 3, 145–155 (2009)
20. Pan, J., Li, J.: MASR: an efficient strong anonymous routing protocol for mobile ad hoc networks. In: Proceeding IEEE MASS, Beijing, China, pp. 1–6 (2009)
21. Jiang, R., Xing, Y.: Anonymous on-demand routing and secure checking of traffic forwarding for mobile ad hoc networks. In: Proceeding IEEE SRDS, Irvine, California, USA, pp. 406–411 (2012)
22. Li, T., Feng, Y., Wang, F., Fu, X.D.: A dynamic pseudonyms based anonymous routing protocol for wireless ad hoc networks. In: Proceeding IEEE MSN, Chengdu, China, pp. 82–86 (2012)
23. Zhang, Y., Liu, W., Lou, W.: Anonymous communications in mobile ad hoc networks. In: Proceeding IEEE INFOCOM, Miami, Florida, USA, pp. 1940–1951 (2005)
24. Zhu, B., Wan, Z., Kankanhalli, M.S., Bao, F., Deng, R.H.: Anonymous secure routing in mobile ad-hoc networks. In: Proceeding IEEE LCN, Tampa, Florida, USA, pp. 102–108 (2004)
25. Kalai Selvi, S., Ganeshkumar, V.: EARP: energy-aware anonymous routing protocol in MANETs. In: Proceeding ICACCCT, Ramanathapuram, India, pp. 1143–1147 (2014)
26. Liu, W., Yu, M.: AASR: authenticated anonymous secure routing for MANETs in adversarial environments. IEEE Trans. Veh. Technol. 63, 4585–4593 (2014)

Parallel Computing of the Adaptive N-Body Treecode Algorithm for Solving Boundary Integral Poisson-Boltzmann Equation

Jiahui Chen and Weihua Geng$^{(\boxtimes)}$

Department of Mathematics, Southern Methodist University, Dallas, TX 75275, USA
wgeng@smu.edu

Abstract. In this paper, we study the parallelization of a Cartesian grid based treecode algorithm in evaluating electrostatic potentials in a charged particle system. The treecode algorithm uses a far-field Taylor expansion to compute $\mathcal{O}(N \log N)$ particle-cluster interactions to replace the $\mathcal{O}(N^2)$ particle-particle interactions. The treecode algorithm is implemented with MPI based parallelization. We design schemes to optimize the implementation adaptive to the particle location. The numerical results show high parallel efficiency. These optimized schemes are further extended to accelerate GMRES iteration in solving boundary integral Poisson–Boltzmann equation in which the discretized linear algebraic system resembles the interactions of the charged system.

Keywords: Parallel computing · N-body problem · Treecode algorithm · MPI · Boundary integral equation

1 Introduction

N-body problem refers to computing the potential or field of a system of N particles with pairwise interactions. These interactions could be Coulombic, screened Coulombic, gravitational, etc. Traditionally, computing N-body problem by direct summation require $\mathcal{O}(N^2)$ amount of work. Fast algorithm such as Fast Multipole Method (FMM) [1] or Treecode [2,3] can efficiently reduce the amount of work to $\mathcal{O}(N)$ or $\mathcal{O}(N \log N)$. The advent of parallel computing brings these fast algorithms a new challenge: since the direct summation has nearly perfect parallel efficiency, how to parallelize fast algorithms with a comparably parallel efficiency?

Recently a Cartesian treecode algorithm was developed in computing electrostatic interactions including Coulombic and screened Coulombic interactions with manageable order of expansion for desired accuracy [3]. In addition, this treecode algorithm is used to accelerate boundary integral Poisson-Boltzmann (PB) equation in which computing one step of matrix-vector product in Krylov subspace iteration resembles the N-body problem [4]. This treecode algorithm is memory saving and parallelization friendly. We recently investigate its parallel performance and optimization on computing N-body problem [5].

© Springer International Publishing Switzerland 2016
J. Xie et al. (Eds.): HPCA 2015, LNCS 9576, pp. 82–89, 2016.
DOI: 10.1007/978-3-319-32557-6_8

In this paper, we further investigate its parallel performance and optimization on solving boundary integral PB equation, which is described below.

In a medium with dielectric constant ε, the Gauss's Law relates the electrostatic potential ϕ in the space to the electrostatic charge density ρ by the classical Poisson's equation $-\nabla \cdot (\varepsilon \nabla \phi) = \rho$. The dielectric coefficient ε in general is a function of the space but can also be simplified as a piecewise constant function with constant value in each particular medium (e.g. for a solvated biomolecule as shown in Fig. 1(a), $\varepsilon = 1\text{--}10$ inside molecule region Ω_1 and $\varepsilon = 70\text{--}80$ in the solvent region Ω_2). The charge density ρ usually contains two components. One is the summation of weighted delta functions representing the partial changes assigned to the atomic centers of the biomolecule. The other is the Boltzmann distribution of the mobile ions (dissolved electrolytes), which takes valence number of the ionic species, electrostatic potential, and temperature into account. In addition, we need to consider interface conditions such as the continuity of electrostatic potential ϕ and flux density $\varepsilon \frac{\partial \phi}{\partial \nu}$ normal to dielectric boundary $\Gamma = \partial \Omega_1 = \partial \Omega_2$ as seen in Fig. 1(a). By combining all these components and assuming the weak ionic strength we have the linearized Poisson-Boltzmann Eq. (1)–(2), its interface jump conditions (2), and the boundary condition (3) as the following.

$$- \varepsilon_1 \nabla^2 \phi_1(\mathbf{x}) = \sum_{k=1}^{N_c} q_k \delta(\mathbf{x} - \mathbf{y}_k), \quad \mathbf{x} \in \Omega_1, \tag{1}$$

$$\varepsilon_2 \nabla^2 \phi_2(\mathbf{x}) + \kappa^2 \phi_2(\mathbf{x}) = 0, \quad \mathbf{x} \in \Omega_2, \tag{2}$$

$$\phi_1(\mathbf{x}) = \phi_2(\mathbf{x}), \quad \varepsilon_1 \frac{\partial \phi_1(\mathbf{x})}{\partial \nu} = \varepsilon_2 \frac{\partial \phi_2(\mathbf{x})}{\partial \nu}, \quad \mathbf{x} \in \Gamma, \tag{3}$$

$$\lim_{|\mathbf{x}| \to \infty} \phi(\mathbf{x}) = 0. \tag{4}$$

where $\varepsilon_1, \varepsilon_2$ are the dielectric constants in Ω_1, Ω_2, respectively, q_k is the partial atomic charge, δ is the Dirac delta function, ν is the outward unit normal vector on Γ, and $\bar{\kappa}$ is the modified Debye-Hückel parameter (modified to dielectric independent) measuring the ionic concentration. We have $\bar{\kappa}^2 = \kappa^2 \epsilon_2$ where κ^2 is Debye-Hückel parameter.

In all work mentioned in this article the interface Γ is the solvent excluded surface (also called the molecular surface) obtained by rolling a solvent sphere over the van der Waals surface of the solute [6,7]. Figure 1(a) gives an illustration in 2-D for the molecular surface. In protein simulation, we use the software MSMS [8] to generate the molecular surface and Figure 1(b) gives the triangulated molecular surface of a sample protein (PDB: 1a63) with 2065 atoms.

Grid based finite difference methods for solving the PB Eq. (1)–(2) subject to its interface and boundary conditions (2)–(3) is challenging due to:

1) the biomolecule is represented by singular point charges,
2) the molecular surface Γ is geometrically complex,
3) the dielectric constant is discontinuous across the molecular surface
4) the domain is unbounded.

(a)   (b)

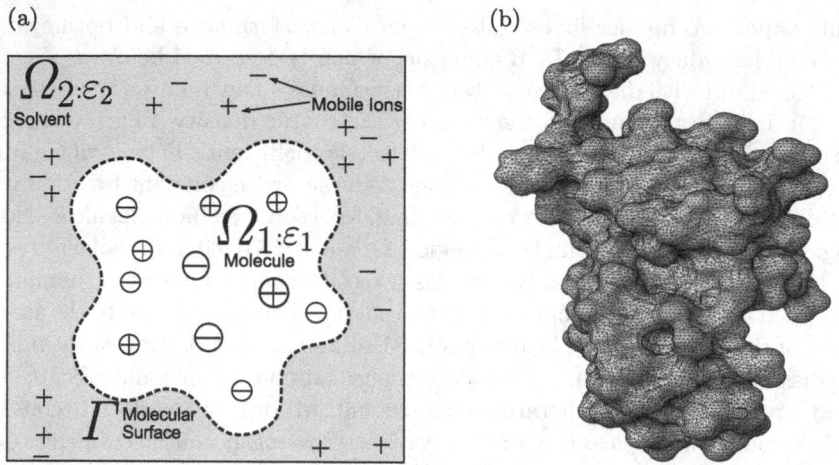

Fig. 1. (a) Poisson-Boltzmann (PB) model: domains Ω_1(`molecule`) and Ω_2(`solvent`) with different dielectric constants ε_1 and ε_2 respectively; (b) the molecular surface is formed by the trace of solvent probe in contact with the solute (molecule).

Boundary element PB solvers bypass above difficulties and have the following advantages:

1) only surface discretizations are needed, rather than volume discretizations,
2) the singular point charges are treated analytically,
3) the molecular surface can be represented accurately using boundary elements,
4) the interface conditions can be explicitly enforced,
5) the far-field boundary condition can be imposed analytically.

Details about Poisson-Boltzmann model, formulation, numerical algorithm and applications can be found in reviews [9–11]. The rest of the paper is organized as the following. In Sect. 2, we introduce the related algorithms of the boundary integral PB solvers including formulation, discretization, treecode algorithm, and parallelization. In Sect. 3, we provide some brief numerical results for parallel efficiency. This paper is ended with a section of concluding remarks.

2   Algorithms

2.1   Boundary Integral PB Formulation

Starting from Eqs. (1)–(2) together with their fundamental solutions, the Coulomb potential $G_0(\mathbf{x}, \mathbf{y})$ and screened Coulomb potential $G_\kappa(\mathbf{x}, \mathbf{y})$ as,

$$G_0(\mathbf{x}, \mathbf{y}) = \frac{1}{4\pi|\mathbf{x} - \mathbf{y}|}, \quad G_\kappa(\mathbf{x}, \mathbf{y}) = \frac{e^{-\kappa|\mathbf{x} - \mathbf{y}|}}{4\pi|\mathbf{x} - \mathbf{y}|}, \tag{5}$$

utilizing the interface jump conditions in Eq. (2), Juffer et al. [12] derived the well-posed integral PB formulation governing the surface potential ϕ_1 and its normal derivative $\frac{\partial \phi_1}{\partial \nu}$ on Γ,

$$\frac{1}{2}(1+\varepsilon)\,\phi_1(\mathbf{x}) = \int_\Gamma \left[K_1(\mathbf{x},\mathbf{y}) \frac{\partial \phi_1(\mathbf{y})}{\partial \nu} + K_2(\mathbf{x},\mathbf{y})\phi_1(\mathbf{y}) \right] dS_\mathbf{y} + S_1(\mathbf{x}), \quad \mathbf{x} \in \Gamma, \quad (6a)$$

$$\frac{1}{2}\left(1+\frac{1}{\varepsilon}\right)\frac{\partial \phi_1(\mathbf{x})}{\partial \nu} = \int_\Gamma \left[K_3(\mathbf{x},\mathbf{y}) \frac{\partial \phi_1(\mathbf{y})}{\partial \nu} + K_4(\mathbf{x},\mathbf{y})\phi_1(\mathbf{y}) \right] dS_\mathbf{y} + S_2(\mathbf{x}), \quad \mathbf{x} \in \Gamma, \quad (6b)$$

where $\varepsilon = \varepsilon_2/\varepsilon_1$. The kernels K_{1-4} are defined by

$$K_1(\mathbf{x},\mathbf{y}) = G_0(\mathbf{x},\mathbf{y}) - G_\kappa(\mathbf{x},\mathbf{y}), \quad K_2(\mathbf{x},\mathbf{y}) = \varepsilon \frac{\partial G_\kappa(\mathbf{x},\mathbf{y})}{\partial \nu_\mathbf{y}} - \frac{\partial G_0(\mathbf{x},\mathbf{y})}{\partial \nu_\mathbf{y}}, \quad (7a)$$

$$K_3(\mathbf{x},\mathbf{y}) = \frac{\partial G_0(\mathbf{x},\mathbf{y})}{\partial \nu_\mathbf{x}} - \frac{1}{\varepsilon}\frac{\partial G_\kappa(\mathbf{x},\mathbf{y})}{\partial \nu_\mathbf{x}}, \quad K_4(\mathbf{x},\mathbf{y}) = \frac{\partial^2 G_\kappa(\mathbf{x},\mathbf{y})}{\partial \nu_\mathbf{x} \partial \nu_\mathbf{y}} - \frac{\partial^2 G_0(\mathbf{x},\mathbf{y})}{\partial \nu_\mathbf{x} \partial \nu_\mathbf{y}}, \quad (7b)$$

The source terms $S_{1,2}$ are defined by

$$S_1(\mathbf{x}) = \frac{1}{\varepsilon_1}\sum_{k=1}^{N_c} q_k G_0(\mathbf{x},\mathbf{y}_k), \quad S_2(\mathbf{x}) = \frac{1}{\varepsilon_1}\sum_{k=1}^{N_c} q_k \frac{\partial G_0(\mathbf{x},\mathbf{y}_k)}{\partial \nu_\mathbf{x}}. \quad (8)$$

Equations (6a) (6b) comprise a set of coupled second kind integral equations for the surface potential ϕ_1 and its normal derivative $\frac{\partial \phi_1}{\partial \nu}$ on Γ. These well-posed boundary integral equations are applied in PB solvers contained in this package. We next introduced related numerical algorithms.

2.2 Discretization

We discretize the integral equations in Eqs. (6a)–(6b) by using purely the flat triangles [4] with centroid collocation.

Let $\mathbf{x}_i, A_i, i = 1, \ldots, N$ denote the centroids and areas of the faces in the triangulation. Then the discretized Eq. (6a)–(6b) have the following form for $i = 1, \ldots, N$,

$$\frac{1}{2}(1+\varepsilon)\,\phi_1(\mathbf{x}_i) = \sum_{\substack{j=1 \\ j\neq i}}^{N} \left[K_1(\mathbf{x}_i,\mathbf{x}_j) \frac{\partial \phi_1(\mathbf{x}_j)}{\partial \nu} + K_2(\mathbf{x}_i,\mathbf{x}_j)\phi_1(\mathbf{x}_j) \right] A_j + S_1(\mathbf{x}_i),$$

$$(9a)$$

$$\frac{1}{2}\left(1+\frac{1}{\varepsilon}\right)\frac{\partial \phi_1(\mathbf{x}_i)}{\partial \nu} = \sum_{\substack{j=1 \\ j\neq i}}^{N} \left[K_3(\mathbf{x}_i,\mathbf{x}_j) \frac{\partial \phi_1(\mathbf{x}_j)}{\partial \nu} + K_4(\mathbf{x}_i,\mathbf{x}_j)\phi_1(\mathbf{x}_j) \right] A_j + S_2(\mathbf{x}_i).$$

$$(9b)$$

Equations (9a)–(9b) define a linear system $\mathbf{Ax} = \mathbf{b}$, where $\mathbf{x}$ contains the surface potential values $\phi_1(\mathbf{x}_i)$ and normal derivative values $\frac{\partial \phi_1}{\partial \nu}(\mathbf{x}_i)$, and $\mathbf{b}$

contains the source terms $S_1(\mathbf{x}_i), S_2(\mathbf{x}_i)$. The linear system is solved by GMRES iteration which requires a matrix-vector product in each step [13]. Since the matrix is dense, computing the product by direct summation requires $O(N^2)$ operations, which is prohibitively expensive when N is large, and in a later section we describe the treecode algorithm used to accelerate the product. The treecode has been successfully applied on the centroid discretization algorithm, achieving significant acceleration compared with the direct summation [4].

2.3   Treecode Algorithm

We here summarize the treecode algorithm and refer to previous work for more details [2,3]. The required sums in Eqs. (9a)–(9b) have the form of N-body potentials,

$$V_i = \sum_{\substack{j=1 \\ j \neq i}}^{N} q_j G(\mathbf{x}_i, \mathbf{x}_j), \quad i = 1, \ldots, N, \tag{10}$$

where G is a kernel as in Eq. (5), $\mathbf{x}_i, \mathbf{x}_j$ are locations of target and source particles, and q_j is a charge associated with $\mathbf{x}_j$. For example, the term involving K_1 on the right side of Eq. (9a) has the form given in Eq. (10) with $q_j = \frac{\partial \phi_1(\mathbf{x}_j)}{\partial \nu} A_j$. To evaluate the potentials V_i rapidly, the source particles $\mathbf{x}_j$'s are divided into a hierarchy of clusters having a tree structure. The root cluster is a cube containing all the particles and subsequent levels are obtained by dividing a parent cluster into eight children [2]. The process continues until a cluster has fewer than N_0 particles (a user-specified parameter).

Once the clusters are determined, the treecode evaluates the potential in Eq. (10) as a sum of particle-cluster interactions,

$$V_i \approx \sum_{c \in N_i} \sum_{\mathbf{x}_j \in c} q_j G(\mathbf{x}_i, \mathbf{x}_j) + \sum_{c \in F_i} \sum_{\|\mathbf{k}\|=0}^{p} a^{\mathbf{k}}(\mathbf{x}_i, \mathbf{x}_c) \, m_c^{\mathbf{k}}, \tag{11}$$

where c denotes a cluster, and N_i, F_i denote the near-field and far-field of particle $\mathbf{x}_i$. The first term on the right is a direct sum for particles $\mathbf{x}_j$ near $\mathbf{x}_i$, and the second term is a pth order Cartesian Taylor approximation about the cluster center $\mathbf{x}_c$ for clusters that are well-separated from $\mathbf{x}_i$. The Taylor coefficients are given by

$$a^{\mathbf{k}}(\mathbf{x}_i, \mathbf{x}_c) = \frac{1}{\mathbf{k}!} \partial_{\mathbf{y}}^{\mathbf{k}} G(\mathbf{x}_i, \mathbf{x}_c), \tag{12}$$

and the cluster moments are given by

$$m_c^{\mathbf{k}} = \sum_{\mathbf{x}_j \in c} q_j (\mathbf{x}_j - \mathbf{x}_c)^{\mathbf{k}}. \tag{13}$$

Cartesian multi-index notation is used with $\mathbf{k} = (k_1, k_2, k_3), k_i \in \mathbb{N}, \|\mathbf{k}\| = k_1 + k_2 + k_3, \mathbf{k}! = k_1! k_2! k_3!$. A particle $\mathbf{x}_i$ and a cluster c are defined to be well-separated if the following multipole acceptance criterion (MAC) is satisfied,

$$\frac{r_c}{R} \leq \theta, \tag{14}$$

where $r_c = \max_{\mathbf{x}_j \in c} |\mathbf{x}_j - \mathbf{x}_c|$ is the cluster radius, $R = |\mathbf{x}_i - \mathbf{x}_c|$ is the particle-cluster distance, and θ is a user-specified parameter [2]. If the criterion is not satisfied, the code examines the children of the cluster recursively until the leaves of the tree are reached at which point direct summation is used. The Taylor coefficients are computed using recurrence relations [3].

2.4   Parallelization

In order to solve the linear algebraic system from Eqs. (9a) and (9b), the matrix-vector product $\mathbf{Ax}$ needs to be computed at each iteration step. This is by nature a straight-forward parallelization. Table 1 is the pseudocode for the MPI based parallelization. Note we designed a cyclic order to assign particles to processors [5], achieving significantly improved parallel efficiency. Here cyclic order means assigning particles that are locally close to each other to different processors instead of one processor (regular order).

Table 1. Pseudocode for parallel TABI solver using replicated data algorithm.

1 on main processor
2   read protein data
3   call MSMS to generate triangulation
4   copy protein data and triangulation to all other processors
5 on each processor
6   build local copy of tree
7   compute assigned segment of source terms by direct sum
8   copy result to all other processors
9   set initial guess for GMRES iteration
10   compute assigned segment of matrix-vector product by treecode
11   copy result to all other processors
12   test for GMRES convergence
13   if no, go to step 10 for next iteration
14   if yes, go to step 15
15   compute assigned segment of electrostatic solvation energy by direct sum
16   copy result to main processor
17 on main processor
18   add segments of electrostatic solvation energy and output result

3   Results

We solved the PB equation on Protein 1a63. Table 2 shows the CPU time and parallel efficiency for both regular order and cyclic order in assigning particles to processors. Initially the parallel efficiency of solving the entire PB equation or computing Ax in each iteration are high. However, due to the fact that several subroutine parts have to be implemented in serial or partially in parallel,

Table 2. CPU time and parallel efficiency regularly paralleled treecode and cyclically paralleled treecode (cpt) for computing electrostatic interactions on molecular surface of protein 1a63 with 265,000 triangles. Treecode parameter $\theta = 0.8$, $N_0 = 500$, $p = 3$.

	Overall				Computing Ax			
	regular		cyclic		regular		cyclic	
# of proc	CPU (s)	P.E. (%)	CPU (s)	P.E. (%)	CPU (s)	P.E. (%)	CPU (s)	P.E. (%)
1	819.93	100.00	819.15	100.00	70.14	100.00	70.11	100.00
2	422.74	96.98	416.49	98.34	36.04	97.29	35.66	98.31
4	231.73	88.46	225.59	90.78	19.77	88.67	19.26	90.99
8	125.86	81.43	120.87	84.71	10.82	81.04	10.27	85.33
16	74.21	69.06	67.59	75.75	6.08	72.15	5.68	77.18
32	44.55	57.51	41.73	61.34	3.72	58.99	3.39	64.56
64	30.87	41.50	29.57	43.29	2.56	42.81	2.27	48.22
128	26.11	24.54	24.93	25.67	2.14	25.58	1.72	31.81

the parallel efficiency are reduced when larger amount of processors are used. For example, from the profiling of the test case as seen in Table 2, forming the linear algebraic matrix in solving PB equation counts for 2.43 % of the total CPU time; computing moments, which happens in each matrix-vector product, counts for 1.24 % of the total CPU time. When more processors are used, this small percentage will weight more and more as they are not parallelized in currently adopted scheme. In addition, we observed the cyclic ordering significantly improves the parallel efficiency in computing Ax with the rate of approximately 5 %.

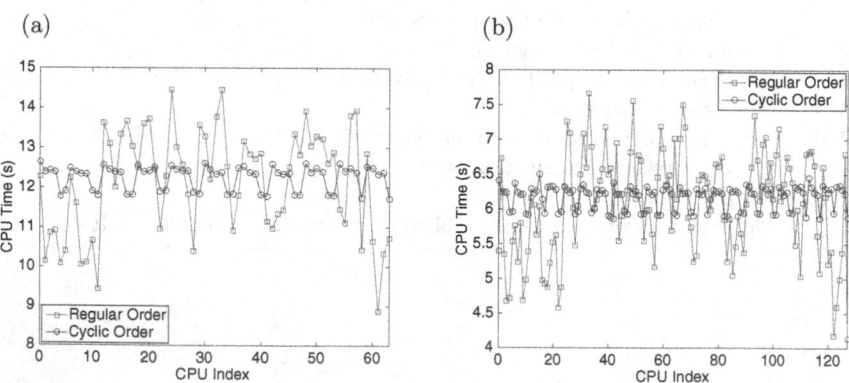

Fig. 2. CPU time consumed on each processor in between the cyclic order (red circle) and regular order (blue square) for 64 processors (a) and 128 processors (b); 1a63 with 265,000 triangles. Treecode parameter $\theta = 0.8$, $N_0 = 500$, $p = 3$. (Color figure online)

Figure 2 compares the load balance of the regular order and the cyclic order. The cyclic order has obviously improved load balance thus improved parallel efficiency as in Table 2.

4 Conclusion

In this paper, we showed that Cartesian treecode with manageable order of accuracy can be efficiently paralleled for solving the boundary integral PB equation. The MPI based parallelization is easy to implement with only a few lines of modification based on the serial version. The parallel efficiency is high initially and gradually reduced with the increase of number of processors because the serial part weights more as parallel part counts less CPU time. The cyclic ordering of assigning particles to processors significantly improved the load balance of the parallelization thus improves the overall parallel efficiency.

References

1. Greengard, L., Rokhlin, V.: A fast algorithm for particle simulations. J. Comput. Phy. **73**(2), 325–348 (1987)
2. Barnes, J., Hut, P.: A hierarchical o(n log n) force-calculation algorithm. Nature **324**(6096), 446 449 (1986)
3. Li, P., Johnston, H., Krasny, R.: A Cartesian treecode for screened Coulomb interactions. J. Comput. Phys. **228**(10), 3858–3868 (2009)
4. Geng, W., Krasny, R.: A treecode-accelerated boundary integral Poisson-Boltzmann solver for electrostatics of solvated biomolecules. J. Comput. Phy. **247**, 62–78 (2013)
5. Chen, J., Krasny, R., Reynolds, D., Geng, W.: Cyclically paralleled treecode for fast computing electrostatic interactions on molecular surfaces. in preparation, 2015
6. Connolly, M.L.: Depth buffer algorithms for molecular modeling. J. Mol. Graphics **3**, 19–24 (1985)
7. Lee, B., Richards, F.M.: The interpretation of protein structures: estimation of static accessibility. J. Mol. Biol. **55**(3), 379–400 (1971)
8. Sanner, M.F., Olson, A.J., Spehner, J.C.: Reduced surface: an efficient way to compute molecular surfaces. Biopolymers **38**, 305–320 (1996)
9. Baker, N.A.: Improving implicit solvent simulations: a Poisson-centric view. Curr. Opin. Struct. Biol. **15**(2), 137–143 (2005)
10. Fogolari, F., Brigo, A., Molinari, H.: The Poisson-Boltzmann equation for biomolecular electrostatics: a tool for structural biology. J. Mol. Recognit. **15**(6), 377–392 (2002)
11. Lu, B.Z., Zhou, Y.C., Holst, M.J., McCammon, J.A.: Recent progress in numerical methods for the Poisson-Boltzmann equation in biophysical applications. Commun. Comput. Phy. **3**(5), 973–1009 (2008)
12. Juffer, A., Botta, E., van Keulen, B., van der Ploeg, A., Berendsen, H.: The electric potential of a macromolecule in a solvent: a fundamental approach. J. Comput. Phys. **97**, 144–171 (1991)
13. Saad, Y., Schultz, M.: GMRES: a generalized minimal residual algorithm for solving nonsymmetric linear systems. SIAM J. Sci. Stat. Comput. **7**(3), 856–869 (1986)

Towards the High Performance Method for Large-Scale Electronic Structure Calculations

Zarko Bodroski[1], Nenad Vukmirovic[2], and Srdjan Skrbic[3(✉)]

[1] Department of Mathematics and Informatics, Faculty of Sciences,
University of Novi Sad, Trg Dositeja Obradovića 3, Novi Sad, Serbia
zarko.bodroski@dmi.uns.ac.rs
[2] Institute of Physics, University of Belgrade, Pregrevica 118, Belgrade, Serbia
nenad.vukmirovic@ipb.ac.rs
[3] Department of Mathematics and Informatics, Faculty of Sciences,
University of Novi Sad, Trg Dositeja Obradovića 3, Novi Sad, Serbia
srdjan.skrbic@dmi.uns.ac.rs

Abstract. Density functional theory is a method for calculation of electronic structure of physical systems with a large number of atoms. In an effort to produce parallel implementation capable of solving systems with tens of thousands of atoms, in the first steps, we use Gaussian orbitals that allow relevant integrals to be calculated analytically. The main goal of this paper is the serial implementation of these integral calculations using C programming language. The analytical solutions consist of a very complex nested summations whose efficient implementation is the main contribution of this paper. We describe challenges encountered during implementation and their solutions. Results show that the given C implementation is at least three orders of magnitude faster than numerical solutions in the best available computational software programs.

1 Introduction

Density functional theory (DFT) [1] is a method of choice for the calculation of the electronic structure of physical systems with a relatively large number (hundreds to about a thousand) of atoms. Within DFT, one has to self-consistently solve the Kohn-Sham equations [2] for the wave functions $\psi_i(\boldsymbol{r})$ and energies ε_i

$$\left(-\frac{\hbar^2}{2m_0}\nabla^2 + V_{ion} + V_H + V_{xc}\right)\psi_i(\boldsymbol{r}) = \varepsilon_i\psi_i(\boldsymbol{r}) \tag{1}$$

where V_{ion} is the potential of the core ions, V_H is the electrostatic (Hartree) potential of the electronic charge density distribution $\rho(\boldsymbol{r})$, and V_{xc} is the exchange correlation potential which, under the local density approximation (LDA), depends only on the charge density at a given point in space. There is a strong interest to develop methods where the cost of solving the system of Eq. (1) would depend linearly on the number of atoms in the system and which will enable electronic structure calculations for systems with even tens of

© Springer International Publishing Switzerland 2016
J. Xie et al. (Eds.): HPCA 2015, LNCS 9576, pp. 90–99, 2016.
DOI: 10.1007/978-3-319-32557-6_9

thousands of atoms. Solving such large systems can only be accomplished using parallel computing techniques.

An overall strategy for tackling this challenging problem for semiconducting materials and nanostructures has recently been introduced [5,6]. Within this approach, the charge patching method (CPM) [5] is used to construct the single-particle Hamiltonian [the operator on the left hand side of Eq. (1)], while the overlapping fragments method (OFM) is used to find its eigenvalues ε_i and eigenfunctions ψ_i. The OFM is based on the idea of representing the Hamiltonian in a localized and physically well motivated basis. The whole system is divided into many small fragments, that are not necessarily disjoint, and the eigenstates of the fragments are chosen as the basis for the representation of the Hamiltonian.

The most demanding computational step in the OFM is the calculation of fragment eigenstates. In current implementation of CPM and OFM [5,6], the plane wave basis was used to represent all relevant quantities (including the fragment eigenstates). While plane wave basis yields numerically accurate results, it comes at a price of high computational cost because a large number of plane waves is needed to accurately represent the wave functions which vary rapidly in the region near the atoms. For this reason, a significant decrease of computational cost can be obtained if some basis of states which are localized is used. One such basis is the basis of Gaussian orbitals. The convenience of Gaussian orbitals is that the relevant integrals involving them can be calculated analytically and that one needs a small number of orbitals to accurately represent the wave functions.

In this paper, we present the implementation of the calculation of all relevant integrals that will be required to implement the CPM and OFM in the basis of Gaussian orbitals.

2   Theoretical Background

To solve the eigenvalue problem given by Eq. (1), one expands the wave function ψ as a linear combination of some predefined orbitals ϕ_m

$$\psi = \sum_m \alpha_m \phi_m. \tag{2}$$

Equation (1) then takes the form of the matrix eigenvalue problem:

$$\sum_n \left[\int \phi_m(\boldsymbol{r})^* \left(-\frac{\hbar^2}{2m_0}\nabla^2 + V_{ion} + V_H + V_{xc} \right) \phi_n(\boldsymbol{r}) \right] \alpha_n$$

$$= \varepsilon_m \sum_n \left[\int \phi_m(\boldsymbol{r})^* \phi_n(\boldsymbol{r}) \right] \alpha_n. \tag{3}$$

As already mentioned, we choose Gaussian orbitals defined as

$$\phi_A(\boldsymbol{r}) = N(x - A_x)^l (y - A_y)^m (z - A_z)^n e^{-\alpha(\boldsymbol{r}-\boldsymbol{A})^2}, \tag{4}$$

where

$$N = (2\alpha/\pi)^{3/4} \sqrt{\left[\frac{(8\alpha)^{l+m+n} l! m! n!}{(2l)!(2m)!(2n)!} \right]} \tag{5}$$

is the normalisation constant, α is orbital exponent, l, m, n are non-negative integers and A_x, A_y, A_z are the Cartesian coordinates of the atom where the Gaussian orbital is centered.

To solve the eigenvalue problem Eq. (3) one needs to calculate all the integrals given in Eq. (3): the overlap integral, the kinetic integral, the nuclear attraction integral and the electron repulsion integral. The definition of these integrals and the analytical formulas used to calculate them are given in the following sections. The main goal of this paper is the implementation of these integral calculations using C programming language. The reader interested in the derivation of the analytical formulas is referred to [4].

2.1   The Overlap Integral

In this section we give correct analytical solutions of the integrals given in Eq. (3). The solution consist of very complex nested summations. Efficient implementation of these sums is the main contribution of this paper.

If $\phi_A(\boldsymbol{r})$ and $\phi_B(\boldsymbol{r})$ are defined as in (4), the overlap integral is defined as:

$$\langle A|B \rangle = \int_{-\infty}^{\infty} d^3 \boldsymbol{r} \phi_A(\boldsymbol{r}) \phi_B(\boldsymbol{r}) \tag{6}$$

Its analytical solution reads:

$$\langle A|B \rangle = N_1 N_2 \left(\frac{\pi}{\gamma_p} \right)^{3/2} e^{-\eta_p (\boldsymbol{A}-\boldsymbol{B})^2} \sum_{i_1,i_2,o} S_x \sum_{j_1,j_2,p} S_y \sum_{k_1,k_2,q} S_z \tag{7}$$

where

$$\gamma_p = \alpha_1 + \alpha_2 \tag{8}$$

$$\eta_p = \frac{\alpha_1 \alpha_2}{\gamma_p} \tag{9}$$

$$\sum_{i_1,i_2,o} S_x = \frac{(-1)^{l_1} l_1! l_2!}{\gamma_p^{l_1+l_2}}$$

$$\sum_{i_1} \sum_{i_2} \sum_{o} \frac{(-1)^o \Omega! \alpha_1^{l_2-i_1-2i_2-o} \alpha_2^{l_1-2i_1-i_2-o}}{4^{i_1+i_2+o} i_1! i_2! o!}$$

$$\frac{\gamma_p^{2(i_1+i_2)+o} (A_x - B_x)^{\Omega-2o}}{(l_1 - 2i_1)!(l_2 - 2i_2)!(\Omega - 2o)!} \tag{10}$$

$$\Omega = l_1 + l_2 - 2(i_1 + i_2) \tag{11}$$

The summation ranges are given as:

$$i_1 = 0 \rightarrow \left[\frac{1}{2}l_1\right], i_2 = 0 \rightarrow \left[\frac{1}{2}l_2\right], o = 0 \rightarrow \left[\frac{1}{2}\Omega\right] \tag{12}$$

The sums $\mathcal{S}_y$ and $\mathcal{S}_z$ are analogously defined.

2.2   The Kinetic Integral

The kinetic integral is defined as:

$$\langle A| - \frac{1}{2}\nabla^2|B\rangle = \int_{-\infty}^{\infty} d^3r\phi_A(r)\left[-\frac{1}{2}\nabla^2\phi_B(r)\right] \tag{13}$$

Its analytical solution is:

$$\begin{aligned}
\langle A| - \frac{1}{2}\nabla^2|B\rangle = \frac{1}{2}[&\alpha_2(4(l_2 + m_2 + n_2) + 6)\langle A|B\rangle \\
&- 4\alpha_2^2(\langle A|B, l_2 + 2\rangle + \langle A|B, m_2 + 2\rangle + \langle A|B, n_2 + 2\rangle) \\
&- l_2(l_2 - 1)\langle A|B, l_2 - 2\rangle \\
&- m_2(m_2 - 1)\langle A|B, m_2 - 2\rangle \\
&- n_2(n_2 - 1)\langle A|B, n_2 - 2\rangle]
\end{aligned} \tag{14}$$

2.3   The Nuclear Attraction Integral

The nuclear attraction integral is defined as:

$$\langle A| - \frac{Z_c}{r_c}|B\rangle = -Z_c \int_{-\infty}^{\infty} d^3r \frac{\phi_A(r)\phi_B(r)}{|r - r_c|} \tag{15}$$

The analytical solution is:

$$\begin{aligned}
\langle A| - \frac{Z_c}{r_c}|B\rangle = \\
- \frac{Z_c N_1 N_2 \pi}{\gamma_p} e^{-\eta_p(A-B)^2} \sum_{i_1,i_2,o} \mathcal{A}_x \sum_{j_1,j_2,p} \mathcal{A}_y \sum_{k_1,k_2,q} \mathcal{A}_z \\
2F_\nu(\gamma_p(P - r_c)^2)
\end{aligned} \tag{16}$$

where

$$\gamma_p = \alpha_1 + \alpha_2, \eta_p = \frac{\alpha_1\alpha_2}{\gamma_P} \tag{17}$$

$$P = \frac{1}{\gamma_p}(\alpha_1 A + \alpha_2 B) \tag{18}$$

$$\sum_{i_1, i_2, o} \mathcal{A}_x = (-1)^{l_1 + l_2} l_1! l_2!$$

$$\sum_{i_1} \sum_{i_2} \sum_{o_1} \sum_{o_2} \sum_{r} \frac{(-1)^{o_2 + r}(o_1 + o_2)!}{4^{i_1 + i_2 + r} i_1! i_2! o_1! o_2! r!}$$

$$\frac{\alpha_1^{o_2 - i_1 - r} \alpha_2^{o_1 - i_2 - r} (A_x - B_x)^{o_1 + o_2 - 2r}}{(l_1 - 2i_1 - o_1)!(l_2 - 2i_2 - o_2)!(o_1 + o_2 - 2r)!}$$

$$\sum_{u} \frac{(-1)^u \mu_x! (P_x - r_{cx})^{\mu_x - 2u}}{4^u u! (\mu_x - 2u)! \gamma_p^{o_1 + o_2 - r + u}} \tag{19}$$

The summation ranges are defined as:

$$i_1 = 0 \rightarrow \left[\frac{1}{2} l_1\right], i_2 = 0 \rightarrow \left[\frac{1}{2} l_2\right]$$

$$o_1 = 0 \rightarrow l_1 - 2i_1, o_2 = 0 \rightarrow l_2 - 2i_2$$

$$r = 0 \rightarrow \left[\frac{1}{2}(o_1 + o_2)\right], u = 0 \rightarrow \left[\frac{1}{2} \mu_x\right] \tag{20}$$

Summations $\mathcal{A}_y$ and $\mathcal{A}_z$ are analogously defined.

$$\mu_x = l_1 + l_2 - 2(i_1 + i_2) - (o_1 + o_2)$$

$$\nu = \mu_x + \mu_y + \mu_z - (u + v + w) \tag{21}$$

Several different methods for the evaluation of the Boys function $F_\nu(u)$ are possible. The best choice of the method depends on ranges of u and ν and on level of accuracy which should be achieved. From the definition of the Boys function, after performing partial integration, one comes at [4]

$$F_\nu(u) = \int_0^1 t^{2\nu} e^{-ut^2} dt$$

$$= \frac{(2\nu)!}{2\nu!} \left[\frac{\sqrt{\pi}}{4^\nu u^{\nu + 1/2}} \operatorname{erf} \sqrt{u} - e^{-u} \sum_{k=0}^{\nu - 1} \frac{(\nu - k)!}{4^k (2\nu - 2k)! u^{k+1}} \right] \tag{22}$$

$F_\nu(u)$ satisfies the following recursion relation [4]

$$F_\nu(u) = \frac{(2\nu - 1) F_{\nu-1}(u) - e^{-u}}{2u} \tag{23}$$

which can also be exploited in its evaluation. Finally, the identity

$$F_\nu(u) = e^{-u} \lim_{N \to \infty} \sum_{i=0}^{N} \frac{(2u)^i}{\prod_{j=0}^{i}(2\nu + 2j + 1)} \tag{24}$$

can be used to evaluate Boys function, as well [3].

2.4 The Electron Repulsion Integral

The electron repulsion integral is defined as:

$$\langle A,C|\frac{1}{r_{12}}|B,D\rangle = \int_{-\infty}^{\infty} d^3 \boldsymbol{r}_1 \int_{-\infty}^{\infty} d^3 \boldsymbol{r}_2 \frac{\phi_A(\boldsymbol{r}_1)\phi_B(\boldsymbol{r}_1)\phi_C(\boldsymbol{r}_2)\phi_D(\boldsymbol{r}_2)}{|\boldsymbol{r}_1 - \boldsymbol{r}_2|} \tag{25}$$

Finally, its analytical solution is:

$$\langle A,C|\frac{1}{r_{12}}|B,D\rangle = -\frac{N_1 N_2 N_3 N_4 \pi^{5/2}}{\gamma_p \gamma_q \sqrt{\gamma_p + \gamma_q}}$$

$$e^{-\eta_p(\boldsymbol{A}-\boldsymbol{B})^2} e^{-\eta_q(\boldsymbol{C}-\boldsymbol{D})^2} \sum_{\substack{i_1,i_2,i_3,i_4,\\o_1,o_2,o_3,o_4,\\r_1,r_2,u}} \mathcal{J}_x \sum_{\substack{j_1,j_2,j_3,j_4,\\p_1,p_2,p_3,p_4,\\s_1,s_2,v}} \mathcal{J}_y$$

$$\sum_{\substack{k_1,k_2,k_3,k_4,\\q_1,q_2,q_3,q_4,\\t_1,t_2,w}} \mathcal{J}_z 2F_\nu(\eta(\boldsymbol{P}-\boldsymbol{Q})^2) \tag{26}$$

where

$$\gamma_p = \alpha_1 + \alpha_2, \gamma_q = \alpha_3 + \alpha_4$$

$$\eta_p = \frac{\alpha_1\alpha_2}{\gamma_p}, \eta_q = \frac{\alpha_3\alpha_4}{\gamma_q}, \eta = \frac{\gamma_p\gamma_q}{\gamma_p + \gamma_q}$$

$$\boldsymbol{P} = \frac{\alpha_1\boldsymbol{A} + \alpha_2\boldsymbol{B}}{\gamma_p}, \boldsymbol{Q} = \frac{\alpha_3\boldsymbol{C} + \alpha_4\boldsymbol{D}}{\gamma_p} \tag{27}$$

$$\sum_{\substack{i_1,i_2,i_3,i_4,\\o_1,o_2,o_3,o_4,\\r_1,r_2,u}} \mathcal{J}_x = \frac{(-1)^{l_1+l_2} l_1! l_2!}{\gamma_p^{l_1+l_2}}$$

$$\sum_{i_1}\sum_{i_2}\sum_{o_1}\sum_{o_2}\sum_{r_1} \frac{(-1)^{o_2+r_1}(o_1+o_2)!}{4^{i_1+i_2+r_1} i_1! i_2! o_1! o_2! r_1!}$$

$$\frac{\alpha_1^{o_2-i_1-r_1}\alpha_2^{o_1-i_2-r_1}\gamma_p^{2(i_1+i_2)+r_1}(A_x - B_x)^{o_1+o_2-2r_1}}{(l_1 - 2i_1 - o_1)!(l_2 - 2i_2 - o_2)!(o_1 + o_2 - 2r_1)!}$$

$$\frac{l_3! l_4!}{\gamma_q^{l_3+l_4}} \sum_{i_3}\sum_{i_4}\sum_{o_3}\sum_{o_4}\sum_{r_2} \frac{(-1)^{o_3+r_2}(o_3+o_4)!}{4^{i_3+i_4+r_2} i_3! i_4! o_3! o_4! r_2!}$$

$$\frac{\alpha_3^{o_4-i_3-r_2}\alpha_4^{o_3-i_4-r_2}\gamma_p^{2(i_3+i_4)+r_2}(C_x - D_x)^{o_3+o_4-2r_2}}{(l_3 - 2i_3 - o_3)!(l_4 - 2i_4 - o_4)!(o_3 + o_4 - 2r_2)!}$$

$$\sum_u \frac{(-1)^u \mu_x! \eta^{\mu_x-u}(P_x - Q_x)^{\mu_x-2u}}{4^u u!(\mu_x - 2u)!} \tag{28}$$

$$\mu_x = l_1 + l_2 + l_3 + l_4 - 2(i_1 + i_2 + l_3 + l_4)$$
$$- (o_1 + o_2 + o_3 + o_4)$$
$$\nu = \mu_x + \mu_y + \mu_z - (u + v + w) \tag{29}$$

Again, $F_\nu(u)$ is the Boys function given by (22).

The summations ranges are defined as:

$$i_1 = 0 \rightarrow \left[\frac{1}{2}l_1\right], i_2 = 0 \rightarrow \left[\frac{1}{2}l_2\right]$$

$$i_3 = 0 \rightarrow \left[\frac{1}{2}l_3\right], i_4 = 0 \rightarrow \left[\frac{1}{2}l_4\right]$$

$$o_1 = 0 \rightarrow l_1 - 2i_1, o_2 = 0 \rightarrow l_2 - 2i_2$$

$$o_3 = 0 \rightarrow l_3 - 2i_3, o_4 = 0 \rightarrow l_4 - 2i_4$$

$$r_1 = 0 \rightarrow \left[\frac{1}{2}(o_1 + o_2)\right], r_2 = 0 \rightarrow \left[\frac{1}{2}(o_3 + o_4)\right]$$

$$u = 0 \rightarrow \left[\frac{1}{2}\mu_x\right] \tag{30}$$

The sums $\mathcal{J}_x$ and $\mathcal{J}_y$ are analogously defined.

3   Implementation

Analytical solutions presented in the previous section have been implemented in C programming language. The complete solution is available at http://www. scorg.pmf.uns.ac.rs/parallel. The code was compiled using the GCC compiler. To test the accuracy of the developed C code, the results were compared to the numerical solutions calculated in Matlab® R2012b and both numerical and analytical solutions calculated in Mathematica® 8. The results of those solutions are used to verify the accuracy and efficiency of C results.

Numerical and analytical formula described in Sect. 2 are implemented and calculated by using different methods. The most relevant testing results are shown in Tables 1, 2 and 3. The calculated values of the integrals are presented and, when it was considered important, the execution time was given in brackets.

Table 1. Test 1 results

Method/int.(value,time)	$\langle A|B\rangle$	$\langle A| - 1/2\nabla^2|B\rangle$
Matlab (numerical)	$-3.2927819 \cdot 10^{-3}$	-
Mathematica (numerical)	$-3.29279 \cdot 10^{-3}$	$-2.30803 \cdot 10^{-1}$
Mathematica (analytical)	$-3.292782 \cdot 10^{-3}$	$-2.30803 \cdot 10^{-1}$
C (analytical)	$-3.292782 \cdot 10^{-3}$	$-2.30803 \cdot 10^{-1}$
Method/int.(value,time)	$\langle A| - Z_c/r_c|B\rangle$	$\langle A, C|1/r_{12}|B, D\rangle$
Matlab (numerical)	$8.4563478 \cdot 10^{-3}(115\,\text{s})$	-
Mathematica (numerical)	$8.45635 \cdot 10^{-3}(10.02\,\text{s})$	-
Mathematica (analytical)	$8.53629 \cdot 10^{-3}(0.8\,\text{s})$	$-6.70602 \cdot 10^{-4}(3545\,\text{s})$
C (analytical)	$8.4563503 \cdot 10^{-3}(<0.01\,\text{s})$	$2.33746748 \cdot 10^{-4}(15.4\,\text{s})$

Table 2. Test 2 results

Method/int(value,time)	$\langle A|B \rangle$	$\langle A| - 1/2\nabla^2|B \rangle$
Matlab (numerical)	$1.043215 \cdot 10^{-1}$	-
Mathematica (numerical)	$1.043215 \cdot 10^{-1}$	2.09594
Mathematica (analytical)	$1.04321 \cdot 10^{-1}$	2.09594
C (analytical)	$1.043215 \cdot 10^{-1}$	2.095937
Method/int(value,time)	$\langle A| - Z_c/r_c|B \rangle$	$\langle A, C|1/r_{12}|B, D \rangle$
Matlab (numerical)	$-3.017343169 \cdot 10^{-1}(68\,\text{s})$	-
Mathematica (numerical)	$-3.01734 \cdot 10^{-1}(9.8\,\text{s})$	-
Mathematica (analytical)	$-2.98633 \cdot 10^{-1}(1.23\,\text{s})$	$1.37929 \cdot 10^7(7334\,\text{s})$
C (analytical)	$-3.017343103 \cdot 10^{-1}(<0.01\,\text{s})$	$3.5954836 \cdot 10^{-3}(34.4\,\text{s})$

Table 3. Test 3 results

Method/int(value,time)	$\langle A|B \rangle$	$\langle A| - 1/2\nabla^2|B \rangle$
Matlab (numerical)	$-2.4587252 \cdot 10^{-2}$	-
Mathematica (numerical)	$-2.45872 \cdot 10^{-2}$	$-1.25781 \cdot 10^{-1}$
Mathematica (analytical)	$-2.45873 \cdot 10^{-2}$	$-1.257808 \cdot 10^{-1}$
C (analytical)	$-2.4587252 \cdot 10^{-2}$	$-1.2578085 \cdot 10^{-1}$
Method/int(value,time)	$\langle A| - Z_c/r_c|B \rangle$	$\langle A, C|1/r_{12}|B, D \rangle$
Matlab (numerical)	-	-
Mathematica (numerical)	$1.43685 \cdot 10^{-1}(10.48\,\text{s})$	-
Mathematica (analytical)	$1.43685 \cdot 10^{-1}(<0.01\,\text{s})$	$1.96543 \cdot 10^{-3}(0.38\,\text{s})$
C (analytical)	$1.4368531 \cdot 10^{-1}(<0.01\,\text{s})$	$1.905432 \cdot 10^{-3}(<0.01\,\text{s})$

Parameters used for the algorithms implemented in C for solving Eqs. (7), (14), (16) and (26) are listed below.

Test 1 (Table 1):
$(l_1, m_1, n_1) = (1, 2, 2)$, $(l_2, m_2, n_2) = (2, 2, 1)$,
$(l_3, m_3, n_3) = (1, 2, 1)$, $(l_4, m_4, n_4) = (2, 1, 2)$.

Test 2 (Table 2):
$(l_1, m_1, n_1) = (3, 2, 1)$, $(l_2, m_2, n_2) = (1, 1, 3)$,
$(l_3, m_3, n_3) = (1, 1, 3)$, $(l_4, m_4, n_4) = (1, 3, 1)$.

Test 3 (Table 3):
$(l_1, m_1, n_1) = (1, 1, 0)$, $(l_2, m_2, n_2) = (1, 1, 1)$,
$(l_3, m_3, n_3) = (1, 0, 1)$, $(l_4, m_4, n_4) = (0, 1, 1)$.

Shared parameters:
$A = (0.15, 0.25, 0.20)$, $B = (0.55, 0.65, 0.33)$,
$C = (0.25, 0.15, 0.23)$, $D = (0.42, 0.72, 0.61)$,
$r_c = (0.35, 0.45, 0.22)$, $Z_c = 3$,
$\alpha_1 = 3.$, $\alpha_2 = 4.$, $\alpha_3 = 4.$, $\alpha_4 = 3.$

Tests were performed running a serial version of the C code on Linux platform with one Xeon 2.4 GHz CPU core and 6 GB of RAM. For fair comparison, Matlab® and Mathematica® results were obtained on the same platform.

4   Results and Discussion

As mentioned in the introduction section, the calculations presented in this paper are meant to be a part of a complex parallel program with calculations described here performed thousands of times. That is why it is important to find a balance between accuracy and efficiency.

During the testing process it was noticed that the most demanding part is the calculation of the Boys function $F_\nu(u)$ (22). Various methods for the evaluation of $F_\nu(u)$ have been developed in the past, but very little is known about the accuracy and efficiency of these methods.

Considering the importance of $F_\nu(u)$ in the calculation of Gaussian integrals we implemented all three methods (22), (23), (24) and tested the accuracy and efficiency of each. First results show that (22) introduces significant errors in the nuclear attraction integral and the electron repulsion integral calculations, especially for larger values of ν. These errors are more obvious in the electron repulsion integral calculation because of larger number of calls and larger values of input parameter ν. The use of recursion (23) reduces the execution time and gives reasonably accurate results for smaller values of ν and therefore accurate results for the nuclear attraction integral.

Complexity of the electron repulsion integral requires a different approach. Values of ν higher than 8 in combination with our range of values for u produce significant errors in $F_\nu(u)$ calculations. As a reference to correct values of the Boys function we used numerical solutions in Matlab and Mathematica. Although the method (23) shows betters results than (22), by increasing ν both methods fail in accuracy.

These issues were solved by implementing (24). Important factor in the calculation of (24) is the proper choice of value for N. The range which gives satisfactory results for our set of input parameters u and ν is $5 \leq N \leq 10$. The example of application of different methods is shown in Table 4. Moreover, for most of the test cases, the execution time is significantly smaller then in first two implementations. This is the case if N is adequately chosen. Correctness of the results was also proven by replacing the part which calculates $F_\nu(u)$ in analytical Gaussian integral calculation algorithm in Mathematica by (24). Since analytical solution in Mathematica uses method (22) for calculation of $F_\nu(u)$, this also explains the divergence in the results for electron repulsion integral calculation in Tables 1 and 2.

Results show that calculations of analytical solutions in C are at least thousand times faster than numerical solutions in best general computational software available. Having in mind that these calculations are to be executed thousands of times, this performance gain is very important.

Table 4. Boys function ($F_\nu(u)$).

Method	$F_{10}(0.08493571428571430)$
Numerical (Mathematica)	0.04406676328867196
(22)	1.20523659261380089
(23)	0.56853261719135277
(24)	0.04406676328867185

Acknowledgements. NV is supported by European Community FP7 Marie Curie Career Integration Grant (ELECTROMAT), Serbian Ministry of Education, Science and Technological Development (project ON171017) and FP7 projects PRACE-2IP, PRACE-3IP, HP-SEE, and EGI-InSPIRE.

The work is partially is supported by Serbian Ministry of Education, Science and Technological Development (project ON174023, Intelligent techniques and their integration into wide-spectrum decision support) and Swiss National Science Foundation (project IZ74Z0_160453/1, Developing Capacity for Large Scale Productivity Computing)

Authors would also like to thank Tomas Petterson for providing help in testing analytical solutions for Mathematica.

References

1. Hohenberg, P., Kohn, W.: Inhomogeneous electron gas. Phys. Rev. **136**, B864 B871 (1964). http://link.aps.org/doi/10.1103/PhysRev.136.B864
2. Kohn, W., Sham, L.J.: Self-consistent equations including exchange and correlation effects. Phys. Rev. **140**, A1133–A1138 (1965). http://link.aps.org//10.1103/PhysRev.140.A1133
3. Mamedov, B.A.: On the evaluation of boys functions using downward recursion relation. J. Math. Chem. **36**(3), 301–306 (2004)
4. Petersson, T., Hellsing, B.: A detailed derivation of gaussian orbital-based matrix elements in electron structure calculations. Eur. J. Phys. **31**(1), 37–46 (2010)
5. Vukmirović, N., Wang, L.W.: Charge patching method for electronic structure of organic systems. J. Chem. Phys. **128**, 121102 (2008)
6. Vukmirovic, N., Wang, L.W.: Overlapping fragments method for electronic structure calculation of large systems. J. Chem. Phys. **134**(9), 8 (2011)

A Dispersion-Relation-Preserving Upwind Combined Compact Scheme for Convection-diffusion Equations with Variable Coefficients

Shouhui Zhang[1,2]($\boxtimes$), Xuanxin Wang[2], and Weidong Zhao[1]

[1] School of Mathematics, Shandong University, Jinan 250100, Shandong, China
ss_zhangsh@ujn.edu.cn
[2] School of Mathematical Sciences,
University of Jinan, Jinan 250022, Shangdong, China

Abstract. In the paper a new dispersion-relation-preserving upwind combined compact difference scheme (DRP-UCCD) to solve a time-dependent convection diffusion equations with variable coefficients is proposed. The developed scheme is constructed by making use of the high-order upwind combined compact difference operators, which can preserve the dispersion relation and enhance the convective stability. The scheme is proved to have the unconditional stability and the error accuracy is six order on space and two order on time. Numerical experiments confirm its high efficiency.

Keywords: Combined compact difference · Convection-diffusion equation · Dispersion-relation-preserving · Variable coefficient · Unconditionally stable

AMS Subject Classifications 2000: 65M06 · 65M12 · 65Y05

1 Introduction

The convection-diffusion equations are commonly used in sciences for governing the transport of a quantity such as concentration, heat and energy [2,6]. It is important to develop numerical methods with high performance and stability to solve the problems. A new research focus of compact difference schemes toward highly accurate numerical schemes of partial differential equations (PDEs) has come into being. Adam [3] and Hirsh [11] proposed Hermitian compact techniques using fewer nodes (three instead of five) at each grid point to solve PDEs. Later on, Adam [4] pointed out, the truncation errors are usually four to six times smaller than the same order noncompact schemes. Since then, much work has come into being about developing compact schemes [10,13,22].

But numerical solving the convection-diffusion equations must consider reducing the indispensable dispersion error, which describe the difference

© Springer International Publishing Switzerland 2016
J. Xie et al. (Eds.): HPCA 2015, LNCS 9576, pp. 100–112, 2016.
DOI: 10.1007/978-3-319-32557-6_10

between the effective and actual wave numbers. So it is important to apply a scheme with good convective stability even for solving a convection-dominated C-D equation with high Reynolds numbers. Many upwind schemes have been proposed [8,14,15,19] to overcome the convective instability. And [17] showed the monotonic upwind schemes are effective in enhancing the convective stability. Another idea to enhance convective stability is to consider the dispersive nature of the investigated first-order derivative term [18].

[21] pointed out that if a scheme accommodates the same dispersion relation as that of the original first order derivative, it can preserve the dispersion relation rigorously. [1] put forward that the relation can characterize the angular frequency relation with respect to the wave number of the spatial derivative term. That some numerical features such as the dispersion, dissipation, group and phase velocities for each wave component supported by the first-order derivative term can be well modeled is the main reason of constructing the dispersion-relation-preserving (DRP) scheme [12].

The combined compact difference(CCD) scheme proposed by Adam [7], is for solving the first and second derivatives simultaneously. The resulting scheme is more compact and accurate than the normal difference schemes constructed on the same stencil points. [5] proposed a new high-order upwind combined compact difference scheme combining with the compact expressions of the first-order and second-order derivative terms, which can keep almost the same dispersion relation as the original convection and diffusion terms of partial differential equation. At the same time, it deals with the boundary condition more easily than the other five point schemes. Most research of high-order CCD schemes was done for solving steady partial difference equations, which indicated their validity and high efficiency. But there is limited research of high-order CCD schemes to solve time-dependent equations with variable coefficients. There is great interest in developing and analyzing the high-order CCD methods for unsteady variable coefficient PDE's.

In this paper, a high order Dispersion-Relation-Preserving upwind CCD scheme is proposed to solve the unsteady convection-diffusion equations with variable coefficients. The proposed scheme can not only solve the numerical solutions of the equations in high accuracy but also has the good convective stability which can preserve the same dispersion relation. The important feature is that we construct the high order upwind compact difference scheme for varying coefficients and time-dependent convection-diffusion equations. The scheme is proved to have unconditional stability and the truncation error is six-order on space and two-order on time. Numerical experiments show the validity of the schemes and confirm the theoretical analysis results.

The following convection-diffusion equations are considered:

$$\frac{\partial u}{\partial t} + k(x)\frac{\partial u}{\partial x} = \varepsilon(x)\frac{\partial^2 u}{\partial x^2}, \quad 0 < x < L, \quad t \in (0, T], \tag{1.1}$$

$$u(0, t) = u(L, t), \quad t \in (0, T], \tag{1.2}$$

$$u(x,0) = u_0(x), \quad 0 \leq x \leq L. \tag{1.3}$$

where $\Omega = [0, L], T > 0$ is time period, $\varepsilon(x)$ is the diffusion functions, and $\varepsilon(x) \geqslant \varepsilon_0 > 0, x \in \Omega$. $k(x)$ is the velocity function. Assume the initial $u_0(x)$ is a smooth function.

The paper is organized as follows: In Sect. 2, we introduce the construction of the upwind combined compact differences. Section 3 gives the DRP upwind combined compact difference method for solving the problems. Section 4 illustrates the unconditional stability and analyzes the truncation errors. Finally, numerical experiments are given in Sect. 5.

2   The DRP Upwind Combined Compact Differences

We first present the construction of the DRP upwind combined compact operators(DRP UCCD) [5]. The first derivative term and the second derivative term, in Eqs. (2.1–2.2), are approximated respectively by the following three-point compact stencil

$$a_1 \frac{\partial \phi}{\partial x}|_{i-1} + \frac{\partial \phi}{\partial x}|_i = \frac{1}{h}(c_1 \phi_{i-1} + c_2 \phi_i + c_3 \phi_{i+1}) - h(b_1 \frac{\partial^2 \phi}{\partial x^2}|_{i-1} + b \frac{\partial^2 \phi}{\partial x^2}|_i + b_3 \frac{\partial^2 \phi}{\partial x^2}|_{i+1}) \tag{2.1}$$

$$\begin{aligned} \overline{b}_1 \frac{\partial^2 \phi}{\partial x^2}|_{i-1} + \frac{\partial^2 \phi}{\partial x^2}|_i + \overline{b}_3 \frac{\partial^2 \phi}{\partial x^2}|_{i+1} &= \frac{1}{h^2}(\overline{c}_1 \phi_{i-1} + \overline{c}_2 \phi_i + \overline{c}_3 \phi_{i+1}) \\ &\quad - \frac{1}{h}(\overline{a}_1 \frac{\partial \phi}{\partial x}|_{i-1} + \overline{a}_2 \frac{\partial \phi}{\partial x}|_i + \overline{a}_3 \frac{\partial \phi}{\partial x}|_{i+1}) \end{aligned} \tag{2.2}$$

Note that the compact schemes for $\frac{\partial \phi}{\partial x}$ and $\frac{\partial^2 \phi}{\partial x^2}$ are rather strongly coupled though terms $\frac{\partial \phi}{\partial x}|_{i-1}, \frac{\partial \phi}{\partial x}|_i, \frac{\partial \phi}{\partial x}|_{i+1}, \frac{\partial^2 \phi}{\partial x^2}|_{i-1}, \frac{\partial^2 \phi}{\partial x^2}|_i, \frac{\partial^2 \phi}{\partial x^2}|_{i+1}, \phi_{i-1}, \phi_i, \phi_{i+1}$. For simplicity, we only consider the positive convective coefficient in the above equation only.

Since the discretization error of $\frac{\partial^2 \phi}{\partial x^2}$ approximated by applying the central schemes will be prevailingly dissipative, the weighting coefficients in Eq. (2.2) were be solved solely for a higher spatial accuracy in [5]. By applying the Taylor series expansions, it can be solved and had an unique solution as $\overline{a}_1 = -\frac{9}{8}, \overline{a}_2 = 0, \overline{a}_3 = \frac{9}{8}, \overline{b}_1 = -\frac{1}{8}, \overline{b}_3 = -\frac{1}{8}, \overline{c}_1 = 3, \overline{c}_1 = -6, \overline{c}_3 = 3$. The presently derived difference scheme approximate $\frac{\partial^2 \phi}{\partial x^2}$ with the spatial accuracy order of sixth

$$\begin{aligned} \frac{9}{8h}(\frac{\partial \phi}{\partial x}|_{i+1} - \frac{\partial \phi}{\partial x}|_{i-1}) + \frac{\partial^2 \phi}{\partial x^2}|_i - \frac{1}{8}(\frac{\partial^2 \phi}{\partial x^2}|_{i+1} + \frac{\partial^2 \phi}{\partial x^2}|_{i-1}) \\ = \frac{3}{h^2}(\phi_{i+1} - 2\phi_i + \phi_{i-1}) - \frac{1}{20160}\frac{\partial^8 \phi}{\partial x^8}h^6, \end{aligned} \tag{2.3}$$

Next, we put a lot attention on the approximation of $\frac{\partial \phi}{\partial x}$. By the same way for Eq. (2.1) as the above procedure, the derived linear algebraic equations for Eq. (2.1) as follows

$$c_1 + c_2 + c_3 = 0, \tag{2.4a}$$

$$-a_1 - c_1 + c_3 = 1, \tag{2.4b}$$

$$-a_1 + b_1 + b_2 + b_3 - \frac{c_1}{2} - \frac{c_3}{2} = 0, \tag{2.4c}$$

$$-\frac{a_1}{2} - b_1 + b_3 + \frac{c_1}{6} - \frac{c_3}{6} = 0, \tag{2.4d}$$

$$-\frac{a_1}{6} + \frac{b_1}{2} + \frac{b_3}{2} - \frac{c_1}{24} - \frac{c_3}{24} = 0, \tag{2.4e}$$

$$\frac{a_1}{24} - \frac{b_1}{6} + \frac{b_3}{6} + \frac{c_1}{120} - \frac{c_3}{120} = 0, \tag{2.4f}$$

All the seven introduced coefficients can't be solved uniquely by the linear systems shown in Eq. (2.1). Next, we conclude the final algebraic equation by embedding the dispersive nature as much as possible. [8] proposed that the dispersion relation governs the relation between the angular frequency and the wave number of the first-order dispersive term. So it is most importance to construct a scheme which accommodates the dispersion relation for the first-order derivative term.

In order to preserve the relation, the Fourier transform and its inverse for ϕ will be applied

$$\widetilde{\phi}(\alpha) = \frac{1}{2\pi} \int_{-\infty}^{+\infty} \phi(x) exp(-j\alpha x) dx \tag{2.5}$$

$$\phi(x) = \int_{-\infty}^{+\infty} \widetilde{\phi}(\alpha) exp(j\alpha x) d\alpha \tag{2.6}$$

where $j = \sqrt{-1}$. Performing Fourier transform on each term shown in Eqs. (2.1–2.2), the actual wavenumber α can be therefore derived as

$$\begin{aligned} j\alpha h(a_1 exp(-j\alpha h) + 1) &\simeq c_1 exp(-j\alpha h) + c_2 + c_3 exp(j\alpha h) \\ &- (j\alpha h)^2 (b_1 exp(-j\alpha h) + b_2 + b_3 exp(j\alpha h)), \end{aligned} \tag{2.7}$$

$$\begin{aligned} (j\alpha h)^2 (-\tfrac{1}{8} exp(-j\alpha h) + 1 - \tfrac{1}{8} exp(j\alpha h)) &\sim 3 exp(-j\alpha h) - 6 + 3 exp(j\alpha h) \\ &- (j\alpha h)^2 (-\tfrac{9}{8} exp(-j\alpha h) + \tfrac{9}{8} exp(j\alpha h)), \end{aligned} \tag{2.8}$$

[23] proposed that the effective wavenumbers α' and α'' have the same expressions as that of Eqs. (2.7–2.8) in an approximation sense. So it's rational to express α' and α'' as follows

$$\begin{aligned} j\alpha' h(a_1 exp(-j\alpha h) + 1) &= c_1 exp(-j\alpha h) + c_2 + c_3 exp(j\alpha h) \\ &- (j\alpha'' h)^2 (b_1 exp(-j\alpha h) + b_2 + b_3 exp(j\alpha h)), \end{aligned} \tag{2.9}$$

$$\begin{aligned} (j\alpha' h)^2 (-\tfrac{1}{8} exp(-j\alpha h) + 1 - \tfrac{1}{8} exp(j\alpha h)) &\simeq 3 exp(-j\alpha h) - 6 + 3 exp(j\alpha h) \\ &- (j\alpha'' h)^2 (-\tfrac{9}{8} exp(-j\alpha h) + \tfrac{9}{8} exp(j\alpha h)), \end{aligned} \tag{2.10}$$

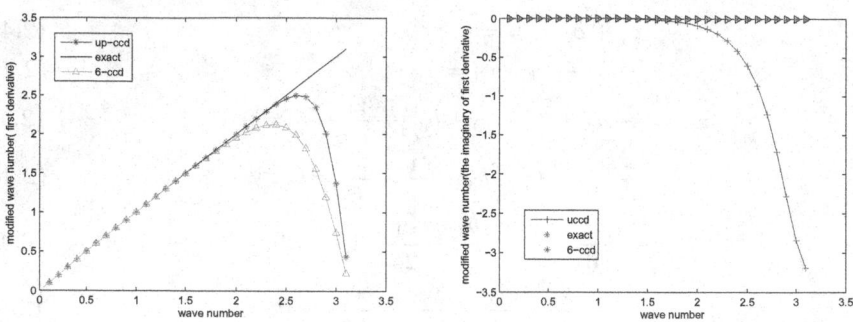

Fig. 1. The comparison of the real part(left) and imaginary part(right) of the modified wave number of first derivative ($\alpha'h$) by two methods

By solving Eqs. (2.9–2.10), the expression for α' and α'' can be derived. That $\alpha h \approx R[\alpha'h]$ is necessary for acquiring a better dispersive accuracy for α', where $R[\alpha'h]$ denotes the real part of $\alpha'h$. This indicates that $E(\alpha)$ defined below should be a very small and positive value

$$E(\alpha) = \int_{-\frac{\pi}{2}}^{\frac{\pi}{2}} [W(\alpha h - R[\alpha h])^2]\alpha h = \int_{-\frac{\pi}{2}}^{\frac{\pi}{2}} [W(\gamma - R[\gamma'])^2]d(\gamma) \qquad (2.11)$$

where $\gamma = \alpha h$ and $\gamma' = \alpha'h$ and the weighting function W shown above is the denominator of $(\gamma - R[\gamma'])$. Making use of the minimum value theorem for E, the following extreme condition is enforced

$$\frac{\partial E}{\partial c_3} = 0. \qquad (2.12)$$

Combining the above equation with Eqs. (2.4), the resulting seven introduced unknowns given below can be uniquely determined as

$$a_1 = 0.875, \quad b_1 = 0.12512823415990895606 \qquad (2.13a)$$

$$b_2 = -0.24871765840091043936, \quad b_3 = 0.00012823415990089560636, \qquad (2.13b)$$

$$c_1 = -1.9359611900810925272, \quad c_2 = 1.9969223801621850545 \qquad (2.13c)$$

$$c_3 = -0.060961190081092527237 \qquad (2.13d)$$

The above upwind scheme developed for $\frac{\partial \phi}{\partial x}$ can be easily proved to have fifth order in spatial from the following modified equation

$$\frac{\partial \phi}{\partial x} = \frac{\partial \phi}{\partial x}\big|_{exact} - 0.00070085615243989224 7h^5 \frac{\partial^6 \phi}{\partial x^6} + O(h^6) \qquad (2.14)$$

Figures 1 and 3 show that the present upwind combined compact difference scheme is much better than the six order CCD in [7] in approximating the derivative and frequency and phase.

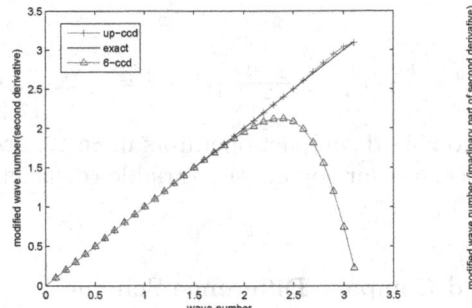 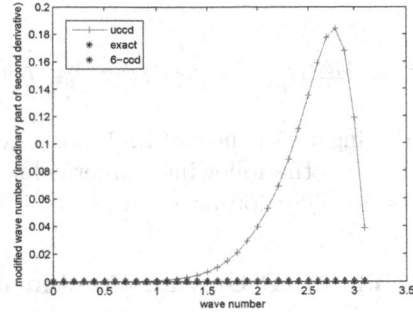

Fig. 2. Comparison of the real part(left) and imaginary part(right) of the modified wave number for second derivative $(\alpha''h)$ by two methods

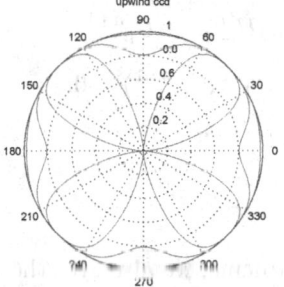 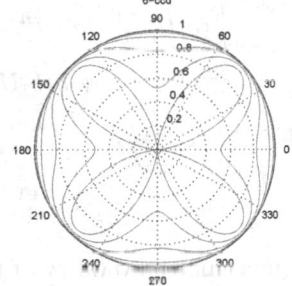

Fig. 3. Comparison of the predicted phase speed anisotropy against θ by the two methods

3   The DRP Upwind Combined Compact Difference Method

Now we construct the high-order combined compact difference scheme for varying coefficient convection-diffusion Eqs. (1.1)–(1.3) by making use of the two CCD operators defined in Sect. 2.

Because the combined compact operators can approximate the function value and its first derivative and second derivative, we only discretize the convection-diffusion problem on time as follows. At the grid point $x_i, i = 1, 2, \ldots, m$, the time Crank- Nicolson difference scheme in $[t^n, t^{n+1}]$ is considered:

$$\frac{u_i^{n+1}-u_i^n}{\Delta t} + \frac{k_i}{2}[u_i^{'n+1} + u_i^{'n}] = \frac{\varepsilon_i}{2}[u_i^{''n+1} + u_i^{''n}] + O(\Delta t^2), \quad i = 1, 2, \ldots, m-1 \quad (3.1)$$

normalsize where $k_i = k(x_i)$, $\varepsilon_i = \varepsilon(x_i)$. Deleting the truncation error term and replacing the u_i', u_i'' by their approximations U_i', U_i'', we can get the following numerical scheme by rearranging:

$$U_i^{n+1} + \frac{k_i \Delta t}{2} U_i^{\prime n+1} - \frac{\varepsilon_i \Delta t}{2} U_i^{\prime\prime n+1} = U_i^n - \frac{k_i \Delta t}{2} U_i^{\prime n} + \frac{\varepsilon_i \Delta t}{2} U_i^{\prime\prime n}, \quad i = 1, 2, \dots, m$$

$$(3.2)$$

Making use of the two high-order combined compact operators in Sect. 2, we can propose the following numerical schemes for solving the variable coefficient convection-diffusion problem (1.1)–(1.3):

3.1 The DRP Upwind Combined Compact Difference Scheme

$$U_i^{n+1} + \frac{k_i \Delta t}{2} U_i^{\prime n+1} - \frac{\varepsilon_i \Delta t}{2} U_i^{\prime\prime n+1} = U_i^n - \frac{k_i \Delta t}{2} U_i^{\prime n} + \frac{\varepsilon_i \Delta t}{2} U_i^{\prime\prime n}, \quad (3.3\text{a})$$

$$- \frac{1}{h}(c_1 U_{i-1}^{n+1} + c_2 U_i^{n+1} + c_3 U_{i+1}^{n+1}) + a_1 U_{i-1}^{\prime n+1} + U_i^{\prime n+1}$$

$$+ h(b_1 U_{i-1}^{\prime\prime n+1} + b_2 U_i^{\prime\prime n+1} + b_3 U_{i+1}^{\prime\prime n+1}) = 0, \quad (3.3\text{b})$$

$$\frac{9}{8h}(U_{i+1}^{\prime n+1} - U_{i-1}^{\prime n+1}) - \frac{1}{8}(U_{i+1}^{\prime\prime n+1} + U_{i-1}^{\prime\prime n+1}) + U_i^{\prime\prime n+1}$$

$$- \frac{3}{h^2}(U_{i+1}^{n+1} - 2U_i^{n+1} + U_{i-1}^{n+1}) = 0. \quad (3.3\text{c})$$

For comparing the validity of the numerical scheme, we also give the numerical scheme based on the four-order combined compact difference scheme for solving problem (1.1)–(1.3):

3.2 The Four-Order CCD C-N Scheme

$$U_i^{n+1} + \frac{k_i \Delta t}{2} U_i^{\prime n+1} - \frac{\varepsilon_i \Delta t}{2} U_i^{\prime\prime n+1} = U_i^n - \frac{k_i \Delta t}{2} U_i^{\prime n} + \frac{\varepsilon_i \Delta t}{2} U_i^{\prime\prime n}, \quad (3.4\text{a})$$

$$U_{i+1}^{\prime n+1} + 4U_i^{\prime n+1} + U_{i-1}^{\prime n+1} = \frac{3}{h}[U_{i+1}^{n+1} - U_{i-1}^{n+1}], \quad (3.4\text{b})$$

$$U_{i+1}^{\prime\prime n+1} + 10U_i^{\prime\prime n+1} + U_{i-1}^{\prime\prime n+1} = \frac{12}{h^2}[U_{i+1}^{n+1} - 2U_i^{n+1} + U_{i+1}^{n+1}]. \quad (3.4\text{c})$$

Because of the periodic boundary condition (1.2), Eqs. (3.3) and (3.4) need the periodical boundary condition. We calculate the initial value of the first- and second- derivatives by making use of $u_0(x)$ for $i = 1, 2, \dots, m$,

$$U_i^0 = u_0(x_i), \quad U_i^{\prime 0} = u_0^\prime(x_i), \quad U_i^{\prime\prime 0} = u_0^{\prime\prime}(x_i). \quad (3.5)$$

4   Theoretical Analysis

[9,13,16,20,23] pointed out that Fourier analysis is commonly used to evaluate various difference schemes extensively. As pointed in [13], discrete Fourier analysis is an effective way to quantify the resolution characteristics of difference approximations.

The solution variable $u(x)$ is assumed to be periodic over the domain [0,L] of the independent variable, i.e., $u_1 = u_{m+1}$ and $h = \frac{L}{m}$, in order to make use of the discrete Fourier analysis. So the solution variable $u(x)$ can be expressed by Fourier series,

$$u(x) = \sum_{l=-\frac{m}{2}}^{l=\frac{m}{2}} \hat{u}_l e^{2\pi jlx/L}, \qquad (4.1)$$

For convenience, a scaled wavenumber $w = 2\pi lh/L = 2\pi l/m$, and a scaled coordinates $s = x/h$ are introduced. Then discretizing (4.1) can produce a function with exact Fourier coefficients

$$\hat{u}_l' = \frac{jw}{h}\hat{u}_l, \quad \hat{u}_l'' = -(\frac{w}{h})^2\hat{u}_l.$$

At the same time, the Fourier coefficients of the derivative approximations obtained by Eqs. (3.3a-c) might not be the same as the exact Fourier coefficients,

$$(\hat{U}_l') = \frac{jw'}{h}\hat{u}_l, \quad (\hat{U}_l'') = -(\frac{w''}{h})^2\hat{u}_l;$$

where $w' = w'(w)$ and $w'' = w''(w)$ are denoted as the modified wavenumber (both real numbers) for the first-order and second-order derivatives. The difference scheme will be better if the difference between the exact and modified wavenumbers is smaller.

The modified wavenumbers w' and w'' in the CCD scheme Eqs. (3.3b,c) can be calculated jointly as follows:

$$u(x) = \sum_l \hat{u}_l e^{(jw(x/h))}, \quad u'(x) = \sum_l \hat{u}_l' e^{(jw(x/h))}, \quad u''(x) = \sum_l \hat{u}_l'' e^{(jw(x/h))}$$
$$(4.2)$$

and

$$U'(x) = \sum_l (\hat{U}_l') e^{(jw(x/h))}, \quad U''(x) = \sum_l (\hat{U}_l'') e^{(jw(x/h))}, \qquad (4.3)$$

$$u(x + h) = \sum_l \hat{u}_l e^{(jw(x/h))} e^{jw}, \quad u(x - h) = \sum_l \hat{u}_l e^{(jw(x/h))} e^{-jw}, \qquad (4.4)$$

$$U'(x + h) = \sum_l (\hat{U}_l') e^{(jw(x/h))} e^{jw}, \quad U'(x - h) = \sum_l (\hat{U}_l') e^{(jw(x/h))} e^{-jw}, \qquad (4.5)$$

$$U''(x + h) = \sum_l (\hat{U}_l'') e^{(jw(x/h))} e^{jw}, \quad U''(x - h) = \sum_l (\hat{U}_l'') e^{(jw(x/h))} e^{-jw}. \qquad (4.6)$$

Substituting of Eqs. (4.2)–(4.6) into Eqs. (3.3b,c), we have:

$$jw'(a_1 exp(-jw) + 1) = c_1 exp(-jw) + c_2 + c_3 exp(jw)$$
$$-(jw'')^2(b_1 exp(-jw) + b_2 + b_3 exp(jw)), \qquad (4.7)$$

$$(jw')^2(-\tfrac{1}{8}exp(-jw) + 1 - \tfrac{1}{8}exp(jw)) \simeq 3exp(-jw) - 6 + 3exp(jw)$$
$$-(jw'')^2(-\tfrac{9}{8}exp(-jw) + \tfrac{9}{8}exp(jw)), \qquad (4.8)$$

Solving Eqs. (4.7)–(4.8), we have that

$$w'(w) = -j[(c_1 + 24b_1)exp(-2jw) + (c_2 - 8c_1 + 24b_2 - 48b_1)exp(-jw)$$
$$+ (c_2 - 8c_3 - 48b_3 + 24b_2)exp(jw) + (c_1 - 8c_2 + c_3 + 24b_1 + 24b_3 - 48b_2)$$
$$+ (c_3 + 24b_3)exp(2jw)]/[(a_1 - 9b_1)exp(-2jw) + (1 - 8a_1 - 9b_2)exp(-jw)$$
$$+ (1 + 9b_2)exp(jw) + (a_1 - 8 + 9b_1 - 9b_3) + 9b_3exp(2jw)],$$
$$(4.9)$$

$$w''(w) = \sqrt{-\frac{3exp(-jw) - 6 + 3exp(jw) - jw'(-\tfrac{9}{8}exp(-jw) + \tfrac{9}{8}exp(jw))}{-\tfrac{1}{8}exp(-jw) + 1 + \tfrac{1}{8}exp(jw)}}. \qquad (4.10)$$

Suppose $w'(w) = a + jb, w''(w) = c + jd$, Fig. 1 shows that $a > 0 \geq b$ and $c \gg d > 0$ and the real part is the main part in approximating to the problem.

Substituting Eqs. (4.6) into (3.3a) and comparing the coefficient of the Fourier basic function, we have

$$(1 + j\frac{k_i\triangle tw'}{2h} + \frac{\varepsilon_i\triangle tw''^2}{2h^2})\widehat{U}_i^{n+1} = (1 - j\frac{k_i\triangle tw'}{2h} - \frac{\varepsilon_i\triangle tw''^2}{2h^2})\widehat{U}_i^n \qquad (4.11)$$

where $\widehat{U}_i^n$ is the i-th component of numerical solution U of Eqs. (3.3). Substituting $w'(w), w''(w)$ into Eq. (4.1), we can obtain the amplification factor is as follows

$$\lambda = \frac{1 - \frac{\varepsilon_i\triangle tw''^2}{2h^2} - j\frac{k_i\triangle tw'}{2h}}{1 + \frac{\varepsilon_i\triangle tw''^2}{2h^2} + j\frac{k_i\triangle tw'}{2h}} = \frac{1 - (\frac{\varepsilon_i\triangle t(c^2 - d^2)}{2h^2} - \frac{k_i\triangle tb}{2h}) - j(\frac{\varepsilon_i\triangle tcd}{h^2} + \frac{ak_i\triangle t}{2h})}{1 + (\frac{\varepsilon_i\triangle t(c^2 - d^2)}{2h^2} - \frac{k_i\triangle tb}{2h}) + j(\frac{\varepsilon_i\triangle tcd}{h^2} + \frac{ak_i\triangle t}{2h})} \qquad (4.12)$$

Because $\varepsilon(x) \geq \varepsilon_0 > 0$ and $b < 0, c^2 - d^2 > 0$, the following result can be obtained

$$|\lambda| = \frac{|1 - (\frac{\varepsilon_i\triangle t(c^2 - d^2)}{2h^2} - \frac{k_i\triangle tb}{2h}) - j(\frac{\varepsilon_i\triangle tcd}{h^2} + \frac{ak_i\triangle t}{2h})|}{|1 + (\frac{\varepsilon_i\triangle t(c^2 - d^2)}{2h^2} - \frac{k_i\triangle tb}{2h}) + j(\frac{\varepsilon_i\triangle tcd}{h^2} + \frac{ak_i\triangle t}{2h})|}$$
$$= \frac{\sqrt{(1 - (\frac{\varepsilon_i\triangle t(c^2 - d^2)}{2h^2} - \frac{k_i\triangle tb}{2h}))^2 + (\frac{\varepsilon_i\triangle tcd}{h^2} + \frac{ak_i\triangle t}{2h})^2}}{\sqrt{(1 + (\frac{\varepsilon_i\triangle t(c^2 - d^2)}{2h^2} - \frac{k_i\triangle tb}{2h}))^2 + (\frac{\varepsilon_i\triangle tcd}{h^2} + \frac{ak_i\triangle t}{2h})^2}} \leq 1 \qquad (4.13)$$

So there is

$$\|U^{n+1}\| \leq \|U^n\| \leq \cdots \leq \|U^0\|. \qquad (4.14)$$

It indicates that the numerical schemes is unconditionally stable.

Theorem 1. *The new six-order CCD C-N scheme (3.3) is unconditionally stable.*

5   Numerical Experiments

In this section, we consider a convection-diffusion equation and solve it by the high order upwind combined compact difference scheme and the Four-order CCD scheme to confirm the validity and higher efficiency.

Consider the following convection diffusion equation

$$\frac{\partial u}{\partial t} + a\frac{\partial u}{\partial x} = b\frac{\partial^2 u}{\partial x^2}, \quad 0 < x < 1, 0 < t < T; \tag{5.1}$$

$$u(0,t) = u(1,t), \quad 0 < t < T; \tag{5.2}$$

$$u_0(x) = sin(2\pi x) \quad 0 < x < 1. \tag{5.3}$$

The exact solution is

$$u(x,t) = e^{-4b\pi^2 t} sin(2\pi(x-t)),$$

where $a = 1$. We fix $\Delta t = h^3, T = 0.01, N = [\frac{T}{\Delta t}]$, let $h = \frac{1}{J}$ being variable according to $J's$ changing. Let $U_{i,j}^N$ be the numerical solution at the $(x_i, t_N), t_N = N\Delta t$, and $u(x_i, t_N)$ be the exact solution at the respective point.
Let

$$e_{l_2} = \{\sum_{i=1}^{J}(U_i^N - u(x_i y, t_N))^2 h^2\}^{\frac{1}{2}}$$

denote the discrete L^2-norm error, and

$$e_m = \parallel U_i^N - u(x_i, t_N) \parallel_\infty = \max_{1 \le i \le J-1} |U_i^N - u(x_i, t_N)|$$

denote the discrete maximum norm error, and the ratios of convergence are

$$R_{m,h} = \frac{log(e_m(h_1)/e_m(h_2))}{log(h_1/h_2)},$$

$$R_{l_2,h} = \frac{log(e_{l_2}(h_1)/e_{l_2}(h_2))}{log(h_1/h_2)}.$$

Table 1 gives the respective errors and ratios in space step. It shows that the ratio of the DPR Upwind CCD is six order. From Table 2, we can see the new CCD is more effective than the four-order CCD for the case of $b = 1$.

The ratio in time step is denoted as follows:

$$R_{m,t} = \frac{log(e_m(\Delta t_1)/e_m(\Delta t_2))}{log(\Delta t_1/\Delta t_2)},$$

$$R_{l_2,t} = \frac{log(e_{l_2}(\Delta t_1)/e_{l_2}(\Delta t_2))}{log(\Delta t_1/\Delta t_2)}.$$

Table 3 gives the numerical results which indicate the errors and the ratios in time step of six-order CCD for the convection-diffusion equation with $a = 1, b = 1$. It indicates that as the convergence of space improves, the convergence of time is second order and more stable than the Four-order CCD.

Table 1. The results of the convergence in space step by the DPR Upwind CCD scheme.

b	J	15	20	25	30	35	40	45	50
		\multicolumn{8}{c}{$(\,h = 1/J, \Delta t = h^3, T = 0.01)$}							
	h	0.067	0.050	0.040	0.033	0.029	0.025	0.022	0.020
1	e_m	5.93e-6	1.26e-6	3.92e-7	1.51e-7	6.75e-8	3.37e-8	1.84e-8	1.07e-8
	order	-	5.379	5.240	5.239	5.220	5.188	5.161	5.154
	e_{l_2}	1.08e-6	2.01e-7	5.55e-8	1.95e-8	8.06e-9	3.77e-9	1.94e-9	1.07e-9
	order	-	5.852	5.773	5.747	5.722	5.686	5.658	5.649
0.001	e_m	3.12e-7	7.28e-8	2.40e-8	9.61e-9	4.42e-9	2.26e-9	1.26e-9	7.41e-10
	order	-	5.056	4.975	5.021	5.042	5.028	4.964	5.028
	e_{l_2}	5.69e-8	1.16e-8	3.40e-9	1.24e-9	5.28e-10	2.53e-10	1.32e-10	7.40e-11
	order	-	5.536	5.498	5.524	5.536	5.518	5.501	5.520

Table 2. The ratios of the convergence in space step by the DPR Upwind CCD and 4-CCD schemes.

Scheme	J	15	20	25	30	35	40	45	50
		\multicolumn{8}{c}{$(\,h = 1/J, b = 1, \Delta t = h^3, T = 0.01)$}							
	h	0.067	0.050	0.040	0.033	0.029	0.025	0.022	0.020
6-CCD	e_m	5.93e-6	1.26e-6	3.92e-7	1.51e-7	6.75e-8	3.37e-8	1.84e-8	1.07e-8
	order	-	5.379	5.240	5.239	5.220	5.188	5.161	5.154
	e_{l_2}	1.08e-6	2.01e-7	5.55e-8	1.95e-8	8.06e-9	3.77e-9	1.94e-9	1.07e-9
	order	-	5.852	5.773	5.747	5.722	5.686	5.658	5.649
4-CCD	e_m	3.11e-5	1.03e-5	4.37e-6	2.13e-6	1.16e-6	6.81e-7	4.26e-7	2.80e-7
	order	-	3.846	3.845	3.935	3.963	3.971	3.974	3.990
	e_{l_2}	5.69e-6	1.64e-6	6.18e-7	2.75e-7	1.38e-7	7.61e-8	4.50e-8	2.80e-8
	order	-	4.315	4.380	4.438	4.467	4.470	4.471	4.486

Table 3. The ratios of the convergence on time by the DPR Upwind CCD and 4-CCD schemes.

Scheme	J	15	20	25	30	35	40	45	50	55
		\multicolumn{9}{c}{$(\,h = 1/J, \Delta t = h^3, T = 0.01)$}								
	Δt	4.44e-3	2.5e-3	1.60e-3	1.11e-3	8.16e-4	6.25e-4	4.94e-4	4.00e-4	3.31e-4
6-CCD	e_m	5.93e-6	1.26e-6	3.92e-7	1.51e-7	6.75e-8	3.37e-8	1.84e-8	1.07e-8	6.55e-9
	order	-	1.793	1.747	1.746	1.740	1.729	1.720	1.718	1.706
	e_{l_2}	1.09e-6	2.01e-7	5.6e-8	1.95e-8	8.06e-9	3.77e-9	1.94e-9	1.07e-9	6.3e-10
	order	-	1.951	1.924	1.916	1.907	1.895	1.886	1.883	1.877
4-CCD	e_m	1.47e-2	8.67e-3	6.48e-3	4.85e-3	3.77e-3	3.04e-3	2.55e-3	2.17e-3	1.88e-3
	order	-	1.836	1.306	1.592	1.621	1.619	1.508	1.524	1.518
	e_{l_2}	1.10e-3	5.55e-4	4.04e-4	2.83e-4	2.04e-4	1.53e-4	1.23e-4	1.01e-4	8.30e-5
	order	-	2.379	1.422	1.955	2.113	2.180	1.813	1.941	2.009

6   Conclusion

In this paper, a six-order combined compact difference scheme for solving convection-diffusion equations with variable coefficients has been presented, where the term $\frac{\partial u}{\partial t}$ is approximated by the C-N scheme and the first and second spatial derivatives are approximated by the high-order combined compact difference operators in space step.

The high-order compact difference method was proved to be unconditionally stable. The truncation error was analyzed and the global truncation error is $O(\triangle t^2 + h^6)$. The numerical experiments showed the efficiency of the theoretical results. The plan of the following research is extend the application to the multi-dimensional convection diffusion problems with variable coefficients.

Acknowledgements. S.H. Zhang was supported by Promotive Research Fund for Excellent Young and Middle-aged Scientists of Shandong Province (BS2013NJ016) and the Project-sponsored by SRF for ROCS, SEM.

References

1. Abalakin, I.A., Alexandrov, A.V., bOBkov, V.G., Kozubskaya, T.K.: HIgh accuarcy methods and software development in computational aeroacoustics. J. Comput. Mth. Sci. Eng. **2**(3), 1–14 (2003)
2. Aziz, K., Settari, A.: Petrolem Reservoir Simulation. Applied Science Publisher Ltd, London (1979)
3. Adam, Y.: A Hermitian Finite-Difference method for the solution of parabolic equations. Comput. Math. Appl. **1**, 393–406 (1975)
4. Adam, Y.: Highly accurate compact implicit methods and boundary conditions. J. Comput. Phys. **24**, 10–22 (1977)
5. Chiu, P.H., Sheu, T.W.H.: On the development of a dispersion-relation-preserving dual-compact upwind scheme for convection-diffusion equation. J. Comp. Phys. **118**, 3640–3655 (2009)
6. Chorin, A.J., Marsdon, J.E.: A Mathematical Introduction to Fluid Mechanics, 2nd edn. Springer-Verlag, Heidelberg (1990)
7. Chu, P.C., Fan, C.E.: A three-point combined compact difference scheme. J. Comput. Phys. **140**, 370–399 (1998)
8. de Felice, G., Denaro, F.M., Meola, C.: Multidimensional single-step vector upwind schemes for highly convective transport problems. Numer. Heat Transf. B **23**(4), 425–460 (1993)
9. Fromm, J.E.: Practical investigation of convective difference approximations of reduced dispersion. Phys. Fluids Suppl. **12**, 2–3 (1969)
10. Goedheer, W.J., Potters, J.H.M.: A compact finite difference scheme on a non-equidistant mesh. J. Comput. Phys. **61**, 269–279 (1985)
11. Hirsh, R.S.: Higher order accurate difference solutions of fluid mechanics problems by a compact differencing technique. J. Comput. Phys. **19**, 90–109 (1975)
12. Hu, F.Q., Hussaini, M.Y., Anthey, J.L.: Low-dissipation and low-dispersion Runge-Kutta schemes for computational acoustics. J. Comput. Phys. **124**, 177–191 (1996)
13. Lele, S.K.: Compact finite-difference schemes with spectral-like resolution. J. Comput. Phys. **103**, 16–42 (1992)
14. Leonard, B.P.: Astable and accurate convective modelling procedure based on quadratic upstream interpolation. Comp. Meth. Appl. Mech. Eng. **19**, 59–98 (1979)
15. Li, Y., Rudman, M.: Assessment of higher-order upwind schemes incorporating FCT for convection-dominated problems. Numer. Heat Transf. B **27**(1), 1–21 (1995)
16. Orszag, S.A.: Numerical simulation of incompressible flows within simple boundaries: accuracy. J. Fluid Mech. **49**, 75–112 (1971)

17. Sheu, T.W.H., Tsai, S.F., Wang, M.M.T.: Monotome multidimensional upwind finite element method fot advection-diffusion problems. Numer. Heat Transf. B **29**(3), 325–334 (1996)
18. Sheu, T.W.H., Tsai, S.F., Wang, S.K.: Monotonic multidimensional flux discretization scheme for all Peclet numbers. Numer. Heat Transf. B **31**(4), 441–457 (1997)
19. Spalding, D.B.: A novel finite difference formulation for differential expressions involving both first and second derivatives. Int. J. Nm. Meth. Eng. **4**, 551–559 (1972)
20. Swartz, B., Wendroff, B.: The relative efficiency of finite difference and finite element methods. I. Hyperbolic problems and splines. SIAM J. Numer. Anal. **11**, 979–993 (1974)
21. Tam, C.K.W., Webb, J.C.: Dispersion-realtion-preserving finite difference schemes for computational acoustics. J. Comput. Phys. **107**, 262–281 (1993)
22. Tolstykh, A.I.: On a class of noncentered compact difference schemes of fifth-order based on Pade approximants. Sov. Math. Dokl. **44**, 69 (1992)
23. Vichnevetsky, R., Bowles, J.B.: Fourier Analysis of Numerical Approximations of Hyperbolic Equations (SIAM Philadelphia 1982)

Performance Optimization of a DEM Simulation Framework on GPU Using a Stencil Model

Ran Xue[1], Yuxin Wang[1(✉)], He Guo[2], Chi Zhang[2], and Shunying Ji[3]

[1] School of Computer Science and Technology, Dalian University of Technology, Dalian, China
wyx@dlut.edu.cn
[2] School of Software Technology, Dalian University of Technology, Dalian, China
[3] State Key Laboratory of Structural Analysis for Industrial Equipment,
Dalian University of Technology, Dalian, China

Abstract. High performance and efficiency for parallel computing has significance in large scale discrete element method (DEM) simulation. After analyzing a simulation framework of DEM built on a Graphic Processor Unit (GPU) platform with CUDA architecture and evaluating the simulated data, we propose three optimization methods to improve the performance of a system. A stencil computation model is applied to the particle searching and calculation of forces based on gridding to formulate the structure in the particle-particle contact and neighboring particle searching. In addition, a reasonable and effective parallel granularity is sought out by altering the number of blocks and threads on GPU. A shared-memory environment is set up for data prefetching and storing the results of intermediate calculations by a rational analysis and calculations. The results of the experiment show that the stencil model is useful for the particle searching and calculation of forces and the rational parallel granularity as well as the fair use of shared memory optimizes the performance of the DEM simulation framework.

Keywords: DEM · GPU computing · Performance optimization · Stencil model

1 Introduction

In the recent years discrete element model (DEM) simulations have been increasingly used to study and analyze flows of particulate systems in the interaction between particles [1]. It is widely accepted that long run times and subsequently high computational costs are major limitations of this method, particularly when a large number of particles are involved. Since a considerable number of particles exist in the simulations of the present study (more than 500,000 particles), an effective solution must be adopted to reduce the run time of simulations [2]. Various numerical simulations in general scientific fields have been implemented by using GPUs. Compared with CPUs, GPUs have a parallel throughput architecture that emphasizes executing many and relatively slow

This work was supported by the National Natural Science Foundation of China (No. 11372067).

J. Xie et al. (Eds.): HPCA 2015, LNCS 9576, pp. 113–119, 2016.
DOI: 10.1007/978-3-319-32557-6_11

concurrent threads, rather than executing a single thread very quickly [3]. Through the past years, the reliability of GPU has been also studied for an accurate application. It is easy to apply GPU calculations for a particle method to an explicit algorithm of the DEM [4]. Elements are grouped together into blocks, and blocks are processed in parallel [5]. The performance of DEM simulation on a GPU was shown to be several dozen times faster than that on a single-thread CPU [6]. However, the main challenges to build the simulation of particle motion in practice still are how to simulate the contact force of particles due to limited computational resources and how to get high computational efficiency.

In this study we apply a stencil computation model to force calculations on the DEM simulation. In addition, we focus on capacity and performance evaluations to ensure the practical use of this simulation by reasonable experiments and analysis.

2   The Simulation Framework of DEM

Our simulation framework of DEM is built on GPU platform with CUDA architecture. According to the characteristics of hardware and DEM, cellular automata method of grid is applied to divide the particles. The algorithm divides calculation area into a series

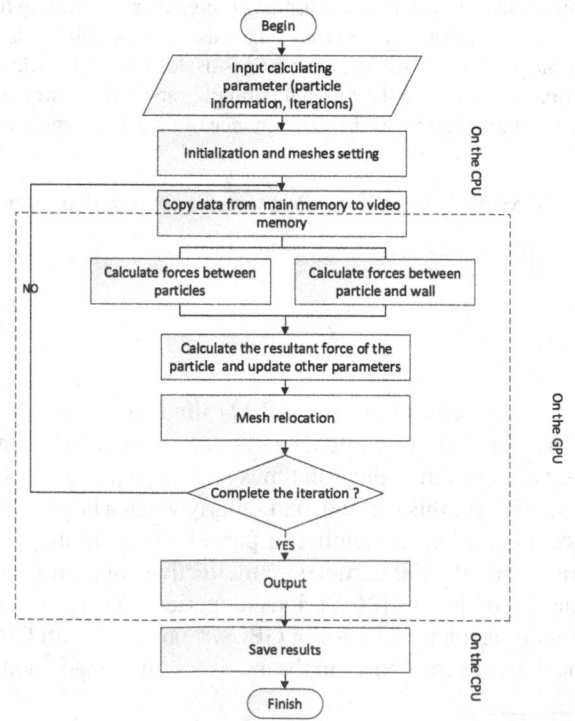

Fig. 1. The overview flow diagram of calculation

of grid cell on the basis of the size of the border area and particle size. Figure 1 shows the overview flow diagram of calculation.

Before computation, a number of calculating parameters such as particle numbers, particle coordinates, grid size, time step, iterations and so on need to be input. Then the calculation data are initialized and the grid mapping of particles is established. After the data are copied from main memory to the video memory, the force computation starts on in parallel on GPU. The calculation of forces between particle and particle is the most important part of the whole process. The computation process is implemented step by step until the iteration is completed. Finally the results are moved to the host and saved in output file.

3   Optimization Methods

3.1   Stencil Computation Model

Stencil programs perform element-wise computations on a fixed neighborhood called the stencil. Stencil computations are important in some computational science applications operating on regular grids. Mapping stencil programs to modern architectures such as GPU is a problem with a growing gap between memory and bandwidth. Such architectures require data-centric optimizations that arrange data.

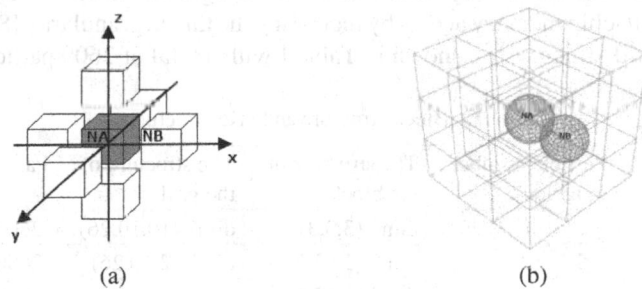

(a)   (b)

Fig. 2.   The contact impact between NA and NB

In many scientific applications stencils are the time-consuming part of particle simulating calculation [7]. As shown in Fig. 2(a) a stencil computation model is applied to the process to improve parallel computing efficiency, in which we add the intermediate results of 27 threads in the three-dimensional space grid to the core particle as shown in Fig. 2(b). In the figure, the core particle which name is "NA" need detect contact and calculate forces with neighbor particles which name is "NB" in 27 neighbor cells. In this program spatial stress analysis of the particle NA is acquired by searching 27 neighbor cells and detecting contact between particle NA and other particles from three different dimensions of the spatial grid to calculate the resultant force. Because there are 27 neighbor cells to be found and calculated by each thread, each particle is put into a thread block and each block has 27 threads to complete the particles contact detection and force calculation according to the space grid. The particle NB could be found by using "threadId" of the particle NA in the grids. The synchronization statement is needed to ensure 27 threads have finished calculation of the NA. The index of each thread can be found by using the thread ID in three different directions for a three-dimensional block of size (3,3,3).

3.2 Changing Parallel Granularity

For the purpose of balancing locality and parallelism and combining GPU resources with the characteristics of the example, different structures of thread block is created in order to seek out a reasonable and effective parallel granularity. On account of temporal and spatial locality of the stencil computation, larger thread granularity could improve the data locality and computation intensity. Before optimization only one particle is put into a block and each block has 27 threads which is based on the "3*3*3" grids to detect the contact in different directions of the three-dimensional grids. The structure of threads per block is defined with dim3 type, which is predefined in CUDA Runtime headers, such as dim3 (3,3,3). The number of thread blocks in a grid is usually dictated by the size of the data being processed or the number of processors in the system, which can greatly exceed. The program should be structured in a way that it exposes as much parallelism as possible and efficiently maps this parallelism to the various components of the system to keep them busy most of the time. Larger thread block could decrease the redundant off-chip memory access by increasing the thread granularity [8]. The block structure and grid structure are shown in Table 1 with a total of 2600 particles.

Table 1. Block structure and grid structure.

Thread number per block	Particle number in a block	The structure of the block	The structure of the grid	Particle number
27	1	dim3 (3,3,3)	dim3 (10,10,26)	2600
135	5	dim3 (15,3,3)	dim3 (2,10,26)	2600
135	5	dim3 (3,15,3)	dim3 (10,2,26)	2600
216	8	dim3 (6,6,6)	dim3 (5,5,13)	2600
270	10	dim3 (30,3,3)	dim3 (1,10,26)	2600
270	10	dim3 (3,30,3)	dim3 (10,1,26)	2600
351	13	dim3 (3,3,39)	dim3(10,10,2)	2600

We put 5, 10 and 13 particles into a thread block from one of the three different dimensions of the spatial grid and construct their spatial structure in with the help of dim3. Combining with the characteristics of the stencil model 8 neighboring particles in the space are put into a thread block to construct a new spatial structure from all of the three different dimensions of the spatial grid.

3.3   Shared-Memory Environment for Prefetching Data and Storing Intermediate Results

In the GPU device, global, local, and texture memory have the greatest access latency. Compared with them, shared memory could not only be used as the buffer for off-chip memory, but also be used to communicate among threads in the same thread block. [8] Shared memory has a read-write access and make all the threads in block to share data with a low latency. In order to hide memory latency a shared memory region is applied for data prefetching. Because there are some calculating data used repeatedly, prefetching data in the shared memory can help to improve the calculation efficiency. The array named "variableGPU[]" is defined to buffer the prefetching data for threads within the block to calculate. And there are also 27 results of intermediate calculations to be stored before the resultant force calculation. Therefore, another shared memory region is applied to buffer the array which helps to storage the intermediate results in order to calculate the resultant force of the NA.

4   Experiment and Evaluation

Considering the optimizing strategies mentioned above, we run the simulation of DEM on the GPU tesla c2050 and tesla k40 with different numbers of threads in a block and use different ways to put particles into blocks. According to the experiment data, the absolute speedup of the results on k40 is 1.414 times comparing to the results on c2050. On both two GPUs there is a consistent performance variation when we read various numbers of particles into a block from three different dimensions. Therefore, we use one line to represent three. The experimental results are shown in Figs. 3 and 4.

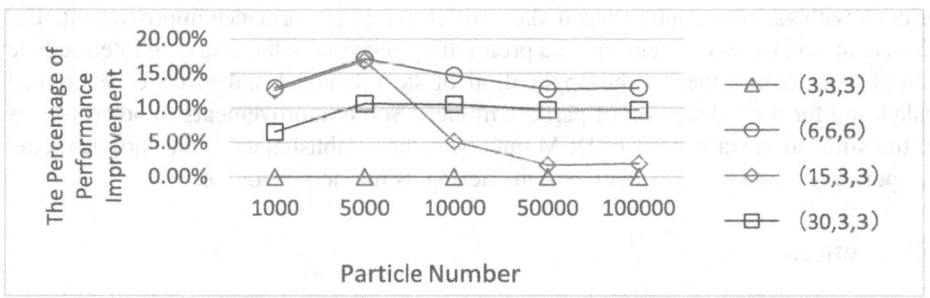

Fig. 3. The optimization results on tesla c2050

There are four comparisons to make with respect to the performance of the simulation framework. Different optimized methods represent different performance when using various parallel granularities to run the system. The three-dimensional thread block (6,6,6), which contains 8 neighboring particles in the spatial grid and 216 theads, always shows a good optimization performance with the increase of particle size on the two different GPUs. The three-dimensional thread block (15,3,3) show a good performance when the particle size is less than 5000 and then declined rapidly with the increase of

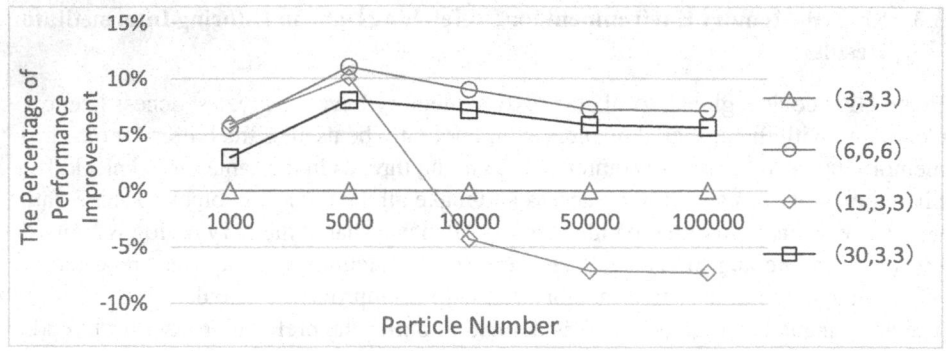

Fig. 4. The optimization results on tesla k40

particle size. However, on the k40 the three-dimensional thread block (15,3,3) presents a negative growth when the particle size is larger than 5000. The reason for this situation may be that the L2 cache of k40 reads small chunks of data from global memory with a lot of switches. Overall, we present different forms of block of threads and their experimental result analysis. showing that the design of parallel granularity is based on a circumstance in which hardware resources and the number of particles should be analysed and balanced.

5   Conclusion

The results of the experiment prove that the stencil model is useful for the particle simulation, especially in the calculation of forces between two particles. And the parallelisms with various granularities make a difference in performance improvement. The shared-memory environment for data prefetching and storing the results of intermediate calculations contributes to the application of stencil model and achieve better load balancing for the calculation of particle models. Some improvements to other aspects of the simulation framework of DEM may be in the establishment of the particle model cooperating with GPU architecture considering its memory resource.

References

1. Radeke, C.A., Glasser, B.J., Khinast, J.G.: Large-scale powder mixer simulations using massively parallel GPU architectures. Chem. Eng. Sci. **65**, 6435 (2010)
2. Hazeghian, M., Soroush, A.: DEM simulation of reverse faulting through sands with the aid of GPU computing. Comput. Geotech. **66**, 253 (2015)
3. Guanghao, J., Toshio, E., Satoshi, M.: A Multi-level Optimization Method for Stencil Computation on the Domain that is Bigger than Memory Capacity of GPU (2013). doi:10.1109/IPDPSW.2013.58
4. Hori, C., Gotoh, H., Ikari, H., Khayyar, A.: GPU-acceleration for moving particle semi-implicit method. Comput. Fluids **51**, 174 (2011)

5. Owens, J.D., Houston, M., Luebke, D., Green, S., Stone, J.E., Phillips, J.C.: GPU computing. Proc. IEEE **96**, 879 (2008)
6. Shigeto, Y., Sakai, M.: Parallel computing of discrete element method on multi-core processors. Particuology **9**, 398 (2011)
7. Yangtong, X., Haohuan, F., Lin, G., Xinliang, W., Yuchen, Q., Peng, H., Wei, X., Chao, Y.: Performance Optimization and Analysis for Different Stencil Kernels on Multi-Core and Many-Core Architectures. HPC China 2013. Guilin, 628 p. (2013)
8. Wang, G., Yang, X., Zhang, Y., Tang, T., Fang, X.: Program optimization of stencil based application on the gpu-accelerated system. In: 2009 IEEE International Symposium on Parallel and Distributed Processing with Applications (2009)

Large-Scale Log-Determinant Computation via Weighted L_2 Polynomial Approximation with Prior Distribution of Eigenvalues

Wei Peng[✉] and Hongxia Wang

College of Science, National University of Defense Technology, Sanyi Avenue, Changsha 410073, Hunan, China
weipeng0098@126.com, whx@lsec.cc.ac.cn

Abstract. Since the classic determinant computation method Cholesky decomposition may devastate sparsity of matrices and cost cubic steps, it is impractical to apply this method to large-scale symmetric positive-definite matrices due to limitation of storage and efficiency. Therefore, a randomized algorithm is proposed to calculate log-determinants of symmetric positive-definite matrices via stochastic trace approximations, implemented by weighted L_2 orthogonal polynomial expansions with efficient recursion formulas and matrix-vector multiplications based on the matrix eigenvalue distribution. As Chebyshev expansions have been applied to this problem before, our main contribution is proposing the strategies of weighted function selection based on prior eigenvalue distribution, which generalizes approximating polynomials for this problem and may accelerate computation.

Keywords: Log-determinant · Best approximation · Eigenvalue distribution · Randomized algorithm

1 Introduction

The problem of large-scale log-determinant computation widely arises from machine learning and data mining applications such as a Gaussian process [4,5] and sparse inverse covariance estimation [6,7]. Previous research has developed several randomized methods to approximate a log determinant of a symmetric positive-definite matrix. Barry and Pace [8], Boutsidis et al. [2], Hunter et al. [9] and Reusken [10] use randomized Taylor expansions for computation in a variety of settings. Randomized Chebyshev expansions are presented to accelerate Taylor seises expansions by Han et al. [3].

Though several randomized polynomial approximations have been proposed for the problem, previous research ignores the relationship between the prior eigenvalue distribution of a symmetric positive-definite matrix and the polynomials used for approximation.

This paper reveals the implicit relationship between the distribution of eigenvalues and the orthogonal polynomials to approximate log-determinants from the perspective of a best approximation in a weighted L_2 space.

© Springer International Publishing Switzerland 2016
J. Xie et al. (Eds.): HPCA 2015, LNCS 9576, pp. 120–125, 2016.
DOI: 10.1007/978-3-319-32557-6_12

2   Preliminaries

Let $\omega : (-1, 1] \to \mathbb{R}$ be a continuous function and be positive almost everywhere on $(-1, 1]$ satisfying $0 < \int_a^b x^{2n}\omega(x)dx < +\infty$, $(\forall n \geq 0)$. Denote $< \cdot, \cdot >_\omega$ as inner product and define weighted L_2 space as

$$L_2(\omega) = \left\{ f| < f(x), f(x) >_\omega = \int_{-1}^{1} |f(x)|^2 \omega(x)dx < +\infty \right\}. \tag{1}$$

It is obvious that $S_k = span\{1, x, x^2, \cdots, x^k\} = \{f(x) \text{ is a polynomial } |deg(f) \leq k\} \subseteq L_2(\omega)$. A family of orthogonal polynomials $\{Q_i(x)|i = 0, 1, 2, \cdots, k\}$ can be obtained by the Gram-Schmidt process such that $deg(Q_i(x)) = i$ and $< Q_i(x), Q_j(x) >_\omega = \delta_{ij}$. It follows that $span\{Q_i(x)|i = 0, 1, 2, \cdots, k\} = span\{1, x, x^2, \cdots, x^k\}$.

Since $L_2(\omega)$ is a Hilbert space, $\forall f(x) \in L_2(\omega)$, we have the best polynomial approximation of $f(x)$ in $L_2(\omega)$, which is the projection of $f(x)$ on $span\{Q_i(x)|i = 0, 1, 2, \cdots, k\} = span\{1, x, x^2, \cdots, x^k\}$.

$$P_N(x) = \arg \min_{p(x) \in S_N} \|f - p\|_\omega = \sum_{i=0}^{N} < f, Q_i(x) >_\omega Q_i(x). \tag{2}$$

A recurrence relation is an alternative method to obtain orthogonal polynomials:

$$Q_{n+1}(x) = \frac{x - < xQ_n(x), Q_n(x) >_\omega}{c_n} Q_n(x) - \frac{< xQ_n(x), Q_{n-1}(x) >_\omega}{c_n} Q_{n-1}(x), \tag{3}$$

where $c_n \in \mathbb{R}^{n \times n}$ is a constant so that $\|Q_{n+1}(x)\|_\omega = 1$. Note that $Q_0(x) = 1$ and $Q_1(x) = px + q$ $(p, q \in \mathbb{R}, p \neq 0)$ through the Gram-Schmidt process. Therefore, we have the recurrence relation of $tr(Q_n(C))$:

$$tr(Q_{n+1}(C)) = tr\left(\frac{C - a_n I_n}{c_n} Q_n(C)\right) - \frac{b_n}{c_n} tr(Q_{n-1}(C)), \tag{4}$$

where C is a symmetric matrix.

The important part of our algorithm includes a randomized algorithm to estimate the trace of a symmetric matrice presented by Avron.

Lemma 1 ([1]). *Let A be an $n \times n$ symmetric matrix. Given $0 < \delta < 1$, $0 < \epsilon < 1$ and $M = 20\ln(2/\delta)/\epsilon^2$, then we have*

$$Pr\left(|tr(A) - \frac{1}{M}\sum_{i=1}^{M} g_i^T A g_i| < \epsilon tr(A)\right) \geq 1 - \delta, \tag{5}$$

where $g_1, g_2, \cdots, g_M \in \mathbb{R}^n$ are independent random standard Gaussian vectors.

Combining Lemma 1 with formula (4), we can estimate $tr(Q_{n+1}(A))$ effectively via a proper arrangement of multiplications.

3   Method

Given sysmetric positive definite $A \in \mathbb{R}^{n \times n}$, where n is usually quite large and A is sparse, we aim to calculate $\log(\det(A))$. Assume the eigenvalue distribution of A is approximated by the density function $g(x)$ and $g(x) = 0$ when x is outside $(0, b]$. Without loss of generality, substitute A with $C := 2A/b - I_n$ so that eigenvalues of C donated as $\{\lambda_1, \lambda_2, \cdots, \lambda_n\}$ are supposed to be lie in interval $(-1, 1]$. We have

$$
\log(\det(A)) = \sum_{i=1}^{n} \log(\lambda_i(A))
$$

$$
= n \log(b) + \sum_{i=1}^{n} \log \frac{(\frac{2\lambda_i(A)}{b} - 1) + 1}{2}
$$

$$
= n \log(b) + \sum_{i=1}^{n} \log \frac{1 + \lambda_i(C)}{2}, \tag{6}
$$

and decompose

$$
\log \frac{1+x}{2} = P_N(x) + r_N(x), \tag{7}
$$

where $P_N(x)$ is the approximating polynomial satisfying $deg(P_N(x)) \le N$. Substitute the last term in Eq. (6) with formula (7), then

$$
\log(\det(A)) = n \log(b) + \sum_{i=1}^{n} P_N(\lambda_i) + \sum_{i=1}^{n} r_N(\lambda_i)
$$

$$
\approx n \log(b) + tr(P_N(C)), \tag{8}
$$

where we have the residual term $r_N(\lambda_i)$ truncated and let $n \log(b) + tr(P_N(C))$ be the approximate value of the log-determinant.

Let eigenvalues of C obeys a distribution with probability density function $\hat{\omega}(x)$ and assume $L_2(\hat{\omega})(-1, 1]$ is Hilbert space. We try to minimize $r_N(\lambda)_i$ with the prior eigenvalue distribution $\hat{\omega}(x)$,

$$
\frac{1}{n} \left| \sum_{i=1}^{n} r_N(\lambda_i(C)) \right| = \frac{1}{n} \left| \log \det(A) - [n \log(b) + tr(P_N(C))] \right|
$$

$$
= \frac{1}{n} \left| \sum_{i=1}^{n} \left[\log \frac{1 + \lambda_i(C)}{2} - P_N(\lambda_i(C)) \right] \right|
$$

$$
\approx \left| \int_{-1}^{1} \left[\log \frac{1+x}{2} - P_N(x) \right] \hat{\omega}(x) dx \right|
$$

$$
\le \left(\int_{-1}^{1} \left| \log \frac{1+x}{2} - P_N(x) \right|^2 \hat{\omega}(x) dx \right)^{\frac{1}{2}}. \tag{9}
$$

Minimizing the right of inequality (9) is relaxed to search for polynomials of degree no more than N, viz. projecting $\log(1/2 + x/2)$ onto the subspace $span\{1, x, x^2, \cdots, x^N\} \subseteq L_2(\hat{\omega})$.

In practice, it is not necessary to use exact $\hat{\omega}(x)$ to be the weight function. Usually, replacing $\hat{\omega}(x)$ with a similar function $\omega(x)$ is enough to obtain results of high quality.

We introduce a family of distributions on $[-1, 1]$ which might be sufficient to approximate various $\hat{\omega}(x)$. Let the probability density function be

$$\omega(x; \alpha, \beta) = J^{\alpha,\beta}(1 - x)^\alpha (1 + x)^\beta \qquad (10)$$

with $\alpha, \beta > -1$ and $J^{\alpha,\beta}$ normalizing the L_2 norm. For a fixed prior distribution $\omega(x)$, we could derive the orthogonal family of Jacobi polynomials [11] $\{J_j^{\alpha,\beta}(x)\}$ in $L_2(\omega(x; \alpha, \beta))$ via recurrence relations. $\omega(x; \alpha, \beta)$ as the weight function corresponds to well known Beta distribution [12] with probability density function:

$$f_{Beta}(x; \alpha, \beta) = \frac{\Gamma(\alpha + \beta)}{\Gamma(\alpha)\Gamma(\beta)} x^{\alpha-1}(1 - x)^{\beta-1}. \qquad (11)$$

Compare formula (10) with (11), we have

$$\omega(x; \alpha, \beta) = f_{Beta}(2x - 1; \alpha + 1, \beta + 1). \qquad (12)$$

Therefore, log-determinants of matrices with eigenvalues of Beta distributions could be well approximated by the Jacobi orthogonal polynomials for the sense of inequality (9). Three special cases are Chebyshev approximation of the first kind with the weight function $w(x) = 1/\sqrt{1 - x^2}$, Legendre approximation with the weight function $w(x) = 1$ and Chebyshev approximation of the second kind with $w(x) = 1/\sqrt{1 - x^2}$.

The family of $w(x) = J^{\alpha,\beta}(1 - x)^\alpha (1 + x)^\beta$ could approximate various kinds of positive functions on $[-1, 1]$, which might be enough to describe the diverse distributions of the target matrices.

Assume eigenvalues of a given symmetric positive definite matrix A lie in interval $(0, b]$ and eigenvalues of A/b obeys Beta distribution $Beta(x; \alpha + 1, \beta + 1)$. According to the weight function $\omega(x; \alpha, \beta)$, a family of Jacobi polynomials $J_i^{\alpha,\beta}(x)$ could be obtained recursively where $J_0^{\alpha,\beta}(x) = 1$ and $J_1^{\alpha,\beta}(x) = px + q$ for $p, q \in \mathbb{R}$. Then calculate coefficients a_i, b_i, c_i in formula (4) and projection coefficients

$$d_i = < \log\frac{1 + x}{2}, J_i^{\alpha,\beta}(x) >_\omega = \int_{-1}^{1} \log(\frac{1 + x}{2}) J_i^{\alpha,\beta}(x)\omega(x; \alpha, \beta)dx \qquad (13)$$

in advance then store these coefficients for future use. According to recursion relation (4), approximation formula (8) and Lemma 1, we have algorithm 1 displayed in Matlab style.

Algorithm 1

```
%%REQUIRE
%%A: sysmetric positive matrix;
%%b: eigenvalues of $A$ lie in (0,b];
%%a[i],b[i],c[i],d[i]: i=1,2,...,N;
%%p,q: coefficients of J1(x);
%%M: number of gaussian vectors;
%%N: the largest degree of approximation polynomials;
G=randn(n,M);C=2*A/b-I;
J[0]G=G;CG=C*G;J[1]G=p*CG+q*G;
detlog(A)=nlog(b)+(d_{0}*sum(sum(G.*J_{0}G))+...
d[1]*sum(sum(G.*J[1]G)))/M;
for i=1:N-1
    J[i+1]G=(C-a[i]*I)/c[i]*J[i]G-b[i]/c[i]*J[i-1]G;
    logdet(A)=logdet(A)+d[i+1]*sum(sum(G.*J[i+1]G))/M;
end
return logdet(A);
```

4 Numerical Experiments

To our knowledge, the randomized algorithm to calculate log-determinant of a positive definite matrix is first presented via Taylor expansions while Han et al. [3] accelerates the procedure using Chebyshev expansions which is a special case of our method with a slight different when computing coefficients. However, Cheybyshev expansions are not always the fast approximations due to the different distributions of eigenvalues.

Three types of diagonal 30000×30000 matrices are generated: diagonal entries are i.i.d. generated from $Beta(0.5, 0.5)$, $Beta(1, 1)$, $Beta(2.5, 2.5)$ respectively.

Chebyshev I expansions, Legendre expansions and Chebyshev II expansions are applied on each type of matrices and the procedure is repeated for 20 times.

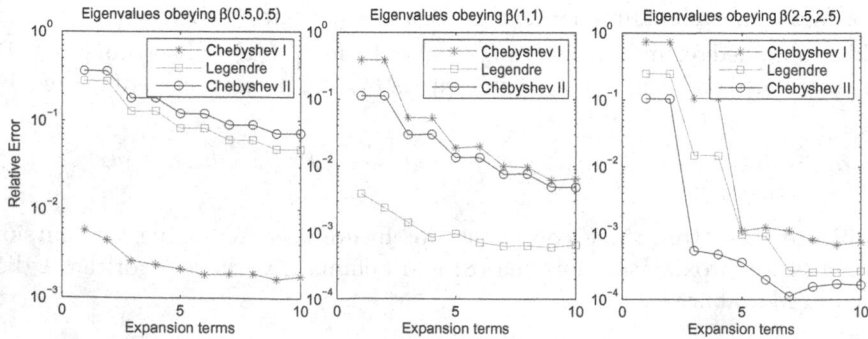

Fig. 1. Algorithm with different weight functions on three types of distributions

The expansions are limited to 10 terms at most. Set $M = 1000$ and $N = 10$ and the results is shown in Fig. 1. The result illustrates that the similarity between distribution function and weight function may effect the convergence speed. An empirical conclusion is that the more similar distribution and weight function are, the faster expansions approximate.

5 Conclusion

We present a randomized method for large-scale log-determinant computation via weighted L_2 polynomial approximation with prior distribution of eigenvalues. Through the theoretical inference and numerical experiments, we illustrate the effects of weight function selection, which extends previous research.

Our method lacks an analysis of convergence rate, which would be complemented in the future. However, the numerical experiments suggests that this method might be an more efficient technique to calculate log-determinant of symmetric positive matrices.

References

1. Avron, H., Toledo, S.: Randomized algorithms for estimating the trace of an implicit symmetric positive semi-definite matrix. J. ACM (JACM) **58**(2), 8 (2011)
2. Boutsidis, C., et al.: A randomized algorithm for approximating the log determinant of a symmetric positive definite matrix. arXiv preprint (2015). arXiv:1503.00374
3. Han, I., Malioutov, D., Shin, J.: Large-scale log-determinant computation through stochastic chebyshev expansions. arXiv preprint (2015). arXiv:1503.06394
4. Leithead, W.E., Zhang, Y., Leith, D.J.: Efficient gaussian process based on BFGS updating and logdet approximation. In: The 16th IFAC World Congress (2005)
5. Zhang, Y., et al.: Log-det approximation based on uniformly distributed seeds and its application to Gaussian process regression. J. Comput. Appl. Math. **220**(1), 198–214 (2008)
6. Kambadur, P., Lozano, A.: A parallel, block greedy method for sparse inverse covariance estimation for ultra-high dimensions. In: Proceedings of the Sixteenth International Conference on Artificial Intelligence and Statistics (2013)
7. Friedman, J., Hastie, T., Tibshirani, R.: Sparse inverse covariance estimation with the graphical lasso. Biostatistics **9**(3), 432–441 (2008)
8. Barry, R.P., Pace, R.K.: Monte Carlo estimates of the log determinant of large sparse matrices. Linear Algebra Appl. **289**(1), 41–54 (1999)
9. Hunter, T., El Alaoui, A., Bayen, A.: Computing the log-determinant of symmetric, diagonally dominant matrices in near-linear time. arXiv preprint (2014). arXiv:1408.1693
10. Reusken, A.: Approximation of the determinant of large sparse symmetric positive definite matrices. SIAM J. Matrix Anal. Appl. **23**(3), 799–818 (2002)
11. Szego, G.: Jacobi polynomials. In: Orthogonal Polynomials, 4th edn, Chap. 5. American Mathematical Society, Providence (1975)
12. Evans, M., Hastings, N., Peacock, B.: Beta distribution. In: Statistical Distributions, 3rd ed, Chap. 5, pp. 34–42. Wiley, New York (2000)

Solar Radio Astronomical Big Data Classification

Long Xu[1(✉)], Ying Weng[2], and Zhuo Chen[1]

[1] Key Laboratory of Solar Activity, National Astronomical Observatories,
Chinese Academy of Sciences, Beijing, China
lxu@nao.cas.cn, chenzhuo.zoom@gmail.com
[2] School of Computer Science, Bangor University, Bangor, UK
y.weng@bangor.ac.uk

Abstract. The Solar Broadband Radio Spectrometer (SBRS) monitors the solar radio busts all day long and produces solar radio astronomical big data foranalysis every day, which usually have been accumulated in mass images for scientific study over decades. In the observed mass data, burst events are rare and always along with interference, so it seems impossible to identify whether the mass data contain bursts or not and figure out which type of burst it is by manual operation timely. Therefore, we take advantage of high performance computing and machine learning techniques to classify the huge volume astronomical imaging data automatically. The professional line of multiple NVIDIA GPUs has been exploited to deliver 78x faster parallel processing power for high performance computing of the astronomical big data, and neural networks have been utilized to learn the representations of the solar radio spectra. Experimental results have demonstrated that the employed network can effectively classify a solar radio image into the labeled categories. Moreover, the processing time is dramatically reduced by exploring GPU parallel computing environment.

Keywords: Solar radio · Big data · Deep learning · Classification

1 Introduction

Solar radio astronomy is an interdisciplinary subject of radio astronomy and solar physics. The discovery of radio waves from the Sun provided a new window to investigate the solar atmosphere. For example, the properties of the solar corona were much more easily determined at radio wavelengths. Solar radio telescopes have been improved a lot recently so that fine structures in solar radio bursts can be detected. In this study, we use the data obtained by Solar Broadband Radio Spectrometer (SBRS) of China [1]. The SBRS is with characteristics of high

L. Xu—This work was partially supported by a grant from the National Natural Science Foundation of China under Grant 61572461, 11433006 and CAS 100-Talents (Dr. Xu Long).

J. Xie et al. (Eds.): HPCA 2015, LNCS 9576, pp. 126–133, 2016.
DOI: 10.1007/978-3-319-32557-6_13

time resolution, high-frequency resolution, high sensitivity, and wide frequency coverage in a microwave region. Its functionality is to monitor solar radio bursts in the frequency range of 0.7–7.6 GHz with time resolution of 1–10 ms. It consists of five 'component spectrometers' which work in five different wave bands (0.7–1.5 GHz, 1.0–2.0 GHz, 2.6–3.8 GHz, 4.5–7.5 GHz, and 5.2–7.6 GHz, respectively). The SBRS monitors the solar radio bursts all day long producing mass of data for researchers to analyze. In the observed data, burst events are rare and always with interference in the meantime. So it seems impossible to identify whether the data contain bursts or not and figure out which type of burst it is by manual operation timely. Thus, classifying the observed data automatically will be quite helpful for a solar radio astronomical study.

Nowadays, for massive data, many algorithms have been developed to learn the representation with unsupervised and supervised methods, especially the deep learning methods. Current methods based on deep learning [2] have demonstrated competitive performance in a wide variety of tasks, including visual recognition [3,4], audio recognition [5,6], and natural language processing [7]. These techniques are especially powerful because they are capable of learning useful features directly from both unlabeled and labeled data, avoiding the need for hand-engineering, which will be much helpful to the automatic analysis of the solar radio spectrum. An autoencoder (AE) can also be employed to learn the representation from the available mass data. AE is an unsupervised learning algorithm that applies backpropagation, setting the target values equal to the inputs. The AE tries to learn a function to make the input similar to the output of the function. There are many other variations of the AE, such as denoising AE [8] and stacked AE (SAE) [9]. In [10], the authors proposed the automatic dimensionality reduction to facilitate the classification, visualization, communication, and storage of high-dimensional data. An adaptive, multilayer "encoder" network to transform the high-dimensional data into a low-dimensional code and a similar "decoder" network to recover the data from the code. With the random weights as the initialization in the two networks, they can be trained together by minimizing the discrepancy between the original data and its reconstruction. Then the representation can be learned in an unsupervised manner. The network can be further named as deep belief network (DBN). With the achievements of these learning methods, we can learn the representations of the solar radio spectra, which will be employed for further solar radio image analysis, such as clustering and classification. In this paper, we make the first attempt to employ the deep learning method, specifically the DBN, to learn the representation of the solar radio spectra. Based on the representation, we can further classify the solar radio spectra into different categories automatically.

The rest of the paper is organized as follows: In Sect. 2, the learning architecture is introduced to learn the representation of a solar radio image. Section 3 gives the experimental results on representation learning and classification. The final section concludes this paper.

2   Representation Learning and Classification for Solar Radio Images

SBRS contains several channels to monitor the solar burst in different frequencies. Therefore, the signal sensed from each channel will be treated individually. In total, there are 120 channels working toward the solar radio information captured at the same time. Moreover, each captured file contains both left and right circular polarization parts, which should be separated and processed individually. We extract the captured data from each channel as a row vector, which is stored according the sensing time. Afterwards, all the vectors from the 120 channels will be assembled together according the frequency values to form a solar radio spectrum, which is used for visualization and further processing. To reduce computational complexity, the solar radio spectrum is down-sampled into 75×30 image with the nearest neighbor sampling method.

We employ DBN to learn solar radio image representation. DBN is a multi-layer, stochastic generative model which is created by stacking multiple restricted Boltzmann machines (RBMs). Each RBM is trained by taking the hidden activities of the previous RBM as its input data. Each time a new RBM is added to the stack, the new DBN has a better variational lower bound on the log probability of the data than the previous DBN, provided the new RBM is learned in the appropriate way [11]

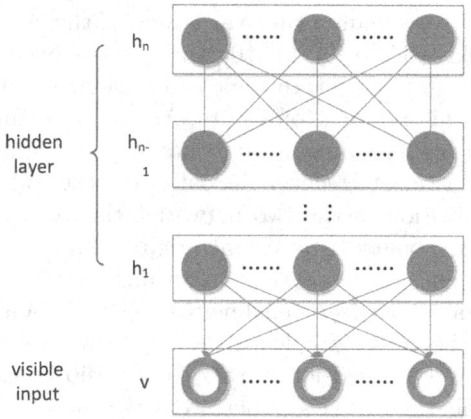

Fig. 1. DBN learning structure

2.1   RBM

RBM is a type of graphical model in which the nodes are divided into two sets, specifically, the visible and hidden. Each visible node is only connected to the hidden nodes. It means that there are no intra-visible or intra-hidden connections, which can be illustrated in each layer of Fig. 1. The energy function of an RBM with V visible units and H hidden units is defined in the following.

$$E(v,h) = -\sum_{i=1}^{V}\sum_{j=1}^{H} v_i h_j \omega_{ij} - \sum_{i=1}^{V} v_i b_i^v - \sum_{j=1}^{H} h_i b_i^h \tag{1}$$

where v is the binary state vector of the visible nodes, h is the binary state vector of the hidden nodes, v_i is the state of visible node i, h_j is the state of the hidden node j, ω_{ij} is the real-valued weight between the visible node i, the hidden node j. b_i^v is the real-valued bias into visible node i, and b_i^h is the real-valued bias into hidden node j. The joint distribution of the visible and hidden nodes is defined in the following:

$$p(v,h) = \frac{e^{-E(v,h)}}{\sum_u \sum_g e^{-E(u,g)}} \tag{2}$$

It can be observed that low energy results in high probability and high energy brings is assigned low probability. Also the probability of a visible node turning on is independent from the states of other visible nodes, given the states of the hidden nodes. Likewise the hidden states are independent from each other given the visible states. The property of RBM makes sampling extremely efficient, as one can sample all the hidden nodes simultaneously and then all the visible nodes simultaneously.

2.2 DBN

As mentioned before, each layer of DBN is composed of an RBM, where the weights in layer l are trained by keeping all the weights in the lower layers constant and taking as data the activities of the hidden units at layer $l+1$. Therefore, the DBN training algorithm trains the layers greedily and sequentially. Layer l is trained after layer $l-1$. If the size of the second hidden layer is the same as the size of the first hidden layer and the weights of the second is borrowed from the weights of the first, it can be proven that training the second hidden layer while keeping the first hidden layer's weights constant improves the log likelihood of the data under the model [12]. Figure 1 illustrates the multilayer DBN. The probability of the DBN assigns to a visible vector is defined as:

$$p(v) = \sum_{h_1,\dots,h_n} p(h_{n-1}, h_n) \prod_{k=2}^{n-1} p(h_{k-1} h_k) p(v|h_1) \tag{3}$$

where n defines the number of hidden layers. In this study, we employ the DBN to learn the representation and perform the classification of the solar radio images.

2.3 Neural Network for Solar Radio Image Classification

Based on the learning architecture in previous section, we propose a simple network for representation learning and classification of solar radio images.

A classification layer with three output nodes is added on top of one RBM layer, which takes learned representation as input and outputs the classification results for each type of the solar radio image. For each type, the classification layer will determine the possibility about how the inputs will result in the specific type.

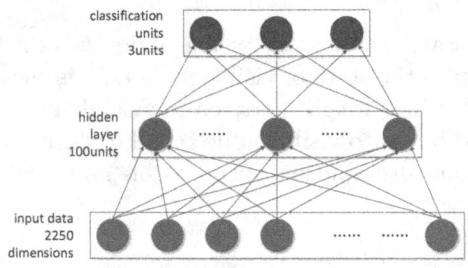

classification
units
3units

hidden
layer
100units

input data
2250
dimensions

Fig. 2. DBN learning structure

The depth of the neural network depends on the problem and the size of the training set. Overfitting will occur with high probabilities if the training samples are insufficient, as the network requires a larger number of parameters. In this case, due to the limit number of solar radio images, only one hidden layer is employed. Then we propose the $I - H - C$ structure network for the experiment, as illustrated in Fig. 2. C, standing for the classification, is defined to give the prediction which most possible type the input is. I, indicating the number nodes of the input layer, is set as 2250 which is the number of dimensions of preprocessed data. H, standing for hidden, is defined as 100 nodes of hidden layer. The bottom layer of the employed network is the RBM and the top layer is a softmax layer for classification. In order to realize the non-linear mapping function for the classification, the object of the learning network is defined as following:

$$\hat{o} = \arg \min p(o|x; \Theta), \tag{4}$$

where Θ include all the parameters in RBM and softmax layers. In order to make the inference, we need to obtain the parameters of the constructed network, i.e., the parameters of RBM and softmax layer, respectively. For the parameters in the RBM layer, the standard contrastive divergence learning procedure is employed for pre-training. Detailed information about the pre-training method can be found in [13]. With the process of pre-training, the constructed network can effectively avoid the risk of trapping in poor local optima. After the pre-training process, the fine-tuning process needs to be further performed to make the network more suitable for solar radio spectrum classification. Thereby, a log-likelihood function is employed as the object function for further training the parameters in the softmax layers and fine-tuning the parameters in the RBM layer:

$$\Theta^* = \arg \max \sum_{t=1}^{k} \log P(\hat{L} = L|x; \Theta), \tag{5}$$

where k indicates the number of categories for determination, L represents the label of the inputs, and $\hat{L}$ represents the outputs of the network. For the parameter training, the traditional back-prorogation (BP) [14] is employed to fine-tune parameters of the constructed deep network. This algorithm is firstly proposed by Rumelhart and McCelland, the essence of which is to minimize the mean squared error between actual output and desired output based on gradient descent. BP algorithm is especially powerful because it can extract regular knowledge from input data and memory on the weights in the network automatically. Furthermore, in order to prevent over-fitting in training neural network, drop-out is introduced. Typically the outputs of neurons are set to zero with a probability of p in the training stage and multiplied with $1-p$ in the test stage. By randomly masking out the neurons, dropout is an efficient approximation of training many different networks with shared weights. In our experiments, we apply the dropout to all the layers and the probability is set as $p = 0.2$.

3   Experimental Results

To evaluate the proposed representation learning and classification of solar radio spectrums, a solar radio spectrum database is established firstly. Then, the representation learning and classification of solar radio spectrums are tested on this database. For GPU acceleration, a high performance computing server with 4 GeForce GTX 780 GPU for computing and one GeForce 210 GPU for display is used in our simulation.

In this database, 4408 observational data files (each one gives two images) are labeled by the experts into six categories ($0 =$ no burst or hard to identify, 1 = weak burst, 2 = moderate burst, 3 = large burst, 4 = data with interference, 5 = calibration). The number of images of each category is listed in Table 1. Since the objective of our experiment is to distinguish the bursts from others, the solar radio image in the database has been selected and relabeled to form a new database for the experiment. Three coarse categories, i.e., 'bursts', 'non-burst', and 'calibrations' are included in the database.

Table 1. The details of the database. $0 =$ no burst or hard to identify, 1 = weak burst, 2 = moderate burst, 3 = large burst, 4 = data with interference, 5 = calibration

Category	0	1	2	3	4	5	total
Image number	6670	618	268	272	570	988	8816

After preprocessing, we input the training set data to the network as batches. The hidden layer is firstly pre-trained to initialize the parameters in an unsupervised way. Then both the hidden layer and the classification layer are fine-tuned with labeled data. After that, the preprocessed testing set data will be input sequentially and the network will output the classification results in possibilities how likely the input data belongs to each category respectively. The model classifies a solar radio image successfully when the category with highest possibility output by the algorithm matches the labeled category of the file input. The classification results can be found in Table 2.

We also exploit the professional line of multiple NVIDIA GPUs to accelerate the computing of neural network. Since the computing of neural network concerns the same processing for the nodes, it is benefited greatly from GPU computing. In our simulation, the computing time by using only CPU (2 Inter(R) Xeon (R) CPU E5-2620 v2 @ 2.10 GHz) is about 1716.64 min, and can be dramatically reduced to 21.90 min by employing GPU acceleration (4 GeForce GTX 780 GPU). Therefore, the GPU acceleration can deliver 78x faster parallel processing power for high performance computing of solar radio spectrum classification.

Table 2. Performance of DBN

	TPR	FPR
Burst	67.4 %	13.2 %
Non-burst	86.4 %	14.1 %
Calibration	95.7 %	0.4 %

References

1. Fu, Q., Ji, H., Qin, Z., et al.: A new solar broadband radio spectrometer (SBRS) in China. Sol. Phys. **222**(1), 167–173 (2004)
2. Bengio, Y.: Learning deep architectures for AI. FTML **2**(1), 1–127 (2009)
3. Le, Q., Ranzato, M., Monga, R., Devin, M., Chen, K., Corrado, G., Dean, J., Ng, A.: Building high-level features using large scale unsupervised learning. In: ICML (2012)
4. Sohn, K., Jung, D.Y., Lee, H., Hero, A.: Efficient learning of sparse, distributed, convolutional feature representations for object recognition. In: ICCV (2011)
5. Lee, H., Largman, Y., Pham, P., Ng, A.Y.: Unsupervised feature learning for audio classification using convolutional deep belief networks. In: NIPS (2009)
6. Mohamed, A.R., Dahl, G., Hinton, G.E.: Acoustic modeling using deep belief networks. IEEE Trans. Audio, Speech, Lang. Process. **20**(1), 14–22 (2012)
7. Collobert, R., Weston, J., Bottou, L., Karlen, M., Kavukcuoglu, K., Kuksa, P.: Natural language processing (almost) from scratch. JMLR **12**, 2493–2537 (2011)
8. Chen, M., Weinberger, K., Sha, F., Bengio, Y.: Marginalized denoising autoencoders for nonlinear representation. In: ICML (2014)
9. Chen, M., Xu, Z., Weinberger, K., Sha, F.: Marginalized stacked denoising autoencoders for domain adaptation. In: 29th International Conference on Machine Learning (ICML) (2012)
10. Hinton, G.E., Salakhutdinov, R.R.: Reducing the dimensionality of data with neural networks. Science **313**(5786), 504–507 (2006)
11. Hinton, G.E., Osindero, S.Y., Teh, Y.: A fast learning algorithm for deep belief nets. Neural Comput. **18**, 1527–1554 (2006)

12. Salakhutdinov, R., Murray, I.: On the quantitative analysis of deep belief networks. In: ICML (2008)
13. Hinton, G.E.: A practical guide to training restricted Boltzmann machines. Technical report, University of Toronto (2010)
14. Deng, L.: Three classes of deep learning architectures and their applications: a tutorial survey. APSIPA Trans. Signal Inf. Process. (2012)

Performance Analysis of Mobile Smart UE-Gateway Assisted Transmission Algorithm for Wireless Sensor Networks

Lianhai Shan[1,2], Weidong Fang[3(✉)], Fengrong Li[3], and Yanzan Sun[4]

[1] Shanghai Research Center for Wireless Communications, Shanghai 200335, China
[2] Shanghai Internet of Things Co. Ltd., Shanghai 201899, China
[3] Shanghai Institute of Microsystem and Information Technology, CAS, Shanghai 200050, China
weidong.fang@mail.sim.ac.cn
[4] Key Laboratory of Specialty Fiber Optics and Optical Access Networks, Shanghai University, Shanghai 200444, China

Abstract. A mobile sink has been exploited for data gathering in Wireless Sensor Networks (WSN), which can reduce and balance energy consumption among sensor nodes. A mobile sink assisted transmission algorithm has become one of the research hotspots for WSN. How to energy-efficiently collect and transmit data by using multiple mobile sinks is one of the hot research topics. In this paper, we propose a mobile smart UE-gateway assisted transmission algorithm for WSN, which considers several parameters to choose an optimized mobile smart UE-gateway as an access point. Then we analyze the WSN system energy cost and transmission delay. The performance evaluation results show that system energy costs, WSNs lifetime and transmission delay can be improved largely by using the optimization of a mobile smart UE-gateway.

Keywords: WSN · Mobile smart UE-gateway · Energy cost · Multi-hop transmission

1 Introduction

With the continued requirement of Internet of Things (IoT) development, Wireless Sensor Networks (WSNs) have played an important role to gather the detected data [1]. WSNs consist of numerous autonomous sensor nodes with limited energy, which constrained the whole WSN system lifetime. Energy becomes one of the most valuable resources, as the WSN size increases. There are energy aware multi-hop routing protocols to use the energy more efficiently. However, some technical issues must be considered with the increasing hop number between the source and the destination nodes [1, 2]. Firstly, nodes close to the sink node consume their energy quickly, which cause the sink node unreachable and data packet loss [3]. Secondly, a data packet buffer will increase in the multi-hop route, which will cause processing overhead and transmission delay. Transmission delay is a great challenge for the real-time requirements for IoT system applications [4]. There is research which utilizes the advantage of mobile sinks

© Springer International Publishing Switzerland 2016
J. Xie et al. (Eds.): HPCA 2015, LNCS 9576, pp. 134–142, 2016.
DOI: 10.1007/978-3-319-32557-6_14

to overcome these problems. A mobile sink is used to prolong the lifetime of WSN and enhance performance metrics in [5–8]. However, as the network size grows, the length of routing will increase, which can cause more challenging. The delay will increase, and the packets will be more possibly dropped. Packet drops will cause retransmissions, which increase the delay excessively. Multiple sinks (multi-sink) appear as an efficient solution for large scale networks. However, deploying more sink nodes cannot resolve the problem directly. Energy-efficient protocols should be researched for multi-sink networks [9–11].

Nowadays, with the development of information and communication technology (ICT), Mobile Cellular Networks (MCN) and WSN convergence appear in many application areas where mobile smart User Equipment (UE) is equipped with a WSN air-interface and can provide data transmission for WSN. Thus the mobile smart UE can be a gateway (UE-gateway) for WSN. WSN can be managed and optimized with a mobile smart UE-gateway of MCN, which can save the WSN's energy consumption, prolong the WSN life time and reduce the transmission delay for WSN services. A mobile smart UE-gateway moves in a WSN area and overhears the sensors in its one-hop range. However, if there are multiple mobile smart UEs acting as mobile gateways to collect data simultaneously in the same WSN area, the sensors may frequently change the data transmission path and cause the extra signaling overhead and energy costs. Hence the technology of convergent interactive control and joint optimization is an important problem, which needs to be researched and developed.

In this paper, in order to solve the aforementioned problems, we propose an optimized mobile smart UE-gateway assisted transmission algorithm for wireless sensor networks in a WSN-MCN converged system. The remainder of paper is organized as follows: We first provide an overview of related work of gathering data by using a mobile sink and a mobile gateway in Sect. 2. Then, in Sect. 3, we introduce a network model and describe the proposed scheme in detail. In Sect. 4, we discuss and analyze the simulation results. Finally, we conclude the work in Sect. 5.

2 Related Works

Since the fundamental advantage of WSNs can be deployed in ad-hoc mode, choosing the suitable cluster head (CH) and sink node is one of the most important things during the process of data aggregation and transmission. In WSN, some different types of mobile sink and gateway with abundant energy provision is proposed to avoid the CH energy going down before other nodes. The research of using mobile sink node generally attempt to prolong the lifetime of the network in [8, 9], which is proven that that mobile sink node improves the lifetime of the network. In the reference [10], repositioning of the sink node to enhance the performance metrics is investigated. There is some work done on the multi-sink wireless sensor networks. Multiple sink location algorithm is proposed to manage the energy efficiently and solutions to these problems [11]. The formulation to find optimal locations of multiple sinks is proposed in [12–14] in order to maximize the network lifetime, however, it is difficult to apply. In current research, some controllably mobile infrastructure for low energy WSN is proposed in reference

[15, 16]. In a WSN, the mobile smart UE gateway moves into the coverage area of WSN, and can provide the backhaul access to these WSN nodes. The mobile smart UEs are also used as UE-gateway to collect the data and transmit to the Base Station (BS), which greatly decrease the traditional transmission energy cost and transmission delay. However, these UE-gateways assisted transmission algorithms just reduce the energy cost, and the serving mobile smart UE-gateway will not tell each WSN node about its leaving when it is leaving its responsible area, which will caused extra energy cast for communications.

This paper proposes an optimized UE-gateway assisted transmission scheme for WSN data to reduce the WSN energy cost and transmission delay. Especially, when an emergency data is detected at a sensor node, it will search the UE-gateway around it, chooses an appropriate UE and make this UE act as its gateway. The UE-gateway will transmit the emergency data to the server directly instead of by using the traditional multi-hop transmission mode to the sink unit. And we analyze the performance of optimized UE-gateway assisted transmission algorithm compared with the traditional multi-hop algorithm and normal UE-gateway assisted transmission algorithm.

3   Network Model and Proposed Scheme

3.1   Network Architecture

The WSN consists of thousands of wireless sensor nodes distributed in a region. In the convergent scenario for WSN and MCN, the mobile smart UEs are under the control of a BS. In the coverage area of a cellular network, there also exists a group of wireless sensor nodes constructing WSN. In the convergence scenario, the mobile smart UEs can act as the mobile smart sinks and gateways for the WSN. The UE-gateways are dual-mode and have WSN and cellular interfaces. Then, the detected data from sensor nodes can be forwarded to the BS via cellular system by the UE-gateways, which is illustrated in Fig. 1.

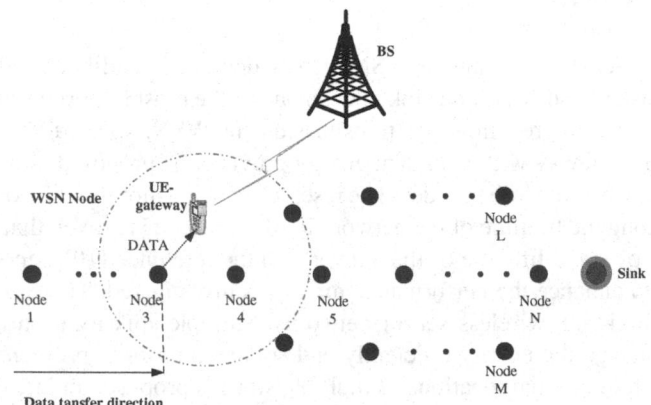

Fig. 1. System architecture of convergent WSN and MCN

3.2 Radio Model

In the proposed system architecture, a sensor network $S(n_0)$ consists of n_0 sensor nodes. We assume a simple model where the power cost $E_{elec} = 50 \ nJ/bit$ to run the transmitter or receiver circuitry, and use $\xi_{amp} = 100 \ pJ/bit/m^2$ or $0.0013 \ pJ/bit/m^4$ according to reference distance for the transmit amplifier to achieve an acceptable E_b/N_0 [17]. Thus, to transmit a k-bit message a distance d using the radio model, the energy expends:

$$E_{Tx}(k, d) = E_{Tx\_elec}(k) + E_{Tx\_amp}(k, d) \tag{1}$$

$$E_{Tx}(k, d) = \begin{cases} E_{elec} \cdot k + \xi_{amp1} \cdot k \cdot d^2, & d < d_0 \\ E_{elec} \cdot k + \xi_{amp2} \cdot k \cdot d^4, & d \geq d_0 \end{cases} \tag{2}$$

and to receive this message, the radio expends:

$$E_{Rx}(k) = E_{Rx\_elec}(k) = E_{elec} \cdot k \tag{3}$$

For the performance, we assume that all sensors are transmitting the sensing data at a fixed rate and thus have k-bit data to send to the UE-gateway for each round. For future versions of the proposed protocol, we will implement event-driven simulation, where sensors only transmit data if some event occurs in the detected area. WSN nodes energy cost is mainly composed of two parts: the end nodes energy cost $E_{Tx}(k, d)$, the intermediate nodes energy cost $E_{Tx\_amp}(k, d) + E_{Rx}(k)$. Node i transmits k-bit data energy cost from j hop to $j + 1$ hop,

$$\begin{aligned} E_{cost}(i,j) &= E_{tran} + E_{rec} = (E_{elec}k + k\xi_{amp1}d^2_{(V(j),V(j+1))}) \quad d < d_0 \\ &+ E_{elec}k = k\xi_{amp1}d^2_{(V(j),V(j+1))}) + 2kE_{elec} \end{aligned} \tag{6}$$

$$\begin{aligned} E_{cost}(i,j) &= E_{tran} + E_{rec} = (E_{elec}k + k\xi_{amp2}d^4_{(V(j),V(j+1))}) \quad d \geq d_0 \\ &+ E_{elec}k = k\xi_{amp2}d^4_{(V(j),V(j+1))}) + 2kE_{elec} \end{aligned} \tag{7}$$

where $0 \leq j \leq m - 1$, $d_{(V(j),V(j+1))}$ denotes distance between the j node and the j + 1 node in transfer process.

Node i transmits k-bit data packet to UE gateway and transferring energy cost for one round is

$$E_{cost}(i) = \sum_{j=1}^{m-1} E_{cost}(i,j) \tag{8}$$

where one round data transferring includes m hops. So for N nodes data packets transmission in the WSN, and the total energy cost for one round is

$$E_{\text{total}}(i) = \sum_{i=1}^{N} E_{\text{cost}}(i) \tag{9}$$

3.3 UE-Gateway Assisted Transmission Scheme

In the convergent network infrastructure, there may be a lot of UE-gateways in the WSN area, how a UE-gateway is selected to be an access point with less signaling is one of the key problems to be solved. There are two basic use procedures: One is that a new capable UE-gateway enters into the WSN area without UE-gateway assisted transmission; The other is that the serving UE-gateway leaves the coverage area of WSN.

When a UE-gateway assisted transmission for WSN and when the current UE-gateway is going to leave the WSN area or disqualified for acting as a gateway, it will cause the UE-gateway reselection process. The procedure of UE-gateway assisted transmission scheme is illustrated in Fig. 2.

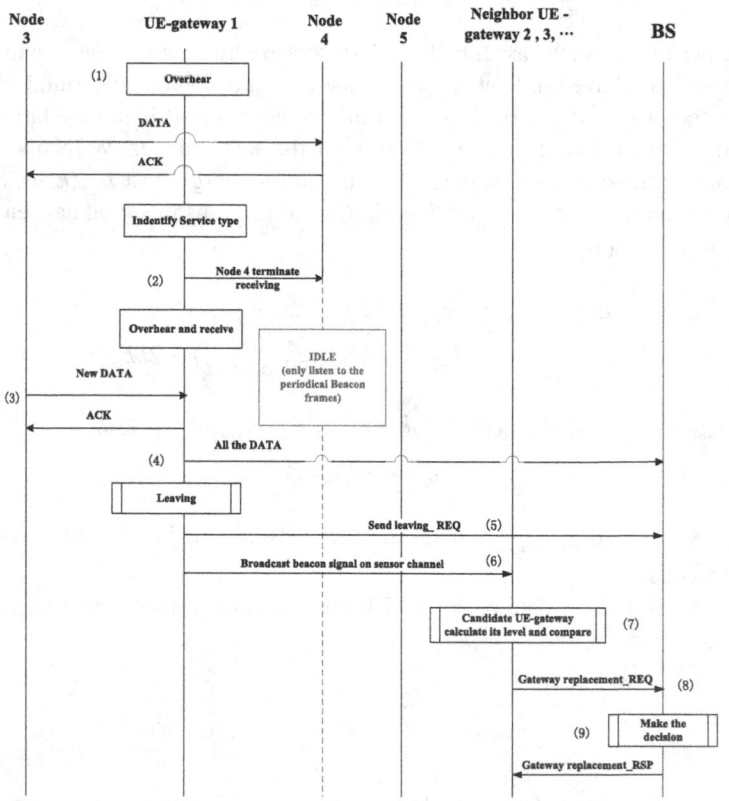

Fig. 2. UE-gateway assisted transmission process

3.4   Optimized UE-Gateway Selection Algorithm

In the UE-gateway assisted transmission scheme, we defined a new parameter named UE-gateway level, which this parameter defines the capability level of a UE-gateway acting as access gateway for WSN. The detailed parameter for calculating the proposed mobile smart UE-gateway level includes but not limited to below elements.

(1) Dwelling time D_t, which means the persistent time of mobile smart UE-gateway for the sensor node acting as a gateway.
(2) Coverage capability C_r, which means the number of sensor nodes of the UE-gateway covering.
(3) Capacity availability C_a, which means load capacity for the UE-gateway to serve sensor nodes.
(4) Channel quality C_g, which means the channel quality between the neighbor UE-gateways and the current serving gateway.
(5) Channel quality C_s, which means the average SNR between the neighbor UE-gateways and sensor nodes.

$$UE - gatewaylevel = aD_t + bC_r + cC_a + dC_g + eC_s \tag{4}$$

where a, b, c, d, e are pre-defined weighting factors in the system parameter during the network system plan process.

4   Performance Analysis

In this section, we analyze the energy cost and transmission delay. And our analysis emphasis is mainly focus on system energy cost of transmitting packets from each sensor node using the traditional multi-hop algorithm, normal UE-gateway assisted algorithm and optimized UE-gateway assisted algorithm (the proposed algorithm), where the traditional transmission algorithm is just using a low energy adaptive clustering hierarchy algorithm.

4.1   Simulation Scenario Description

The radio model and the energy cost method of each round (simulation time) have been presented in Sect. 2, which we have described in details. The remained simulation parameters are shown in Table 1.

Table 1. Simulation parameters

Parameter	Value
Field size	200 m × 200 m
Initial energy of nodes	0. 5 J
Number of nodes	100 nodes, 200 nodes
Data packet size	random(10,100) Byte
ξ_{elec}	50 nJ/bit
ξ_{amp}	100 pJ/bit/m^2

4.2 Simulation Results

The system energy cost with simulation time (rounds) can be described as follows. The energy cost of each transmission is based on the transmission distance, which the energy cost is exponentially incremental according to the transmission distance. In additional, the transmission hops is another important factor and more energy will cost for the extra hops. From Figs. 3(a) and (b), we can see that the proposed algorithm can reduce the system energy cost because we use the optimized UE-gateway to forward detected data.

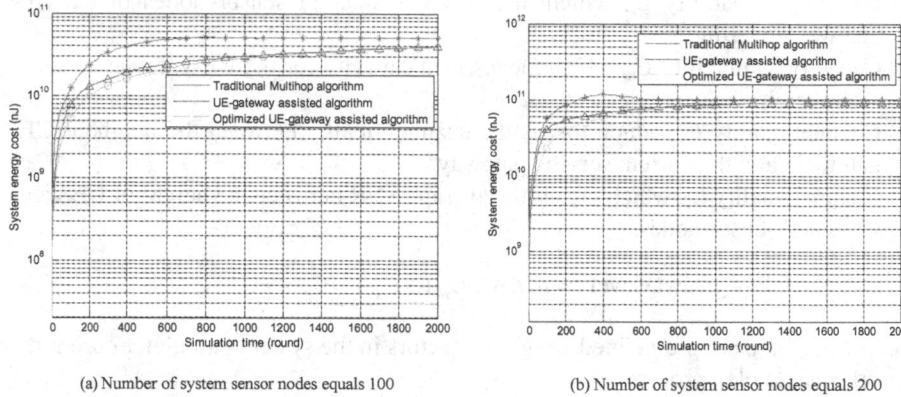

(a) Number of system sensor nodes equals 100   (b) Number of system sensor nodes equals 200

Fig. 3. System energy cost in WSN

The number of alive nodes with simulation time (rounds) is shown as Figs. 4(a) and (b) for 100 and 200 sensor nodes. After 600 rounds, the remain nodes of using traditional multi-hop algorithm, UE-gateway assisted algorithm and optimized UE-gateway assisted algorithm are respectively 16, 70, and 83 for 100 system sensor nodes. The number of remain nodes respectively is 5, 80, and 101 for 200 system sensor nodes after 600 rounds. The reason is that the proposed algorithm can select the optimal UE-gateway to assist the WSN data transmission which not only reduced the system energy cost but also balanced the other sensor nodes energy cost. At the same time, the traditional multi-hop algorithm cannot have a better energy balance because the sensor nodes near to the gateway will cost more energy for forwarding data.

Table 2. Performance comparison of 100 sensor nodes

Performance Metrics		WSN with no UE-gateway	WSN with 4 normal UE-gateways	WSN with 4 optimized UE-gateways
Network Lifetime (rounds)	FND	34	69	108
	HND	346	1579	1803
Energy Consumption (10^{-3} J/round)		4.14	2.21	2.05
Delay (slots/round)		51.5	21.4	18.6

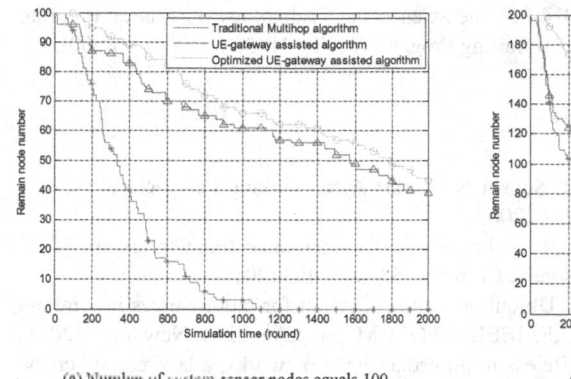

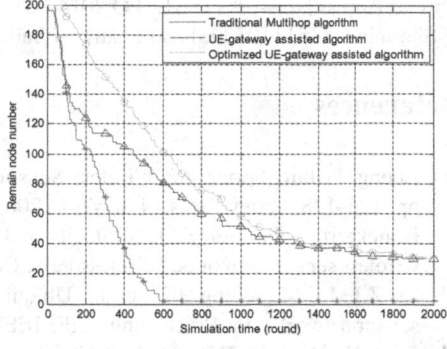

(a) Number of system sensor nodes equals 100   (b) Number of system sensor nodes equals 200

Fig. 4. System alive nodes in WSN

The main numerical results of energy cost and transmission delay are shown in Tables 2 and 3 for different WSN size. The average energy consumption and transmission delay have the same trendline. (FND: First Node Dies, HND: Half Node Dies.)

Table 3. Performance comparison of 200 sensor nodes

Performance Metrics		WSN with no UE gateway	WSN with 4 normal UE gateways	WSN with 4 optimized UE gateway
Network Lifetime(rounds)	FND	23	42	65
	HND	235	434	602
Energy Consumption (10^{-3} J/round)		7.85	4.12	4.03
Delay (slots/round)		103.5	36.8	29.8

5 Conclusions

Since the traditional multi-hop transmission algorithm cannot perform a better lifetime for sensor nodes, in this paper, we proposed a novel method considering several parameters to choose the optimized UE-gateway as the access gateway for the WSNs. For a request, we design some new additional signaling for the convergence of WSN and MCN. Performance analysis results verify that the proposed algorithm can prolong the lifetime and reduce the transmission delay for WSN. In the future, we will consider that sensor nodes have the capability to know themselves positions and this will optimize the WSN data transmission and decrease the energy consumption much more.

Acknowledgment. This work is partially supported by the National Natural Science Foundation of China (61302113), the Shanghai Natural Science Foundation (13ZR1440800), the Shanghai Rising-Star Program (14QB1404400), Shanghai Key Laboratory of Specialty Fiber Optics and

Optical Access Networks (SKLSFO 2014-03), the Science and Technology Innovation Program of Shanghai (14511101303) and Shanghai Sailing Program (15YF1414500, 14YF1408900).

References

1. Zheng, J., Jamalipour, A.: Wireless Sensor Networks: A Networking Perspective, 1st edn, pp. 125–138. Wiley Press, New York (2009)
2. Bouckaert, S., Poorter, E.D.: Strategies and challenges for interconnecting wireless mesh and wireless sensor networks. Wireless Pers. Commun. **53**, 443–463 (2010)
3. Li, Z.J., Li, M., Wang, J.L., et al.: Ubiquitous data collection for mobile users in wireless sensor networks. In: Proceeding of the IEEE INFOCOM, pp. 2246–2254, New York (2011)
4. Zara, H., Hussain, F.B.: QoS in wireless multimedia sensor networks: a layered and cross-layered approach. Wireless Pers. Commun. **75**, 729–757 (2014)
5. He, L., Pan, J.P., Xu, J.D.: A progressive approach to reducing data collection latency in wireless sensor networks with mobile elements. IEEE Trans. Mobile Comput. **12**, 1308–1320 (2013)
6. Xing, G.L., Wang, T., Jia, W.J., et al.: Rendezvous design algorithms for wireless sensor networks with a mobile base station. In: Proceeding of the ACM MobiHoc, New York, pp. 231–240 (2008)
7. Gao, S., Zhang, H., Das, S.K.: Efficient data collection in wireless sensor networks with path-constrained mobile sinks. Mobile Comput. **10**, 592–608 (2011)
8. Marta, M., Cardei, M.: Using sink mobility to increase wireless sensor networks lifetime. In: Proceeding of International Symposium on a World of Wireless, Mobile and Multimedia Networks, CA, pp. 1–10 (2008)
9. Anastasi, G., Borgia, E., Conti, M., et al.: A hybrid adaptive protocol for reliable data delivery in WSNs with multiple mobile sinks. Comput. J. **54**, 213–228 (2011)
10. Xu, X., Luo, J., Zhang, Q.: Delay tolerant event collection in sensor networks with mobile sink. In: Proceeding of the IEEE Infocom, New York, pp. 2471–2479 (2010)
11. Basagni, S., Carosi, A., Melachrinoudis, E., Petrioli, C., Wang, Z.M.: Controlled sink mobility for prolonging wireless sensor networks lifetime. Wireless Netw. **14**, 831–858 (2008)
12. Gatzianas, M., Georgiadis, L.: A distributed algorithm for maximum lifetime routing in sensor networks with mobile sink. IEEE Trans. Wireless Commun. **7**, 984–994 (2008)
13. Luo, J., Hubaux, J.P.: Joint sink mobility and routing to maximize the lifetime of wireless sensor networks: the case of constrained mobility. IEEE/ACM Trans. Networking **18**, 871–884 (2010)
14. Liang, W.F., Luo, J., Xu, X.: Prolonging network lifetime via a controlled mobile sink in wireless sensor networks. In: Proceeding of the IEEE GlobeCom, New York, pp. 1–6 (2010)
15. Zhang, J., Shan, L.H., Hu, H.L.: Mobile cellular networks and wireless sensor networks: toward convergence. IEEE Commun. Mag. **50**, 164–169 (2012)
16. Crosby, G.V., Vafa, F.: Wireless sensor networks and LTE-a network convergence. In: Proceeding of the 38th Annual Conference on Local Computer Networks (LCN 2013), Australia, pp. 731–734 (2013)
17. Puccinelli, D., Haenggi, M.: Wireless sensor networks: applications and challenges of ubiquitous sensing. IEEE Circuits Syst. Mag. **5**, 19–31 (2005)

A Platform for Routine Development of Ternary Optical Computers

Xianshun Ping[1], Junjie Peng[1(✉)], Shan Ouyang[1,2], Yunfu Shen[1], and Yi Jin[1,2]

[1] School of Computer Engineering and Science, Shanghai University, Shanghai, 200072, China
jjie.peng@shu.edu.cn
[2] High Performance Computing Center, Shanghai University, Shanghai, 200072, China

Abstract. A ternary optical computer (TOC) has many advantages compared with its electronic counterpart such as huge data bits, excellent parallelism, and reconfigurable data bit. However, traditionally, to use a TOC, the user has to get to know some details about it. This does not benefit to exert the advantages of TOCs. One of the most attractive solutions is to develop a kind of platform for routine development by shielding the underlying hardware and let the user uses a TOC just like using electronic computers without needing to understand the details of an optical system. As a preliminary attempt, we put forward the idea of how to design an application routine platform and present the implementation process of the platform. Meanwhile, we design a basic version of the application routine platform and execute a MSD parallel addition routine on it. Experiment results show that the routine platform is correct and feasible. It can mask the details about a TOC and the internal operational logic of the platform can quite exert the advantages of the TOC.

Keywords: TOC · MSD adder · Routine platform · Operational logic

1 Introduction

With the rapid development of science and technology, the requirements on performance and capability of computer systems are increasing. To meet these needs, computers have become more and more complex, which leads to many obvious bottlenecks or deficiency, such as very limited data bits, high energy consumption, and lack of parallel processing capability. To solve these problems, people have to try to develop new computer systems to adapt to the needs of future applications. Compared with electronic computers, optical computers have many advantages, such as high speed [1], giant parallelism [2], multi-values and low-energy consumption brought by the physical properties of light. These make more and more researchers have set focuses on the study of optical computers. In addition, many achievements and progresses have been obtained. Among these research achievements one of the branches is to use polaroid and liquid crystal to achieve a three-valued logic and try to build optical computer systems.

In 2000, Jin proposed a ternary optical computer (TOC) architecture, which applied two orthometric polarizations of light and no-light states to express information [3]. Based on this theoretical system, thousand-data-bits experimental systems were

© Springer International Publishing Switzerland 2016
J. Xie et al. (Eds.): HPCA 2015, LNCS 9576, pp. 143–149, 2016.
DOI: 10.1007/978-3-319-32557-6_15

successfully constructed and a first practical TOC is coming soon. For better development, not only a perfect computer architecture but also a wide variety of applications in a TOC are needed. Each specific routine, from relegation it belongs to the underlying software, and from the operational functions and user point of view it is a separate entity, but in view of processing it needs to interact with multiple functional modules, such as a task scheduling module, the reconstruction processor modules, a memory management module, the control module of optical components and the control module of data flow. We are sure that it is a challenge for people to know so many modules and let alone developers to develop routines with a combination of these. To solve this problem, we propose a routine development platform that allows users to use a TOC like an electronic computer, without specifically understanding the underlying details of a TOC. In this paper, combining the theory of parallel MSD addition and the advantage of the characteristics of a computer, we will implement the first platform of routine development for a new type of photoelectric computer and verify the feasibility of the platform.

2   Related Work

2.1   Features of TOC

A ternary optical computer (TOC) has the following characteristics: the numbers of data bits is not only large but also easy to expand, the resources of data bits can be allocated by bit, and computing capabilities of optical processors can be reconfigured by bit. Such as the data bits of the latest generation of experimental system for TOC which being named SD11 has reached 1024 and expandable to 16,384 [4], every data bit can separate from other data bits to configure three-valued (binary) logic unit [5]. On the basis of reconfigurable processor and numerous of data bits, TOC has constructed parallel MSD adder [6, 7], and then create a multiplication routine [8] and a division routine. These works laid the foundation for develop a platform for routine development of TOC.

2.2   Modified Signed-Digit Number

In 1961, Avizienis proposed MSD number system representation for the first time [9]. Later, Draker et al. introduced MSD number system to optical computer [10]. What is different from that of binary system is that MSD number system is a redundant number system. There are three characters in the system. And the symbol set of MSD is $\{\overline{1}, 0, 1\}$, where $\overline{1}$ denotes the number -1. Obviously, due to the characteristic of redundancy, a value may have several representations in the MSD system. To any decimal number X, it can be expressed in the MSD system as follows:

$$X = \sum_i x_i 2^i$$

where the symbol set of x_i is $\{-1, 0, 1\}$, and -1 denotes the number -1. 2^i show that MSD is still a binary system. However, it is an abnormal binary system. It is a three-valued binary system. This means MSD number system is a redundant number system. In this system, a number can be expressed in different forms. For example, number 6 and -6 can be represented as the following different forms.

$$(6)_{10} = (110)_{MSD} = (1\ \overline{1}\ 10)_{MSD} = (10\ \overline{1}\ 0)_{MSD},$$

$$(-6)_{10} = (\overline{11}\ 1)_{MSD} = (\overline{1}\ 1\ \overline{1}\ 0)_{MSD} = (\overline{1}\ 010)_{MSD}.$$

3   A Platform for Routine Development

Before the concept of the application routine platform is put forward, the relationships between the user and the TOC as shown in dotted lines in Fig. 1. That is, user has to communicate with TOC directly. It means that user has to know some details about the TOC before he can efficiently use the optical computing system. This brings a lot of inconvenience to the user of TOC, also bring safety problem to TOC at the same time. Once we have a routine development platform, the platform takes a role as a bridge between TOC and the routine developers or users. It can send the routine that is developed by the developer according to certain steps with the platform to TOC, can let users call the routine which has been store in TOC through the platform and feedback operation result to the routine caller. For these, the platform plays a supervisory role to prevent the illegal routines to operate in TOC. But by considering of the complexity of the supervision function, this article will do not conceive. The operation interface of the platform for routine development is shown in Fig. 2.

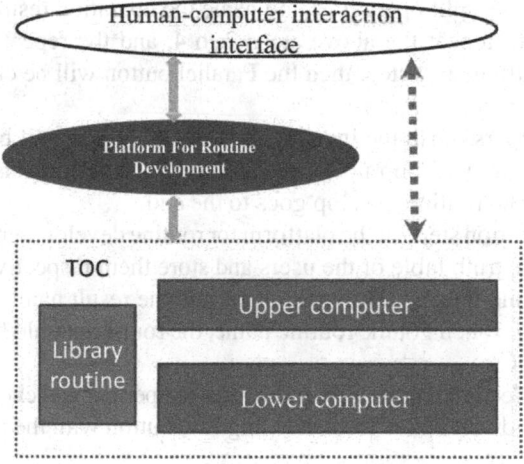

Fig. 1. The location of the platform for routine development

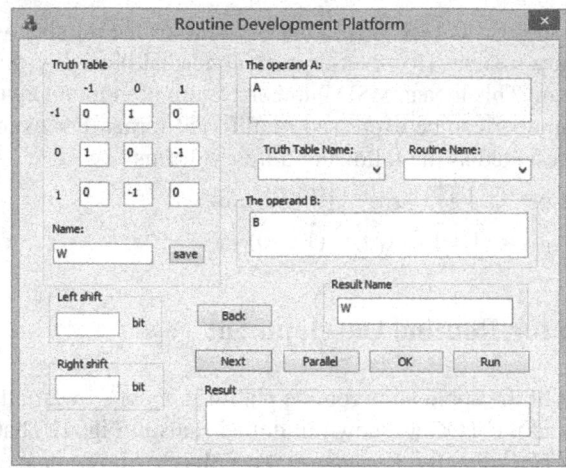

Fig. 2. The operation interface of the platform for routine development

The steps for develop the Routine are as following:

Step 1: routine developers fill in the table to provide all truth tables that routines require and name the corresponding truth tables;

Step 2: select operation type. If it is the shift operation jump to step 4, otherwise, operate the next step;

Step 3: import the name of two groups of operands. Operands can be the variables of previous operating result have ever. Select the corresponding operation truth table of operands or the routines which already exist and name the results. Please note that all name cannot be began with numbers;

Step 4: import the single operand or the variables of operand, then import number of bit for the left or the right operations and name the operation result;

Step 5: if need to repeat the above steps 2 to 4, and the repeated content can be operated parallel with the last step, then the Parallel button will be chosen, or the Next button will be;

Step 6: if developers finish the input steps then OK button will be selected and the routine named window will pop up to let developers name it. Finishing naming and confirm means that the routine develop goes to the end.

The internal operation steps of the platform for routine development are as following:

Step 1: get all the truth table of the users and store them respectively by name;

Step 2: get operand names, truth table name and the result name input by the users to store them by step. When got the routine name, the routine should be stored to library routine which in TOC.

You can get the desired results after input a set of operand and choosing the required routines by the drop-down boxes then choosing Run button with the routine platform to invoke routine.

After the users select the Run button, the routine platform firstly combing truth table and operands, then send to upper computer of TOC in SZG file format which specific of TOC. Then, the task processing module (SZG_RWCL) of monitoring system, generates and sends restructuring instructions to lower computer. The operation control module (SZG_YSKZ) reconstructing instruction and send it to restructuring instruction latch of ternary Optical Computer. Obviously, the research content of these two modules does not belong to this article. Finally the result of TOC feedback the number of MSD is got and shown.

4   Simulation and Results

The Hardware Configurations for the simulation experiment: Processor Pentium(R) Dual-Core CPU E5700 @ 3.0 GHz 3.0 GHz, 4 GB RAM, 64 - bit operating systems, the simulation of the hardware portion of ternary optical computer using C language, for example, Shift and reconstruction operations.

In order to verify the feasibility of the platform preliminary, we use the MSD addition theory to construct an Addition routine. Specific steps are as following:

Step 1: input the truth table used in the MSD addition as is shown in Table 1, name it as T, W, _T, _W;

Table 1. The truth table of MSD adder

T	-1	0	1	W	-1	0	1	T'	-1	0	1	W'	-1	0	1
-1	-1	-1	0	-1	0	1	0	-1	-1	0	0	-1	0	-1	0
0	-1	0	1	0	1	0	-1	0	0	0	0	0	-1	0	1
1	0	1	1	1	0	-1	0	1	0	0	1	1	0	1	0

Step 2: select the truth table of transform W, the two operands are named add_A and add_B, the result is named w, select Parallel key;

Step 3: select the truth table of transform T, the two operands are named add_A and add_B, the result is named t, select Next key;

Step 4: input "t" on the operand window A, input 1 on the left shift window, meaning left shift one bit. And name the result as t1, select the Next button;

Step 5: select the truth table of transform _W, fill w and t1 into two operands window, naming the results as _w, select Parallel key;

Step 6: Select the truth table of transform _T, fill w and t1 into two operands window, naming the results as _t, select Next key;

Step 7: input "_t" on the operand window A, input 1 on the left shift window, meaning left shift one bit. And name the result as _t1, select the Next button.

Step 8: Select the truth table of transform W, fill _w and _t1 into two operands window, naming the result as "result", select the OK button;

Step 9: input the name of routine Add, select the OK button;

Then we create the routine successfully, input binary number 101011 and 101110 in the input window. The result is correct, as is showed in Fig. 3. $(101011)2 = 43$, $(101110)2 = 46$, $(101101\text{-}1) MSD = 89$.

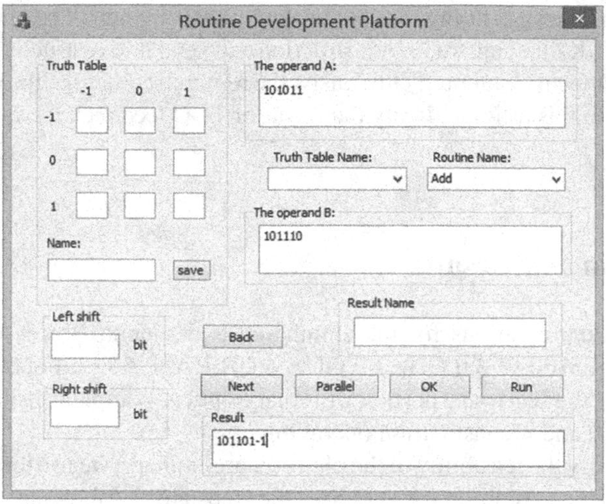

Fig. 3. Call routine of adder

Figure 4 is W-transform generated SZG files. Left part of the figure is the zone of file parameters and area of information page. Respectively show IP addresses, file names, character within the code mapping, truth tables and other information; right part of the figure is area of data: from the 289,233th bytes to the end is the zone of operand. Two operands are hexadecimal string FF FF FF FF as the end identifier. The hexadecimal string 02 01 02 02 02 01 FF FF FF FF means the code mapping of operand b which is 101011, 02 01 02 01 02 02 FF FF FF FF means the mapping of operand b which is 101110.

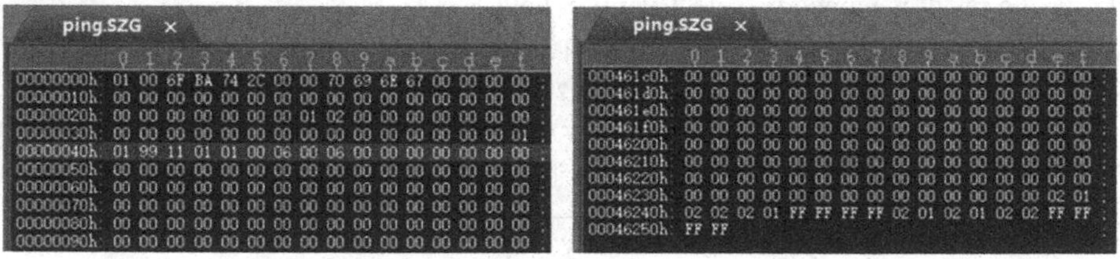

Fig. 4. W-transform generated SZG file

5   Conclusion and Future Work

This paper introduces the use method and the internal operational logic of Routine development platform. By constructing the MSD parallel adder routine and getting operation result with specific examples in adder routine, we verifies the feasibility and handleability of the Routine development platform, laying a solid foundation for the construction of the next generation routine development platform. As the first routine development platform, the routine of the platform haven't been checked so that the routine developers need to have a clear understanding about the specific steps of the routines. We believe in the second generation, these problems will be effectively solved. Besides, future version will gradually add powerful supervising function to improve the development efficiency of the routine developers effectively, having a better connection with underlying system gradually and promoting the operation efficiency of the routine.

As the first routine development platform, it does not check the routine so that the routine developers need to have a distinct acquaintance with specific steps to implement routines. This routine failed to realize iterative management which then will lead to time-consuming for the user to develop the routine that having the function of the iteration. We believe in the second generation, these problems will be effectively solved. Besides this, future version will gradually add up powerful supervising function to improve the development efficiency of routine developers effectively, obtain a better connection gradually with more underlying system and promote efficiency of the routine operation.

Acknowledgment. This work is supported by the National Natural Science Foundation of China (No. 61103054 and No. 61572305).

References

1. Wong, W.M., Blow, K.J.: Design and analysis of an all-optical processor for modular arithmetic. Opt. Commun. **265**, 425–433 (2006)
2. Nishimuraa, N., Awatsujib, Y., Kubota, T.: Two-dimensional arrangement of spatial patterns representing numerical data in input images for effective use of hardware resources in digital optical computing system based on optical array logic. J. Parallel Distr. Comput. **64**, 1027–1040 (2004)
3. Jin, Y., He, H.C., Lü, Y.T.: Ternary optical computer principle. Sci. China Ser. F **46**, 145–150 (2003)
4. Shan, O.: Design and Implementation of Ternary Optical Processor Control Circuit. PhD. Dissertation of Shanghai University, Shanghai China (2012)
5. Jin, Y., Wang, H.J., Ouyang, S., et al.: Principles, structures, and implementation of reconfigurable ternary optical processors. Sci. China Inf. Sci. **54**(11), 2236–2246 (2011)
6. Jin, Y., Shen, Y.F., Peng, J.J., et al.: Principles and construction of MSD adder in ternary optical computer. Sci China Inf Sci **53**, 2159–2168 (2010)
7. Peng, J., Shen, R., Jin, Y., Shen, Y., Luo, S.: Design and implementation of modified signed-digit adder. IEEE Trans. Comput. **63**(5), 1134–1143 (2014)
8. Hu, X.J., Jin, Y., Ouyang, S.: A 40-bit multiplication routine of ternary optical computer. J. Shanghai Univ. (Nat. Sci.) **20**(5), 645–657 (2014)
9. Avizienis, A.: Signed-digit number representations for fast parallel arithmetic. IRE Trans. Electron. Comput. **10**, 389–400 (1961)
10. Draker, B.L., Bocker, R.P., Lasher, M.E., Patterson, R.H., Miceli, W.J.: Photonic computing using the modified signed-digit number representation. Opt. Eng. **25**, 38–43 (1986)

Principle of a Computing Request File
of Ternary Optical Computers

Sulan Zhang[1], Yuexing Han[1(✉)], Yunfu Shen[1], and Yi Jin[2]

[1] School of Computer Engineering and Science, Shanghai University, Shanghai 200444, China
hanyuexing@gmail.com
[2] High Performance Computing Center, Shanghai University, Shanghai 200444, China

Abstract. A ternary optical computer (TOC) has three prominent features, numerous data bits, reconstruction of each bit's function and allocation bit by bit. The numerous data bits determine that a TOC is particularly suitable to processing large amounts of data, especially in high-performance computing where data is more and more. In order to organize large amounts of data which is entered into a TOC, a new kind of file is defined, which includes all input operands and calculating rules. The file is called SZG file because it has a suffix. SZG. The paper introduces the demands, significance, construction principles and usage method of a SZG file. Finally, an example of using a SZG file in high-performance computing is given.

Keywords: SZG file · Numerous data bits · Reconstruction · Allocation bit by bit · High performance computing

1 Introduction

In 2000, a ternary optical computer (TOC) was proposed, where information is expressed by three light states: two mutually orthogonal polarized light states and one no-light state [1–3]. There are three prominent features of a TOC: numerous data bits, reconstruction of each bit's function and severability of data bits. Based on the large number of data bits, a TOC is especially suitable to processing large amounts of data and structured data, such as some applications of high-performance computing which process large amounts of data.

During the last ten years, some studies about data bits allocation and reconstruction for a TOC have been proposed. These studies include the dynamically reconfigurable theories and technologies of optical components of a TOC [4], address a space allocation plan and technology of the TOC data bits [5], and include the techniques and strategies to effectively manage a large number of data bits [6].

2 Demands of User Request File

There are three differences between a TOC and an electronic computer:

© Springer International Publishing Switzerland 2016
J. Xie et al. (Eds.): HPCA 2015, LNCS 9576, pp. 150–157, 2016.
DOI: 10.1007/978-3-319-32557-6_16

(1) Number of data bits

Currently, the number of data bits in main trend electronic computer is 32 or 64; however, in the TOC, the number of data bits is numerous. For instance, SD11, the third generation of hardware systems of the TOC, has 16,384 data bits.

(2) Allocability of data bits

When executing an arithmetic operation in electronic computer, the digits must be byte (8 bits), word (2 bytes), double word, quad word or octa-word. The data bits of the electronic computer cannot be split. For instance, while computing a 5 bits digit in a 64 bit electronic computer, a 64 bit processor is used instead of a 5 bits processor. Thus, 59 bits are wasted in the process. Although the TOC has many data bits, the allocability of data bits can avoid the wasted of ternary optical processor (TOP). For example, when a user computing some 60-bit digits, the processor manage software of TOC is only assigned a 60-bit section of TOP to the user, and the rest is assigned to other users.

(3) Reconstruction

In electronic computer, functions of arithmetic unit are fixed and processor cannot be reconfigured too. However, in the TOC, the processor can be reconfigured following the user's requests. The contents of the reconstruction include to allocate data bits and to reconfigure TOP according to the needs of the user. Thus, the data processing methods are significantly different between the TOC and electronic computer. We should propose a new technology to organize user's data for the TOC.

When using TOC to compute so much data, three new questions are encountered as follows:

- In order to reconstruct of the TOP, Operation Rules needs to be described before calculating any data.
- In order to allocate the data bits in the TOC, the scale of the task needs to be perceived. Then, the processor management software of TOC may decide how many data bits allocated to the task.
- In order to improve the efficiency of the TOP, the all of original data have to be sent into the processor before calculating any one data.

In order to solve the three questions, we set a package file which includes the user's operation rules and all of original data, defined as SZG file. The SZG file is timely transferred to the ternary optical processors by the user's program. With the received SZG file, the TOC can obtain the heavy of the task and allocate an appropriate number of data bits, i.e., a section of TOP, for the task. After getting the calculation rules of the user from the SZG file, the TOP's section allocated to the task is reconstructed to meet the use's demand. As soon as the TOP is reconstructed, all original data in the SZG file is calculated one by one via the specialized TOP. After finishing all calculating, the results of every calculating are organized into a new SZG file denoted by *_R. SZG and it is returned to the user's program. Since the SZG file includes calculation rules and all original data, it is called computing request file of the TOC. Generally, SZG file has name as *.SZG, the "*" is wildcard of file name given by user.

The "SZG" are the first letter of "San Zhi Guang" which is Chinese pronunciation of a Ternary Optical Computer.

3 Effect of the SZG File

The SZG file is a bridge between the user and the TOC, and its effects are shown as follows:

(1) Keeping the user's programming habits
Comparing with the electronic computer, only a method of organizing the data file, i.e. SZG file, is increased in the TOC. In other aspects of programming both TOC and electronic computer is very simile. For example, a mathematical modeling is first set for the attention problem; then, the primary data is organized to form the operands and to select operation rules; then, the according program is designed following to the program flow chart; finally, the instruction sequence of program is written. Generally, a program includes some steps, i.e. inputting data, setting the computer status, sending data into processor, analyzing result, deciding next process and outputting results. The only difference is that electronic computer sends one date into a fixed adder or logical unit through one operate instruction, but the TOC send the SZG file into the TOP through one operate instruction too.

(2) Sharing TOP by multiple users
Each user's Operation Rules are recorded in the SZG file header respectively. Thus, the users can be grouped according to the same or similar Operation Rules. So long as TOP is reconstructed, the specific optical processor can compute all data belong to one user group.

(3) Improving system efficiency
Comparing with sending one data into processor through one operation instruction in electronic computer, the TOC has more efficiency via sending a SZG file which includes lots of data through one instruction because in one communication, and the more the data is, the higher its efficiency is.

(4) TOC and electronic computer work together
The SZG file is stored in the electronic computer and is sent into the TOP when it is used. In the same time of TOP handling the SZG file, the electronic computer can do other things of the program. So, both the electronic computer and TOC are working together for one program.

4 SZG File Format

In order to accurately understand the user's calculation and data through a SZG file for the TOP, we defined every field of SZG file to form its format, shown in Fig. 1. In the format, a SZG file has two segments: the file header and data area. The file header contains the parameters which be used to allocate data bits and to reconfigure the TOP. An overview of the main fields of the file header is given as follow.

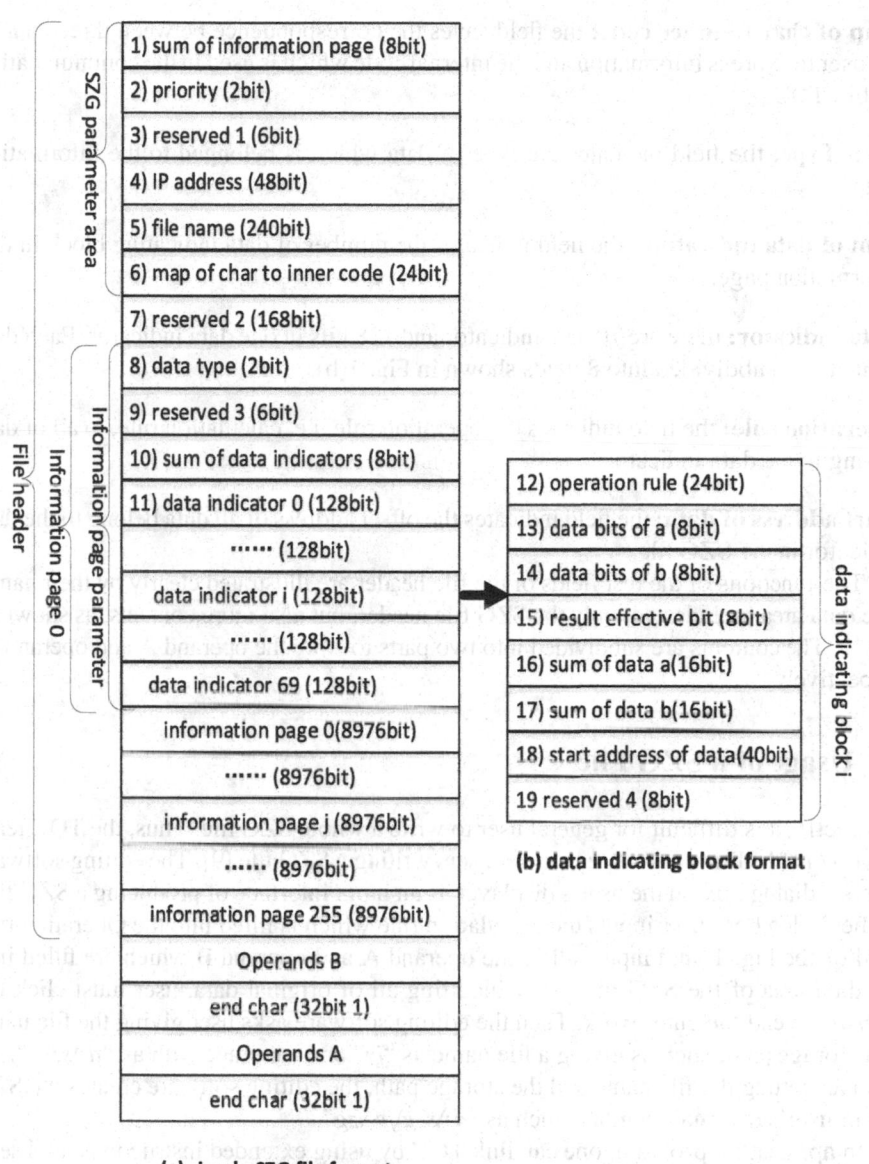

SZG parameter area

1) sum of information page (8bit)

2) priority (2bit)

3) reserved 1 (6bit)

4) IP address (48bit)

5) file name (240bit)

6) map of char to inner code (24bit)

7) reserved 2 (168bit)

Information page parameter

8) data type (2bit)

9) reserved 3 (6bit)

10) sum of data indicators (8bit)

11) data indicator 0 (128bit)

······ (128bit)

data indicator i (128bit)

······ (128bit)

data indicator 69 (128bit)

information page 0(8976bit)

······ (8976bit)

information page j (8976bit)

······ (8976bit)

information page 255 (8976bit)

Operands B

end char (32bit 1)

Operands A

end char (32bit 1)

data indicating block i

12) operation rule (24bit)

13) data bits of a (8bit)

14) data bits of b (8bit)

15) result effective bit (8bit)

16) sum of data a(16bit)

17) sum of data b(16bit)

18) start address of data(40bit)

19 reserved 4 (8bit)

(b) data indicating block format

(a) simple SZG file format

Fig. 1. 2015 version of SZG file format

Sum of information page: the field indicates the sum of information pages in the file header. A file header contains 1 to 256 information pages, and all pages has same structure.

IP Address: this field saves the IP address from that the SZG file is submitted and the result is sent back to.

Map of char to inner code: the field saves the correspondence between three char of the user to express information and the internal code which is used in the communication within TOC.

Data Type: the field indicates the type of data which is belonged to the information page.

Sum of data indicators: the field indicates the number of data indicating block in this information page.

Data indicator: there are 70 data indicator and 128 bits in one data indicator. Each data indicator is subdivided into 8 fields shown in Fig. 1(b).

Operation rule: the field indicates the operation rule, i.e. calculation rule, to all of data belong to the data indicator.

Start address of data: the field indicates the offset address of all data belong to the data indicator in the SZG file.

The functions of the rest fields of the file header are illustrated clearly by their name. The data area includes not only the SZG file header, but also more contents, as shown in Fig. 1. The contents are subdivided into two parts to store the operand A and operand B, respectively.

5   Usage of a SZG File

Distinctly, it is difficult for general user to write a whole SZG file. Thus, the TOC team has invented editing software to assist users writing a SZG file [9]. The editing software offers a dialog box on the user's displayer as an input interface of producing a SZG file. In the dialog box, user inputs the calculation rule which is filled into the Operation rule field of the Fig. 1, and inputs all of the operand A and operand B which are filled into the data area of the SZG file. After inputting all of original data, user must click the "*finish*" to end the enter work. Then the editing software asks user giving the file name and storage path, such as giving a file name as "*jy*" and a storage path as "*d:\szg*". As soon as getting the file name and the storage path, the editing software creates the SZG file in user's external memory, such as "*d:\szg\jy.szg*".

In application program, one can link TOC by using extended instructions, and send a SZG file to TOC by using an operating order. The SZG file is running in a TOC, and the other parts of the program can be running in an electronic computer. So the TOC and the electronic computer are cooperative work for one program.

The extended instructions of MPI have been completed in reference [7]. The extended instructions of C completed in reference [9]. The extended instructions of C++ and FORTRAN are being making.

For example, the expanded instructions of C are offered in the small plug-in, named SZGX. The plug-in must be installed to the client's computer before programming.

The application program must include the header file: "# SZG.h", and four expanded instructions, as fellows, can be written in anywhere in the program [9].

(1) **void SZG_Init ()**
Establish work foundation of expanded instructions.
(2) **int SZG (char * path)**
Send a SZG file stored in the path to optical processors.
(3) **int SZG_SearchResult (char * path)**
Inquire state of SZG file sent to TOC.
(4) **void SZG_Suspend ()**
Suspend the program itself until the result file, *-r.szg, be received.

6   An Example

In real work, computing a lot of data with several different calculation rules is frequently met, especially in high performance computing the data and calculation rules are more and more. In this case the TOC is higher efficiency than electronic computer. In order to illustrate the computing method of TOC and the role of SZG file, we survey a simplified example which including four calculation rules: $f1 = a+b$, $f2 = c - d$, $f3 = e \wedge g$ and $f4 = h \vee i$, and computing 100000 groups of original data. Meanwhile, we assume that a and b have 32 bits, c and d 16 bits, e and g 5 bits, and h and i 7 bits.

Step 1: Organizing Calculation Rule and Original Data into a SZG File. After running the editing software referred in Sect. 5, user select the calculation "+" and input 100000 values of a and b as 32 bit data in the dialog box of the editing software. The data of a and b are filled into the data area of SZG file and other information inputted is filled into "data indicator 0" field in Fig. 1. Then user select the "−" and input 100000 values of c and d as 16 bits data. The data of c and d is filled into the data area behind the data of b and other information is filled into "data indicator 1". It is similar, users select the "∧" and input 100000 values of e and g as 5 bits data, the data of e and g filled into data area behind d and other information filled into "data indicator 2". At last user selects the "∨" and input 100000 values of h and i as 7 bits data, the data of h and i filled into data area behind g and other information filled into "data indicator 3". Until inputting all data, the *"finish"* button cannot be clicked. As soon as clicking the *"finish"*, the SZG file is created in user's path and file name, such as $d:\backslash szg\backslash y.szg$.

Step 2: Sending the SZG File to TOC in Program. In application program which is run in an electronic computer in generally, a SZG file is sent to TOC by a special expanded instruction, and the computing tasks of SZG file are completed by TOP instead of electronic CPU. For example, we can write a C application program in which sending the $d:\backslash szg\backslash y.szg$ to TOC, as follows.

```
#include <SZG.h>        //Including the header file about SZG expanded instructions
......
main ()
{
......
void SZG_Init ()        //Setting the compiler and work base for SZG expanded instructions
......
int SZG (d:\szg\jy.szg)    //Sending the SZG file to TOC
void SZG_Suspend ()    //Suspending the program itself, awakened by SZG result file
......
}
```

Step 3: Handling the SZG File in TOC. After receiving a SZG file, the TOP is reconfigured into a special compound processor according to the information get out from the data indicators included in the SZG file header. Once reconfiguring TOP is finished the all of original data included in data area of the SZG file is calculated via the special compound processor in high efficient.

For instance, according to the data indicator 0, 1, 2 and 3 of the file $jy.szg$, a compound processor which possesses 32 bits adder, 16 bits subtracter, 5 bits $\wedge$ unit, 7 bits $\vee$, and total at 60 bits, is built in the TOP to meet the need of user. The calculating every data of 100000 a and b, c and d, e and g, and h and i in the data area of $jy.szg$ ensues in parallel. After finishing the computing to all data, a SZG result file, such as $jy\_r.szg$ corresponding to $jy.szg$, is created in TOC's storage, and the result file is sent back to the program which sent the SZG file to TOC as quickly as possible.

To take into account the TOC has many data bits, dozens of 60 bits compound processor can be built in one TOP. As a result, the time of calculating all data is shortened to several tenths of using one compound processor. So TOC has high value to reduce the computing time in high performance computing.

Step 4: Receiving the SZG result file from TOC. While TOC handling the SZG file, the electronic computer can suspend the application program or run other parts irrelevant with the SZG file or wait the SZG result file by repeatedly executing the inquiring instruction. Once receiving the SZG result file, electronic computer awakes the program or runs the remainder base on the SZG result file. By the SZG file, it is realized that two different architecture computer cooperative work for one program. It is very importance to high performance computing and super computer system.

For example, the program of step 2 is suspended by instruction "void SZG_Suspend ()", after sending the $jy.szg$ to TOC. And the program is awakened as receiving the $jy\_r.szg$.

7   Conclusions

Up to now, we have known that the TOC is super than electronic computer in many number of data bits, reconfigurable of processor's function and allocability of each data bit. In order to apply the three advantages of TOC, it is necessary to send the all original data and calculation rules to TOC before computing those data by TOP. This is a new problem brought by TOC. SZG file is an efficient method to solve the new problem for it including all of original data and calculation rules and being send to TOC in the application program by special expanding instructions. Based on SZG file and expanding the instruction of a programming language, one can use the TOC in application program written in the form of habit. The SZG file is a bridge and foundation of applying the TOC.

References

1. Jin, Y.: Structure and principles of ternary optical computer. Ph.D. thesis. Xi'an: Northwestern Polytechnical University (2002)
2. Yi, J., Hua-can, H., Yang-tian, L.: Ternary optical principle. Sci. China Ser. F **46**(2), 145–150 (2003). (in Chinese)
3. Jin, Y., He, H., Lu, Y.T.: Ternary optical computer architecture. Phys. Scr. **T118**, 98–101 (2005)
4. XianChao, W., JunJie, P., Shan, O.: Control method for the optical components of a dynamically reconfigurable optical platform. Appl. Optics **50**(5), 662–670 (2011)
5. Shan, O.: Design and Implementation of Ternary Optical Processor Control Circuit Doctoral dissertation. Shang-hai University, Shanghai (2012)
6. Yi, J., Shan, O., Kai, S., YunFu, S., JunJie, P., XueMin, L.: The management theory and technology of data bits of the optical processor of TOC. Chin. Sci. Inf. Sci. **43**(3), 361–373 (2013)
7. Qian, Z., Yi, J., Kai, S., Huan, G.: Use of MPI programming of ternary optical computer in supercomputing cluster. Shanghai Univ. (Natural Science) **20**(2), 180–189 (2014)
8. Kai, S.: Overall architecture and prototype implementation of the task management software of the ternary optical computer. Ph.D. thesis. Shanghai University, Shanghai (2014)
9. Huan, G., Yi, J., Kai, S.: The extension of the C program for ternary optical computer. Shanghai Univ. (Natural Science) **19**(3), 280–285 (2013)

High-Efficiency Realization of SRT Division on Ternary Optical Computers

Qun Xu[1,2], Yunfu Shen[1(✉)], and Yi Jin[1]

[1] School of Computer Engineering and Science, Shanghai University,
99 Shangda Road, Shanghai 200444, China
yfshen@mail.shu.edu.cn
[2] State Grid Huangdao Power Supply Company,
369 Ningbo Road, Tsingtao, Qingdao 266400, China

Abstract. Based on the characteristics of a huge number of data bits and reconfigurable optical processors of a ternary optical computer, a high-efficient division algorithm and realization are presented in this paper. The division algorithm adopts the SRT division to simplify operation steps and uses a two-step parallel M+B adder to speed up calculations. A number of rigorous tests for this algorithm are carried out through software simulation, which proves that the accuracy and performance of division in a ternary optical computer is superior to that of an electronic computer.

Keywords: Ternary optical computer · SRT division · Ternary optical processor · M+B adder

1 Introduction

In an electronic computer, division is completed by addition, subtraction, and comparison under the control of software. Compared to other elementary arithmetic operations, division is more complex and has a longer time delay. Thus how to speed up the process of division is a subject that has received great attention in computer science.

In a ternary optical computer (TOC), information is expressed with the three states of light, i.e., vertical polarized light, horizontal polarized light, and no light. A ternary optical processor is composed of polarizer and a liquid crystal array under the control of electrical signals. So it has a great number of data bits [1]. In 2007, according to the decrease-radix design principle, researchers designed a ternary optical processor that has many data bits and can be reconstructed at any time [2]. At present, each data bit of optical processor can be constructed into a ternary or binary logic unit or a MSD binary parallel adder [3]. There is no correlation among the logic units or the bits of a MSD adder, so each data bit in the ternary optical processor can be used independently and every data bit can be distributed to meet the needs of the user.

With many data bits and a reconfigurable ternary optical processor, the authors proposed a high-speed realization method of a SRT division algorithm. In the realization, a two-step M+B adder is used to speed up the division calculations. Moreover, a large number of software simulation tests are carried out to verify the validity and

J. Xie et al. (Eds.): HPCA 2015, LNCS 9576, pp. 158–169, 2016.
DOI: 10.1007/978-3-319-32557-6_17

feasibility of the algorithm and the experimental results show that division calculating performance of a ternary optical computer is superior to that of an electronic computer in data width and calculating steps.

2 MSD System and Parallel Addition

2.1 MSD System

In MSD system, an n-bit number N (N_n......N_{k+1} · N_k......N_1) which consists of (n−k)-bit integer and k-bit fractional part can be represented by:

$$N = \sum_{i=0}^{n-k-1} N_{k+1+i} \times 2^i + \sum_{i=1}^{k} N_i \times 2^{i-k-1}$$

N_i may be a value like 0, 1 or $\bar{1}$ where $\bar{1}$ represents the number −1. A value can have several forms due to the redundancy of MSD system, e.g.

$$(4.625)_{10} = (101.\bar{1}01)_{MSD} = (100.101)_{MSD} = (1\bar{1}01.\bar{1}01)_{MSD}$$

Some problems have to be clarified about MSD system here:

- There is no sign bit in a MSD number and the most significant bit is used to determine whether positive or negative.
- The negative can be obtained by reversing each bit of a MSD number.
- Comparison of two MSD numbers is made through subtracting them and then determining sign of the difference.

2.2 M+B Parallel Addition and Subtraction

The M+B addition is applicable to adding a MSD number M and a binary number B [4]. It completes addition operation by applying the ternary logic transforms C, P, and R shown in Table 1 to each bit in parallel. Each of the three transforms can be accomplished in one pulse, and the addition is always finished in two clock cycles whether how length the two operands are. Before an M+B addition is called, M (M_p... M_{k+1} · M_k...M_1) and B (B_q...B_{g+1} · B_g...B_1) should be adjusted into the same length by zero padding. Then the M+B addition is operating through the following steps:

Step 1. Press transforms C and P to each bit of M and B at the same time, and notate the results with c and p correspondingly. Fill the highest order of c and the lowest order of p with one zero respectively.

Step 2. Press transform R to each bit of c and p in parallel, and notate the result with r. The r is the sum.

When two p-bit operands are added, p+1-bit sum is got from M+B addition. So, p-bit C, P function units and p+1-bit R function unit have to be constructed simultaneously in ternary optical processor for one p-bit M+B parallel adder.

Obviously, any subtraction, M−B, can be achieved through performing an addition, (−M)+B, and negating each bit of the difference at last.

Table 1. The truth table of M+B addition

B_i	M_i	C (c)	P (p)	R
0	$\bar{1}$	0	$\bar{1}$	$\bar{1}$
0	0	0	0	0
0	1	1	$\bar{1}$	
1	$\bar{1}$	0	0	
1	0	1	$\bar{1}$	0
1	1	1	0	1

3 SRT Division

In order to improve floating-point division, SRT algorithm is proposed and named after three mathematicians, Sweeney, Robertson and Tocher. In every iteration of SRT algorithm, the divisor is subtracted from partial remainder and one or several bits of the quotient are obtained [5]. There are two key operations of this algorithm, one is to calculate the partial remainder, and the other is to select the value of quotient bit and the value of partial remainder.

The relation among the dividend N, the divisor D, the quotient Q and the remainder W can be expressed as follows:

$$N = D \times Q + W$$

Here, N and D have the same sign and W meets the condition $0 < W < D$. N (N_n......N_{k+1} • N_k......N_1) is one n-bit MSD number with k-bit fractional part and D (D_m......D_{x+1} • D_x......D_1) is one m-bit binary number with x-bit fractional part.

It is necessary to complete some pre-operations before SRT division operation, they are that (a) Determine the sign of Q according the symbol of N and D. (b) Compute the absolute value of N and D. (c) Make N and D satisfy the condition $\frac{1}{2} \leq N < 1$ and $\frac{1}{2} \leq D < 1$ by shift. Denote the numbers of bits to shift N with Noffset and D with Doffset. For Noffset and Doffset, the negative represents left shift and the positive represents right shift.

SRT algorithm is an iterative process. In the i-th iteration, Q_i is one digit of quotient Q, W_i is the partial remainder and U_i is an intermediate variable to compute the W_i. According to the comparison of W_{i-1} with $\frac{1}{2}$ and $-\frac{1}{2}$ respectively, U_i is calculated from (1), W_i is from (2), and Q_i is selected from (3) [5–8]. W_0 is initialized to N. It is important to point out that the dividend N, the divisor D, the quotient Q, the intermediate variable U_i and the remainder W are all MSD binary numbers.

$$U_i = \begin{cases} (W_{i-1} + D); & W_{i-1} \leq -\dfrac{1}{2} \\[2ex] W_{i-1}; & -\dfrac{1}{2} < W_{i-1} < \dfrac{1}{2} \\[2ex] (W_{i-1} - D); & W_{i-1} \geq \dfrac{1}{2} \end{cases} \tag{1}$$

$$W_1 = 2 \times U_i \tag{2}$$

$$Q_i = \begin{cases} \bar{1}; & W_{i-1} \leq -\dfrac{1}{2} \\[2ex] 0; & -\dfrac{1}{2} < W_{i-1} < \dfrac{1}{2} \\[2ex] 1; & W_{i-1} \geq -\dfrac{1}{2} \end{cases} \tag{3}$$

The iteration time of division algorithm is decided by F, which is also bit number of binary significant figure of quotient. In generally, users customarily give a decimal significant figure of operands, which is recorded by G. The relation between G and F can be expressed by formula (4).

$$\lceil (G-1) \times \ln 10 \div \ln 2 \rceil + 1 < F \leq \lceil G \times \ln 10 \div \ln 2 \rceil + 1 \tag{4}$$

We use the following formula (5) to compute F from G [9] so as not to reduce the accuracy of the corresponding decimal number.

$$F = \lceil G \times \ln 10 \div \ln 2 \rceil + 1 \tag{5}$$

After F iterations, digits of quotient Q are obtained and written in the following format $Q_1 \cdot Q_2 \ldots \ldots Q_F$. Then we shift $Q_1 \cdot Q_2 \ldots \ldots Q_F$ to Doffset-Noffset bits owing to that N and D have been shifted. So far, the final quotient is got.

4 Implementation of SRT Division by Two-Step M+B Adder

4.1 Parallel Iteration Steps Designed by M+B Adder

Each iteration needs MSD addition to realize comparison operation and calculation of partial remainder in SRT algorithm. As mentioned earlier, when M+B addition is performed, one of the operands is a MSD number and the other is required to be a binary number. It is easy to find out that there is always a fixed value, such as D or $\frac{1}{2}$, in the input data of each addition operation in the SRT algorithm. Considering that D is the initial data entered by the user and $\frac{1}{2}$ can be set as desired, we can make D or $\frac{1}{2}$ adopt binary numeration. Then M+B adder is suitable to perform division operation.

Assume four operations, W1, W2, W3 and W4 are as follows:

$$W1 = \frac{1}{2} + W_{i-1},\ W2 = \frac{1}{2} - W_{i-1},\ W3 = D + W_{i-1},\ W4 = D - W_{i-1}$$

The four operations run in parallel in an iteration step. W1 and W2 are used for comparison of W_{i-1} and $\frac{1}{2}$ or $-\frac{1}{2}$ to select Q_i. W3 and W4 are used to calculate the intermediate variable U_i. Laws of judgment are listed below:

If W1 $\leq$ 0, we can get $Q_i = \bar{1}$, $U_i = W3$;
If W1 > 0 and W2 > 0, we can get $Q_i = 0$, $U_i = W_{i-1}$;
If W2 $\leq$ 0, we can get $Q_i = 1$, $U_i = -W4$;

Then we can get the partial remainder W_i by left shift U_i one bit to meet the formula (2).

Assume that the bits of W_0, N and D is n, n and m respectively. In the first iteration, $\frac{1}{2}$ and n-bit W_0 are sent into the M+B adder and the subtractor. Meanwhile, m-bit D and n-bit W_0 are adjusted to two p-bit operands, then they are sent to the M+B adder and the subtractor, here p = max{n−k, m−x} + max{k, x}. According to operation laws of M+B adder, the output data W3 and W4 are p + 1-bit values. U_1 will be one of W3, W_0 or −W4 and W_1 will be got through left shifting the U_1 one bit. So the data bits of W_1 are up to p + 2. In a similar way, the data bits of the partial remainder will also increase two bits after each of iteration. Then, after the i-th iteration, the data bits of W_i will be up to p + 2i at most. In the last iteration, $\frac{1}{2}$, D and W_{F-1} which having p + 2F − 2 bits are send to the M+B adder and the subtractor respectively. Considering the utmost size of M+B adder in all of iterative process, we should construct four V_A-bit M+B adders and distribute V_T data bits of ternary optical processor for performing the SRT division in parallel. Here,

$$V_A = p + 2F - 2$$

$$V_T = 4(3(p + 2F - 2) + 1 = 12p + 24F - 20)$$

4.2   Computational Complexity Related Time and Data Bits

Comparing with the three-step MSD adder which be used in reference [9], the M+B adder can often accelerate the calculating process by eliminating one cycle in each iteration. SRT division need iterate F times for calculating quotient with F significant figures, so the total amount of clock cycles can be reduced by F.

On other hand, a V_A-digit three-step MSD adder must occupy $5V_A + 4$ bits of the ternary optical processor [9], but a V_A-digit M+B adder only occupies $3V_A + 1$ bits. Obviously, the M+B adder uses fewer data bits of the ternary optical processor and runs faster.

5 Implementation Steps of SRT Division Routine in TOC

Ternary optical computer is a photo-electronic hybrid computer as a whole and the optical constituents keep increasing with the continuous progress of the optical components. At present, ternary optical computer is possessed of restructuring optical processor and still uses the electronic computer to run its underlying software, such as hardware monitoring program, task scheduler and user interface, etc. SRT division routine described in this paper is a part of ternary optical computer's underlying software and is an independent body in calculation function. SRT division routine appears as a complete routine in the face to users, but it is decomposed into several functional modules that cooperate with task scheduling module, reconfigurable processor module, memory management module, optical components control module and data flow control module, respectively.

When implementing SRT division, ternary optical computer adopts the operational data file (*.SZG) to transmit users' requests [11]. This file consists of not only all pairs of the divisors and the dividends, but also the parameters for constructing ternary optical processor, such as m, n and F. Here, m is the maximum number of digits held by divisors, n is the maximum number of digits held by dividends and F is the significant figure of quotient. n and m can be obtained from initial data inputted by the users through the computer software.

The implementation steps of SRT division routine are as follows:

Step 1. Get m, n and G from initial data inputted by the users. Calculate F according to formula (5). Then save these parameters for constructing optical processors. The software module to do this step is integrated into the task scheduling module of ternary optical computer.

Step 2. Construct M+B adders A_1 and A_2 and M+B subtractors S_1 and S_2. The data management module of TOC's monitoring system will look for a V_T-bit free data bits section in optical processor [3, 12]. If an appropriate section is found, it will be assigned to SRT division to construct the A_1, A_2, S_1 and S_2 in accordance with the strategy shown in Table 2.

Table 2. Reconstruction strategy of data bits from h to $h+V_T$

M+B adders A1 and A2		M+B subtractors S1 and S2	
Range of data bits	Type	Range of data bits	Type
h–h + p + 2F − 3	C transformer	h + 6p + 12F − 10–h +7p + 14F − 13	C transformer
h + p + 2F − 2– h + 2p + 4F − 5	P transformer	h + 7p + 14F − 12–h +8p + 16F − 15	P transformer
h + 2p + 4F − 4– h + 3p + 6F − 6	R transformer	h + 8p + 16F − 14–h +9p + 18F − 16	R transformer
h + 3p + 6F − 5– h + 4p + 8F − 8	C transformer	h + 9p + 18F − 15–h +10p + 20F − 18	C transformer
h + 4p + 8F − 7– h + 5p + 10F − 10	P transfomer	h + 10p + 20F − 17–h +11p + 22F − 20	P transformer
h + 5p + 10F − 9– h + 6p + 12F − 11	R transformer	h + 11p + 22F − 19–h +12p + 24F − 21	R transformer

Step 3. Take calculating path distribution, iteration time and the original data (several pairs of dividends and divisors) to substratum control software. This step calls directly relevant function modules of ternary optical computer's monitoring system.

Step 4. Define variables. Define variables D and N to hold the divisor and the dividend. Define a variable i to hold iteration time and initialize i to 1. Define a variable W to hold the partial remainder W_i generated in the i-th iteration. Define a variable half to hold $\frac{1}{2}$. Define a variable W1 to hold the sum of $\frac{1}{2}$ and W_{i-1} generated in the i-th iteration. Define a variable W2 to hold the difference between $\frac{1}{2}$ and W_{i-1} generated in the i-th iteration. Define a variable W3 to hold the sum of D and W_{i-1} generated in the i-th iteration. Define a variable W4 to hold the difference between D and W_{i-1} generated in the i-th iteration. Define variables W1Value and W2Value to hold the most significant bit of W1and W2. Define a variable U to hold an intermediate variable of the partial remainder U_i. Define a variable Q to hold one bit of the quotient Q_i generated in the i-th iteration. Define a variable sign to hold the quotient's sign. Define a variable Noffset to hold shift amount of normalizing N. Define a variable Doffset to hold shift amount of normalizing D. Since the iterative process runs in ternary optical processor, the algorithm sets all the variables, such as D, N, W, Half, W1, W2, W3, W4, W1Value, W2Value, U, Q, sign, Noffset and Doffset in the underlying software directly controlling the ternary optical processor. It is important to point out that these variables including D, N, W, W1, W2, W3, W4, W1Value, W2Value, U, and Q are ternary variables represented by MSD binary numbers, and the rest are normal binary numbers.

Step 5. Iterative operations of SRT division. Get input data N and D from substratum control software. If all operations have been completed, then jump to step 8. Taking into account that the iterative process uses the M+B adders and subtracters repeatedly, this algorithm integrates the software module executing this step smoothly into the underlying control software of ternary optical computer. This module uses ternary optical processor and variables defined in step 4 to finish division operations.

Step 5–1. Determine Q's sign. If N and D are with the same sign, sign equals 1 and if not, sign equals −1. Then compute the absolute values of N and D.

Step 5–2. Shift N and D to make them fall in the interval $[\frac{1}{2}, 1)$. The bits shifting N and D are recorded in Noffset and Doffset. The results of shifting are still held in variables N and D.

Step 5–3. Dividend N as the initial value W_0 is stored in W and i is initialized to 1.

Step 5–4. Calculate W1, W2, W3 and W4. Send $\frac{1}{2}$ and W_{i-1} into A_1 and S_1. The returned results are stored in W1 and W2. Then send D and W_{i-1} into A_2 and S_2. The returned results are stored in W3 and W4.

Step 5–5. Calculate Q_i and W_i. According to W1, W2 and the formula (3), Q_i is determined. In the meantime, U_i is calculated based on W3, W4 and the formula (1). Q_i and U_i are stored in Q and U. W_i is obtained by shifting U_i one bit to the left and is stored in W, which prepares the input value for the next iteration.

Step 5–6. Increase i by 1. Repeat step 5–4 and step 5–5 until i = F. Then the iterative operations are completed.

Step 5–7. Obtain the final quotient Q by adjusting the sign first and then shifting (Noffset-Doffset) bits.

Step 6. Save the result of this division. Then send a group of input data N and D together with corresponding output data Q to the calculated result queue.

Step 7. Calculate the next pair of input data. Jump to step 5 and repeat step 5–step 6 until all the data have been calculated. At this time, the underlying control software no longer provides the input data, but delivers the completer.

Step 8. Send the calculated result queue to the task scheduling module by the underlying control software.

Step 9. Send the calculated results to the users by task scheduling module of ternary optical computer.

6 Software Simulation of SRT Division Algorithm Based on M+B Adder

6.1 Overview of Experiment

A function MSD_Add_MB is constructed to simulate the M+B adder. This function gives definition of truth tables of transforms C, P and R through two-dimensional integer arrays C, P and R. The core codes are as follows:

```
int C[2][3] = {0,0,1,0,1,1};
int P[2][3] = {-1,0,-1,0,-1,0};
int R[2][2] = {0,1,-1,0};
```

When adding an n-bit MSD number M and an n-bit binary number B, MSD_Add_MB calls three subfunctions CC, PP and RR. These subfunctions use the formula $c_i = C[b[i]][m[i] + 1]$, $p[i + 1] = P[b[i]][m[i] + 1]$ and $s[i] = R[-p[i + 1]][c[i + 1]]$ to realize transform C, transform P and transform R respectively, here $i = 1, 2, ...,n$ [4]. The core codes are as follows:

```
Void MSD_Add_MB(int m[], int b[],int s[])
{
    inti,n=MAX_LENGTH;
    int c[MAX_LENGTH+1],p[MAX_LENGTH+1];
    c[n]=0; p[0]=0;
    CC(m,b,n,c); // Accomplish transform C
    PP(m, b, n, p); //Accomplish transform P
    RR(c,p,n,s); //Accomplish transform R
}
```

A function MSD_Sub_MB is constructed to simulate the M+ B subtracter. When subtracting M from B, MSD_Sub_MB reverses each digit of M and then calls the function MSD_Add_MB.

A function MSD_Div is constructed to perform iterative steps. For each iteration, Half and W are provided to MSD_Add_MB and MSD_Sub_MB as the input parameters and the results returned by two functions are W1 and W2. D and W are provided to MSD_Add_MB and MSD_Sub_MB as the input parameters and the results returned by two functions are W3 and W4. Then W1Value and W2Value are obtained by scanning arrays W1 and W2. Based on laws of judgment presented in Sect. 4, Q and U are determined. W is obtained by shifting U one bit to the left. The core codes are as follows:

```
for(inti=0;i<F;i++)
  {
    MSD_Add_MB(W,Half,W1);// Compute W1 and W2
    MSD_Sub_MB(Half,W,W2);
    MSD_Add_MB(W,D,W3);// Compute W3 and W4
    MSD_Sub_MB(D,W,W4);
    Scan(W1,MAX_LENGTH,W1Index,W1Value);
    Scan(W2,MAX_LENGTH,W2Index,W2Value);
    if(W1Value<=0) // Determine Q and U
    { Q[INTEGER-1+i]=-1;
      memcpy(U,W3,sizeof(int)*MAX_LENGTH);
    } else if(W1Value>0&&W2Value>0)
    { Q[INTEGER-1+i]=0;
      memcpy(U,W,sizeof(int)*MAX_LENGTH);
    } else if(W2Value<=0)
    { Q[INTEGER-1+i]=1;
      for(int k=0;k<MAX_LENGTH;k++)
      {  W4[k]*=-1;  }
      memcpy(U,W4,sizeof(int)*MAX_LENGTH);
    }
    ShiftLeft(U,MAX_LENGTH);//Generate new W
    memcpy(W,U,sizeof(int)*MAX_LENGTH);
  }
```

6.2 Results Analysis

The original data with different scales are input and different significant figures of quotient are set to carry out simulation experiments. Five groups are randomly selected and their simulation results are shown in Table 3. The last column of Table 3 is the experiment result. When all the bits of Q agree with its theoretical calculating value exclusive of the last bit, we confirm that the result is accurate and a sign "$\sqrt{}$" is marked. When there is more than one inaccurate bit in Q, a sign "×" is marked. Several pairs of the dividends and the divisors randomly generated are input to make the simulation experiments and all the results are consistent with their theoretic calculations. So it can be concluded that the method and theory for SRT division are correct and feasible. The six groups of Table 3 are sent to the electronic computer to carry on contrast computation, and the results are shown in Table 4.

Table 3. Simulating experiment results of SRT division

Group	Input	MSD binary system	Decimal	Parameter	Result
1	N	10-10010-101-1010-10110-101-10	6497970	n = 24	√
	D	10100110100010101010001010	10914442	m = 24	
	Q	0.10011000100-1-1001010-1010-10	0.5953552	G = 7	
2	N	110-1010-10010-10110-1010-10-1010-1011-1	3004877621	n = 32	√
	D	10010100111010111001000100010010	4996932114	m = 32	
	Q	0.10011010000-10001101101101000000-1	0.601344495	G = 9	
3	N	10-10-101-1001-10100-10110-10010-1001-1000 -10010-10	765164307398	n = 40 m = 40	√
	D	10100100100001001000100010000100100101 0	353299087946	G = 12	
	Q	10.00101010100-1000000-100-10-100-10-1-100 1000100	2.16576926888		
4	N	1-10-101-1011011-1001 1 1-1000-1-1001-10-10 -1001-1-1011011-1-1-10	55886358087074	n = 48 m = 48	√
	D	10001010010011100101001010100100111100 10 1010010	76034499311954	G = 14	
	Q	0.11000-1000010100111010010101010011101100 00000-10-1-100	0.73501316629683		
5	N	10000-1-1001-1-1-100010-101-1-10010-101-1-1 001-1-1001-1-10011-1001-1-1-1001	34349164981144072	n = 56 m = 56	√
	D	100100100001001000110001100011100011000110 0 0000001000100110 1	41115347307725904	G = 16	
	Q	0.1101011000-10000-100000011000101100011 10000-1-1000010110101	0.8354341439477416		
6	N	1-1-1001-1-1000-10-1001-100011-1001-1001-1 0001-1-1001-1-1-1001-100-1-1-100-100-10-1-1	593086760775594421	n = 62 m = 62	√
	D	100100011100000010000010000100011000010000000 10000100000100000	2625634335692228640	G = 18	
	Q	0.01000-1-1000-10-1-100-10000-1000-100-1000 -100-1-10-100001100010000000111000	0.225883228564358174		

Table 4. The compared calculation of TOC and the electronic computer

Group	TOC	The electronic computer	Theoretical calculating value
1	0.5953552	0.59535521834281591000	0.59535521834281587643...
2	0.601344495	0.60134449547176694000	0.60134449547176697946...
3	2.16576926888	2.16576926888345510000	2.16576926888345531341...
4	0.73501316629683	0.73501316629683722000	0.73501316629683721229...
5	0.8354341439477416	0.83543414394774163000	0.83543414394774157740...
6	0.225883228564358174	0.22588322856435822000	0.22588322856435817476...

After analyzing of calculation results shown in the Tables 3 and 4, we can find the following rules. To begin with, ternary optical computer computes the quotient in accordance with the significant digits G, while the electronic computer always computes the quotient at the fixed precision. Next, two types of computer are all adequate for calculating when calculation accuracy of division required by users is low. However, the results returned by the electronic computer become inaccurate as calculation accuracy of division is rising and the maximum number of decimal digits that the electronic computer can calculate up to is 18 digits. By contrast, ternary optical computer can always ensure that G bits of the quotient are exactly calculated.

168 Q. Xu et al.

In fact, owing to electronic CPU with fixed data bits, the electronic computer only provides limited computing power. For example, in the programming environment of C language, float type can guarantee an accuracy of 7 digits and double type can guarantee an accuracy of 15 digits. So the electronic computer is unable to meet the computational requirements when users request high precision. In comparison with the electronic computer, ternary optical computer's great strength lies in many data bits and the reconfigurable optical processor, leading ternary optical computer to distribute the data bits to construct the parallel arithmetic units based on users' need. After analyzing compared calculation results, we can draw a conclusion that ternary optical computer appears more powerful in computing capacity.

7 Conclusion and Outlook

This paper studies and improves division strategy of ternary optical computer based on two-step M+B adder and SRT division. Two-step M+B adder is used to parallel implement SRT division, reduce the computational time and decrease consumption amount of data bits. The paper gives a detailed description of implementation steps for the SRT division. Then the paper demonstrates the correctness and effectiveness of the theory through simulation experiment. The research is of practical importance in theory and practice, on one hand it provides a new technical route for the engineering algorithm and it promotes development on application of ternary optical computer on the other.

In this paper, the research is sponsored by the Nature Science Foundation of China (61103054), Natural Science Foundation of Shanghai, China (13ZR1416000), and Innovation Program of Shanghai Municipal Education Commission (13ZZ074).

References

1. Jin, Y., He, H.C., Lu, Y.T.: Ternary optical computer principle. Sci. China Ser. F-Inf. Sci. **46**(2), 145–150 (2003)
2. Yan, J.Y., Jin, Y., Zuo, K.Z.: Decrease-radix design principle for carrying/borrowing free multi-valued and application in ternary optical computer. Sci. China Ser. F-Inf. Sci. **51**, 1415–1426 (2008)
3. Jin, Y., Wang, H.J., Ouyang, S., et al.: Principles, structures and implementation of reconfigurable ternary optical processors. Sci. China Ser. F-Inf. Sci. **54**, 2236–2246 (2011)
4. Shen, Y., Jiang, B., Jin, Y., et al.: Principle and design of ternary optical accumulator implementing M-K-B addition. Opt. Eng. **53**(9), 095108 (2014). doi:10.1117/1.OE.53.9.095108
5. Robertson, J.E.: A new class of digital division methods. IRE Trans. Electron. Comput. **7**, 88–92 (1958)
6. Hooman, N.: Architectures for floating-point division. Dissertation for Ph.D. Degree. Adelaide University of Australia, Adelaide (2005)
7. Atkins, D.E.: The theory and implementation of SRT division. Technical Report UIUCDCS-R-67-230 (1967)

8. Tocher, K.D.: Techniques of multiplication and division for automatic binary computers. Q. J. Mech. Appl. Math. **11**, 364–384 (1958)
9. Xu, Q., Jin, Y., Shen, Y.F., et al.: MSD iterative division algorithm and implementation technique for ternary optical computer. Sci China Ser F-Inf. Sci. doi:10.1360/N112014-00391
10. Jin, Y., Shen, Y.F., Peng, J.J., et al.: Principles and construction of MSD adder in ternary optical computer. Sci. China Ser. F-Inf. Sci. **53**, 2159–2168 (2010)
11. Gao, H., Jin, Y., Song, K.: Extension of C language in ternary optical computer. J. Shanghai Univ. (Nat. Sci.) **19**, 280–285 (2013). (in Chinese)
12. Wang, H.J., Jin, Y., Ouyang, S.: Design and implementation of 1-bit reconfigurable ternary optical processor. Chin. J. Comput. **37**, 1500–1507 (2014). (in Chinese)

A Limited Incremental Clustering Algorithm with Respect to Cluster Stability

Wenhao Zhu[1], Wenxin Yao[1], Song Dai[1], and Zhiguo Lu[2(✉)]

[1] School of Computer Engineering and Science, Shanghai University, Shanghai, China
[2] Shanghai University Library, Shanghai University, Shanghai, China
luzg@staff.shu.edu.cn

Abstract. As one of the important techniques of data analysis, a clustering algorithm is widely used in data mining, image recognition, information extraction, pattern recognition and other fields. In the era of big data, with the rapid development of web applications, much of the data to be processed is characterized by massive and dynamic growth. Under this background, how to cluster the incremental data becomes a challenging problem that clustering algorithms face. In this paper, we proposed a limited incremental clustering algorithm with respect to cluster stability. Based on an assumption that the categories of data are limited, we take advantage of an existing clustering structure and deal with incremental data steadily with respect to cluster stability. Cluster reconstruction will be triggered when the stability does no longer hold or a buffer pool for undetermined data is full. At the end of the paper, we implement the limited incremental clustering algorithm with K-means. Meanwhile, we use an average density of clusters and the global stability to choose a proper value of K.

Keywords: Incremental data · Clustering · K-value

1 Introduction

Clustering is a popular unsupervised learning method which organizes a data point into groups whose members are similar in the same way according to the features of data. The characteristics of automatically dividing data into different groups imply the potential structure in a collection of unlabeled data and save a lot of labor costs. Therefore, it has been widely used in statistics, pattern recognition, bioinformatics and machine learning [1]. We can use clustering to find groups of customers with similar behavior given their properties and past buying records. In biology, clustering is used to classify plants and animals. We can also use it to cluster weblog data to discover groups of similar access patterns. So we can consider it as one of the most useful algorithms. There are two main clustering methods: hierarchical clustering and partitioning clustering. K-means and K-centroids are two common partitioning clustering algorithms. Their main idea is to partition a data set into different clusters to make the distance of data points in the same cluster as close as possible and the distance between different clusters as far as possible. BIRCH and Chameleon are typical Hierarchical clustering. Their main idea is to divide the data into different layers from top to bottom or from the bottom up, at

© Springer International Publishing Switzerland 2016
J. Xie et al. (Eds.): HPCA 2015, LNCS 9576, pp. 170–177, 2016.
DOI: 10.1007/978-3-319-32557-6_18

last generating a dendrogram. Generally, calculation complexity of Hierarchical clustering is higher than that of partitioning clustering and is more time consuming [2]. So we often use hierarchical clustering to cluster small data sets [3].

With the rapid development of the internet technology, a data set is growing incrementally and largely. However, traditional clustering algorithms cannot handle this condition properly because the cluster of a data set needs to be reconstructed again every time when a new data is coming. Obviously, it is repetitive, time-consuming and impractical especially when the size of data becomes larger. Considering this situation, we are inspired by [4] and try to cope with the increase of data in an incremental way. It is intuitive that in many applications, the categories of data cannot grow infinitely, such as character recognition and biometric identification. Under this precondition, we consider the structure of dataset's clusters kept mostly unchangeable until the amount of data is big enough and reconstructing the clusters of data sets is not necessary. So we will divide new data into the closest existing clusters if the similarity between them is above the threshold; otherwise, we reserve it in a buffer pool. When the buffer pool is full we construct the clusters on the whole dataset. We use this idea to avoid the computational cost of the frequent reconstructed data set and also guarantee the validity of clustering in some degree. The main contribution of this paper is to propose an incremental clustering algorithm for clustering dynamic growth data based on the assumption that the category of incremental data is limited. Moreover, the algorithm is proved to be feasible by realizing our methods based on K-means. In the end, a new method for choosing the K-values is proposed.

The rest of this paper is organized as follows: We discuss related work on clustering algorithms in Sect. 2. The algorithms of incremental clustering based on K-means and the selection of K-values are introduced in Sect. 3. In Sect. 4, we show the results of clustering using K-means and our limited incremental clustering separately. Section 5 concludes this paper and gives some directions for future research.

2 Related Work

With more and more applications need processing large amounts of data, incremental clustering has gradually into people's view and attracted wide attention. [4] proposed an incremental clustering algorithm which is applied in relational database, because in a database insert operation is frequent, reconstruct the cluster when insert operation occurs is impractical. HIREL algorithm firstly divides the whole data set into a series of sub clusters, so that the variance of each cluster is lower than the threshold, then form a balanced search tree based on these sub clusters. When new data come, the similarity between the data and the clustering will be computed. If the similarity is lower than threshold, dividing this data into the closest cluster, otherwise creating a new cluster contains the new data. Finally, we adjust the balanced search tree according to the insert data. [5] present a single pass incremental clustering algorithm GenIc, and applies it to the network monitoring data. For each new data, it can be classified into the nearest cluster, meanwhile the location of the clusters' center are adjusted. When the number of processing data reaches the window's size, the probability of survival is calculated.

If the probability is bigger than a random threshold between 0 and 1, the clustering center is preserved. Otherwise, select a random alternative from the current existing data as the cluster center. [6] use the method of incremental clustering to handle the problem of dynamic growth data in the classification of text and images, and it is proved that the result is better than the traditional clustering algorithm in this case. News of an event is incremental at a period of time. Using complex language model or method of combining multiple clustering to process this kind of news data has high computational complexity and is infeasible. [7] take K-means as the prototype to create an incremental clustering to classify the news about different events. For new news, according to the similarity between the news and the existing clusters, we decide which cluster it belongs to, whether the new cluster is generated.

Categories of news events are vastly different, while there are also many applications has limited categories. We assume that in some applications the number of clusters will not increase when the size of samples is big enough. Under this hypothesis, we proposed an incremental clustering algorithm base on K-means, which defines the membership degree to measure the categories of incremental data, take use of buffer mechanism to achieve a limited incremental clustering algorithm. We chose K-means as the basic algorithm, because it can classify large data sets efficiently. Clustering speed is much faster than hierarchical clustering algorithm. Firstly, the new sample is deposited in the buffer. We calculate the membership degree of each sample when the number of samples reached a certain size. We decided to reserve the sample in the buffer or subsume the sample into the existing cluster according to whether its member degree is lower or higher than threshold. We will adjust the structure of clustering unless every sample in buffer cannot be classified.

The defect of K-means algorithm based on partition is that it is necessary to initialize k value, and the selection of K largely determined the results of clustering to a great degree. Paper [8] mentioned using Silhouette coefficient and Partition coefficient to evaluate the clustering method. We are inspired by the thought of Silhouette coefficient, and define two concepts: average density of cluster and the global stability, separately considered the compact degree of intra-cluster and the separation degree of inter-cluster. Furthermore, we propose a new method to confirm which K value is better so that our method can overcome the problem of the selection of K to some extent. In the end we compare our method with the traditional K-means, which shows our idea is feasible.

3   Limited Incremental Algorithm

Clustering is to divide data points into groups and meets the requirement that the similarity between the data points in the same group as higher as possible, while in different groups as lower as possible [9]. In this paper, K-means algorithm is used as the basis of incremental clustering.

3.1 Selection of K-values

K-means need the user set the K-values according to their experience, which not only bring a lot of burden to the user, but also increase the randomness and uncertainty of the algorithm. The selection of K value will affect the performance of the algorithm to a large extent. Rezaee et al. [10] believe the optimal number of clusters is range from 2 to $\sqrt{N}$ in accordance with empirical regularity, here n is the number of all the data points in data space. We conducted a study on the K value, and proposed a clustering validity function to evaluate the effectiveness of clustering. Select K value within a given interval individually, use cluster validity function to evaluate the clustering, and get the best K value ultimately. Given the interval of K is much easier than chose the value of K.

Definition 1: Suppose N spatial objects were clustered into K clusters, using Euclidean distance to calculate the average distance of cluster:

$$\bar{d}_i = \frac{\sum_{p \in C_i} \sqrt{(p - m_i)^2}}{n_i} \tag{3.1}$$

In the formula, $\bar{d}_i$ is the average distance within the cluster. p represents the object in the space. m_i is the center of cluster, namely, the mean value of the cluster C_i. n_i represents the number of object in C_i.

Definition 2: Suppose that the N objects in the space are clustered into K clusters, and the average distance between the clusters is:

$$\bar{D} = \frac{\sum_{i=1,j=1}^{K} \sqrt{(m_i - m_j)^2}}{2K} \tag{3.2}$$

In the formula, $\bar{D}$ is the mean of distance within cluster, m_i and m_j are the mean values of C_i and C_j respectively.

Definition 3: Suppose that the N objects in the space are clustered into K clusters, the cluster density is the number of objects in the average distance of the cluster.

$$f_i = \frac{n_i}{\bar{d}_i} \tag{3.3}$$

$$\bar{f} = \frac{\sum_{i=1}^{K} f_i}{K} \tag{3.4}$$

In the formula, f_i is the cluster density. n_i and $\bar{d}_i$ have the same meaning in formula 3.1. $\bar{f}$ is the average density of all clusters.

Clustering effectiveness is evaluated from two aspects. First, use average density to measure the stability and compactness of cluster. Second, use global stability to measure the similarity of inter-cluster. S denotes the global stability.

$$S = \frac{\bar{D}}{K} \tag{3.5}$$

From the above formula, we can find that the higher the average density $\bar{f}$, the more compact cluster. And when the average distance between the clusters is far and the number of cluster is little, the value of S will become big, which means cluster is steady.

To sum up, we define the cluster effectively function as follows:

$$\text{Function} = S\bar{f} \tag{3.6}$$

The selection process of K: Select K value within a given interval individually, calculate the value, find a K value make the value of the Function maximum.

3.2   Incremental Clustering

Incremental clustering is proposed under the background of insufficient memory space. At present, there are two main types of incremental clustering: One is to cluster all of the data again when new data comes. Nevertheless, this method is inefficient and costly. The other is to use the results of the original clustering, add new data to the existing cluster. That is to say, we assign new data points to the nearest cluster, meanwhile the center of cluster be recalculated. The advantage is that it is not necessary to re-cluster every time when new data comes. However, this method cannot detect the outlier and the structure of the cluster will be changed with more and more new data added. For example, the new data point in a particular sequence may be assign to a cluster of the existing K clusters, may be assign to a new cluster, or lead to cluster merging. There is no better way to judge the changes of cluster structure when a new data is added.

Definition 4: Suppose that the N objects in the space are clustered into K clusters, the membership degree of spatial object p with respect to the cluster C_i is the ratio of average distance of cluster C_i and distance from p to the center of cluster C_i.

$$\gamma_i = \frac{\bar{d}_i}{\sqrt{(p - m_i)^2 + \bar{d}_i}} \tag{3.7}$$

In the formula, γ_i is the membership degree of object P with respect to the cluster C_i. $\bar{d}_i$ is the average distance of cluster C_i. m_i is the center of cluster C_i. When the distance from p to cluster C_i is more than $\bar{d}_i$, p is not belong to cluster C_i, which means the value of γ_i is less than 0.5. When the value of γ_i is more than or equal to 0.5, the smaller the distance from p to cluster C_i, the higher the value of γ_i, that is to say the more likely p belongs to cluster C_i.

We combine two methods and use buffer mechanism to realize the incremental clustering. The main procedures as following:

1. Set up the buffer to store the new samples.
2. When here comes a new sample, put it in a buffer.
3. Detecting buffer, when the number of new samples is bigger than the minimum size of the existing clusters, calculate γ_i for every samples in buffer. If the value of γ_i is

more than 0.5, add the sample to the cluster which value of γ_i is maximum, keep the center of cluster unchanged and delete it from buffer. Otherwise, go to step 4.
4. When samples remaining in buffer cannot be assigned to any existing clusters, re-cluster all the samples.

In the step 3, we keep the center of cluster unchanged to prevent the newly added sample affect the cluster structure. We keep the samples which cannot be assigned to any existing clusters in the buffer, and re-cluster all samples to adjust the whole cluster structures only once when the buffer is full. This incremental clustering method is relatively simple but can achieve the incremental clustering well and improve the incremental efficiency to some extent.

4   Experiment

We extracted 400 different types of news from the six mainstream news sites: Sohu, Sina, QQ, People, 163, ifeng. In the incremental clustering, 3/5 of the training samples are used to cluster the k-means, and then the remaining 2/5 of the data is clustered according to the incremental clustering method we proposed. Samples are different type of news. The clustering effect before and after the increment is shown in the following Figs. 1 and 2.

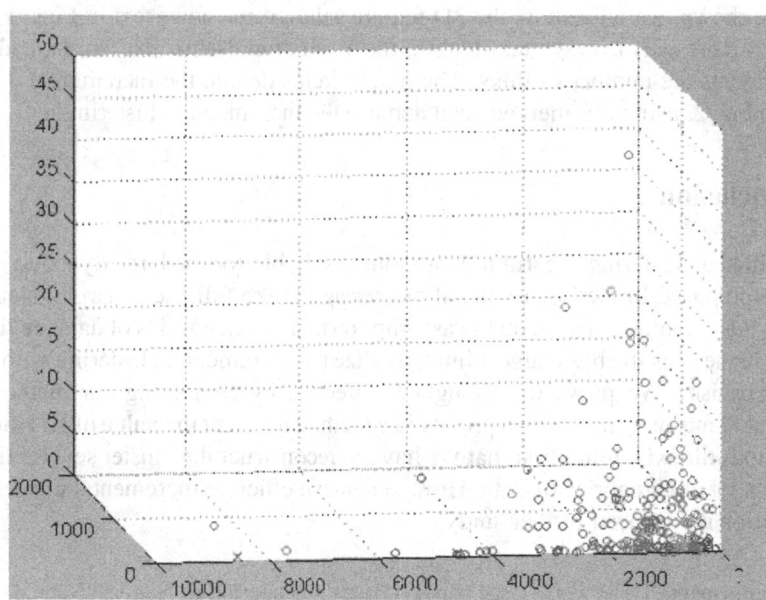

Fig. 1. k = 9, traditional clustering

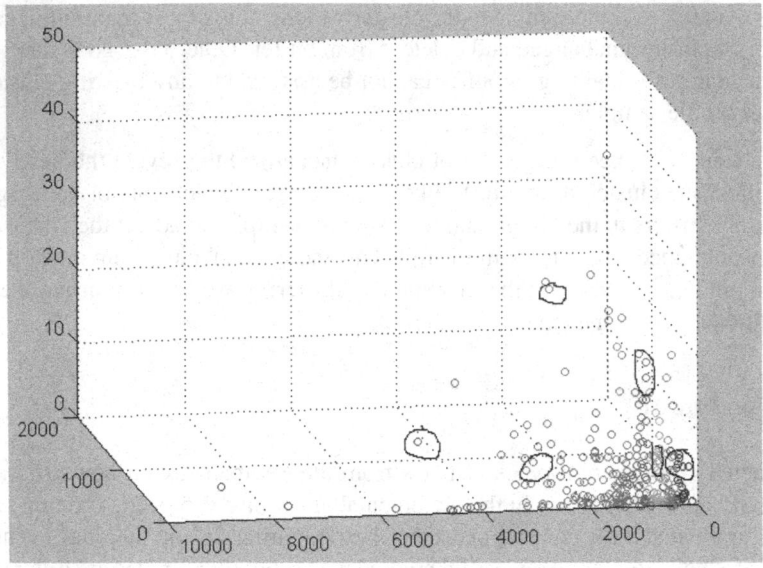

Fig. 2. k = 9, incremental clustering

According to the cluster effectively function in Sect. 3.1, we take the mode of 20 k-means test set the value of K equal to 9. Because the four-dimensional effect diagram cannot be shown, we only show the 3D feature value of the news text in Figs. 1 and 2, the X axis represents average text length, the Y axis represents text length, and the Z axis represents the number of links. The black circles denote the incremental data. As shown in Fig. 2, using our methods can achieve the incremental clustering.

5   Conclusion

The traditional clustering algorithm is no longer suitable for the large dynamic growth data. We proposed limited incremental clustering to take full use of large amounts of web data. Our method is based on the assumption that the categories of data are limited, and take K-mean as the basic algorithm to realize the incremental clustering with buffer pool mechanism. We prove our thought is effective by comparing our method with traditional K-means. And we also proposed a method to select the value of K. However, this method still exist limitation that we have to reconstruct the cluster several times if there are a lot of categories of data. How to achieve efficient incremental clustering in this situation is still need further study.

Acknowledgements. The work of the paper is partially supported by National Natural Science Foundation of China (No. 61303097) and Ph.D. Programs Foundation of Ministry of Education of China (No. 20123108120026).

References

1. Xu, R., Wunsch, D.: Survey of clustering algorithms. IEEE Trans. Neural Netw. **16**(3), 645–678 (2005)
2. Steinbach, M., Karypis, G., Kumar, V.: A comparison of document clustering techniques. In: Proceedings of the KDD Workshop on Text Mining, Boston, MA, USA, 20–23 August 2000
3. Sun, J., Liu, J., Zhao, L.: Clustering algorithms research. J. Softw. **19**(1), 48–61 (2008)
4. Li, T., Anand, S.S.: Hirel: an incremental clustering algorithm for relational datasets. In: Eighth IEEE International Conference on Data Mining, ICDM 2008, pp. 887–892. IEEE (2008)
5. Gupta, C., Grossman, R.L.: GenIc: a single-pass generalized incremental algorithm for clustering. In: SDM 2004, pp. 147–153 (2004)
6. Charikar, M., Chekuri, C., Feder, T., et al.: Incremental clustering and dynamic information retrieval. In: Proceedings of the Twenty-Ninth Annual ACM Symposium on Theory of Computing, pp. 626–635. ACM (1997)
7. Azzopardi, J., Staff, C.: Incremental clustering of news reports. Algorithms **5**(3), 364–378 (2012)
8. Berkhin, P.: A Survey of Clustering Data Mining Techniques. Grouping Multidimensional Data, pp. 25–71. Springer, Heidelberg (2006)
9. Jing, L., Ng, M.K., Huang, J.Z.: An entropy weighting k-means algorithm for subspace clustering of high-dimensional sparse data. IEEE Trans. Knowl. Data Eng. **19**(8), 1026–1041 (2007)
10. Rezaee, M.R., Lelieveldt, B.P., Reiber, J.H.: A new cluster validity index for the fuzzy C-means. Pattern Recogn. Lett. **19**(3–4), 237–246 (1998)

Prediction on Performance of Age Group Swimming Using Machine Learning

Jiang Xie[1(✉)], Junfu Xu[1], Celine Nie[2], and Qing Nie[3]

[1] School of Computer Engineering and Science, Shanghai University,
99 Shangda Road, Shanghai 200444, China
{jiangx,xujunfu}@shu.edu.cn
[2] University High School, 4771 Campus Drive, Irvine, CA 92612, USA
nie.celine@gmail.com
[3] Department of Mathematics, Center for Mathematical and Computational Biology,
University of California at Irvine, Irvine, CA, USA
qnie@math.uci.edu

Abstract. Time for swimming at young ages may be a good indicator for swimmers' future performance. Through analyzing a large data set on swimming time, we use the machine learning algorithms to explore swimmers' performance on four different strokes in a 100 m long course for both males and females. For each stroke, we divide swimmers' performance into four levels according to their time at the ages of 12–13, and predict their performance levels at the age of 18 using two well-known machine learning methods with optimal parameters. Based on the existing data, we predict the probability from each level at a young age to the top 25 % at the age of 18. The predictions obtained by the machine learning approach are very close to a statistical analysis result, indicating that our approach is effective in predicting swimming performance based on swimmers' past records.

1 Introduction

Competitive swimming is an old and popular sport. Multiple analyses on swimming, including on oxygen uptake kinetics [1], swimming performance and technique evaluation with wearable acceleration sensors [2], an age of peak swim speed, and the effect of sex on stroke performance [3], have been performed. Additionally, Eichenberger et al. investigated performance trends at the Zurich 12-h Swim in Switzerland from 1996 to 2010 and studied sex differences in peak performance in ultra-endurance swimming [4]. Tanaka analyzed the peak exercise performance of highly trained athletes as a function of age [5]. In particular, a regression analysis showed that for both men and women, endurance swimming performance (i.e., 1,500 m) declined linearly from peak levels at 35–40 years of age until 70 years of age, whereupon performance declined exponentially thereafter [5]. A greater understanding of the characteristics of male and female performance at different ages in different strokes may result in better training methods and improved performance.

© Springer International Publishing Switzerland 2016
J. Xie et al. (Eds.): HPCA 2015, LNCS 9576, pp. 178–184, 2016.
DOI: 10.1007/978-3-319-32557-6_19

During the past thirty years, a large amount of swimming performance data has been recorded. In this study, we predict swimmers' performance levels using machine learning tools, including the support vector machine (SVM) method [6–8], which solves pattern recognition problems, and the artificial neural network (ANN) method, which has been widely used in many applications such as drug classification and weather classification [9–11].

2   Data Set

2.1   Data Set Description

A large observational data set of swimmers' performance was obtained from the USA Swimming website (http://www.usaswimming.org/DesktopDefault.aspx). The USA Swimming website is the national governing body for competitive swimming in the United States. It is charged with selecting the United States Olympic Swimming team and any other teams that officially represent the United States, as well as the overall organization and operation of the sport within the country, in accordance with the Amateur Sports Act [12].

To study the performance of the top swimmers in the USA, we chose the top 5512 male swimmers and 2218 female swimmers based on their swimming times in the 100 m (100 M) long course freestyle. We then collected all the available swimming times of those swimmers for all the swimming meets listed on the USA Swimming websites dating back to as early as age 10. The result is a data set containing 2,762,237 records for 7730 swimmers.

2.2   Data Representation

A vector model is used to describe the record of each data point. This vector has five elements, namely, swimming stroke, course, age, time, and power point, and takes on the following form:

$$record = (stroke, course, age, time, powerpoint) \tag{1}$$

There are four swimming strokes, namely, freestyle (FR), butterfly (FL), backstroke (BK) and breaststroke (BR), with different distances. The swimming course includes two options: long-course, measured in meters (LCM), and short-course, measured in yards (SCY). The time of each performance is always measured in seconds. The power point is a Hy-Tek (http://www.usaswimming.org/DesktopDefault.aspx?TabId=757) value that allows for a comparison of the quality of performances across strokes, distances and events, as well as between age groups.

3   Machine Learning

3.1   Introduction of SVM and ANN Methods

We use two machine learning methods, an artificial neural network (ANN) and a support vector machine (SVM), to classify swimming performance and to predict whether a swimmer will go to top 25 % with age. The SVM method is largely based on the structural risk minimization principle and statistical learning theory [13]. The ANN method assumes that nodes and the connections among them are similar to the neurons and synapses in the human brain [14]. Both methods can be used to recognize patterns to generate classification of data.

3.2 Data Preprocessing

To determine if performance at older ages depends on performance at younger ages (12–13). For each swimmer, we denote x_i as the average time at the age of i. Based on the swimming time performance of the data sets at age 13, we divide the athletes into four groups from fastest to slowest, as shown in Table 1. And, the level at age 13 is defined as swimming level at younger ages. In addition, we divide the performance at age 18 into four levels in a similar way.

Table 1. Definition of swimming level labels

Level labels	Description (Mean time at age X in a stroke)
level_1	Top 25 %
level_2	25 %–50 %
level_3	50 %–75 %
level_4	Bottom 25 %

3.3 Training and Learning Model

Similar to the standard machine learning approach, the data set is divided into two portions at random with a training set and a testing set. In our trials, for data set, 80 % of the data for each young age is selected as the training set, and the remainder is the testing data. We next apply both machine learning methods to the data set. The average swimming times for young ages in groups are used as the inputs to produce a classification model for ANN or SVM. With the classification models, we predict swimming performance in terms of levels at the age of 18. In this paper, exhaustive search method is utilized to select the optimal parameters (penalty parameter c and kernel function parameter g) of SVM, which we give the original range the range of this parameters from 1 to 2000. The Gaussian radial basis function kernel, or RBF kernel, is a popular kernel function used in SVM learning algorithms. For the ANN method, the iteration parameter epochs is set to be 2000, and the learning rate is set to be 0.001.

3.4 Evaluating Performance

The predicted outcomes using the two machine learning methods will be tested by direct calculation. As seen in Fig. 1, any swimmer in the top 25 % at age 18 must come from one of the four levels in their younger ages. This ratio of the swimmers in the top level at age 18 from a certain level at a young age is referred to as "Level Change Ratio (LCR)". This ratio can be estimated by ANN or SVM, and it can also be directly calculated based on the data in the following way. First, we define N_{11} as the number of swimmers who are in level_1 (top 25 %) at a young age and who join level_1 at the age of 18. Similarly, we define N_{i1} as the number of swimmers who are at level_i (i=2,3,4) at a young age but who join level_1 at age 18. The percentage of swimmers at the top level at age 18 coming from each level at a young age can be defined as

$$LCR_i = \frac{N_{i1}}{N_{11} + N_{21} + N_{31} + N_{41}} \quad i = 1, 2, 3, 4 \qquad (2)$$

This quantity, based on a statistical method (SM) analysis of the original data, will be compared with the predictions made by the two machine learning methods.

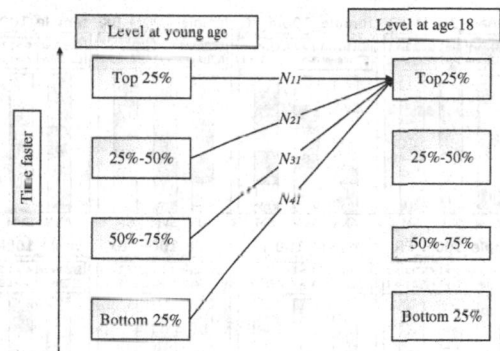

Fig. 1. An illustration of the change in performance level from a younger age to the age of 18.

3.5 Result

Here, we show the predicted probability using the ANN and SVM and the percentage of swimmers (SM) going from one level (level_1, level_2, level_3 or level_4) at a young age to level_1 (top 25 %) at the age of 18. We will present the results for four different strokes in 100M LCM for both females and males.

When using swimming performance in LCM at ages 12 and 13 to predict performance at age 18 (shown in Fig. 2), we observe that three methods, ANN, SVM, and SM, produce similar results for 100 FR. Male and female swimmers in the top level at ages 12–13 have an approximately 40 % chance of remaining in the top level at age 18. There is a more than 20 % chance that swimmers in level_2 and level_3 will move to the top level once they reach the age of 18. This trend is similar for the Fly and Backstrokes, although the ANN and SVM predict somewhat lower percentages than do the statistical methods for both males and females. Interestingly, for the Breaststroke, the SM shows that over 60 % of the level_1 female swimmers at ages 12–13 remain in the top, and this is true for nearly 60 % of males. However, the ANN and SVM predict that approximately 40 % of both males and females at the top level come from the top level at a younger age, while the same portion at level_4 can move to the top level, which is not shown in the SM analysis. On the one hand, this suggests that the data for the Breaststroke at younger ages are less useful in predicting future performance than for the other three strokes; this may in part be because the Breaststroke is a timing stroke, which may present challenges to further development as the swimmers, females in particular, become older. As indicated in Fig. 2, the predictions for females using the ANN and SVM are less accurate those for the male for the breaststroke. On the other hand, the direct computation based on the SM shows that if one swimmer does not perform well at the breaststroke to begin with (in level_4), it is difficult to move to the top level, suggesting the importance of breaststroke training at younger ages for both males and females.

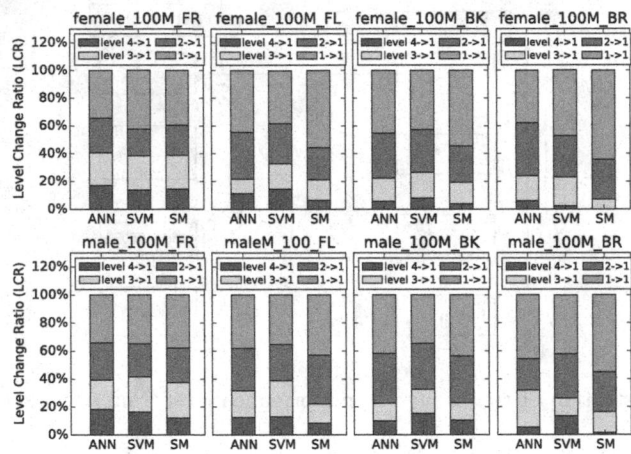

Fig. 2. Predictions of level change ratio (LCR) of LCM for ages 12–13 to age 18.

4   Summary and Outlook

In this paper, the ANN (a high-dimension nonlinear classification method) and SVM (a high-dimension linear classification method) are used to forecast swimming level performance. Our study and approaches may be used and modified to predict future swimming times using different swimming data sets. The data in this study can be applied to the swimming world, giving both parents and swimmers the opportunity to be proactive in future training. As is known to all, besides the age, there are many impact factors which can affect the scores, such as, weight, height, and so on. If we can add this impact factors in the future, maybe we can draw a better conclusion. As the increasing of data size, swimming data mining requires a large amount of computation time for solving large size problems and highly parallel computing technologies should be applied.

Acknowledgments. This work was partially supported by the Major Research Plan of NSFC [No. 91330116], and the Scientific Research Foundation for the Returned Overseas Chinese Scholars, State Education Ministry.

References

1. Reis, J.F., Alves, F.B., Bruno, P.M., Vleck, V., Millet, G.P.: Oxygen uptake kinetics and middle distance swimming performance. J. Sci. Med. Sport **15**(1), 58–63 (2012)
2. Bächlin, M., Tröster, G.: Swimming performance and technique evaluation with wearable acceleration sensors. Pervasive Mob. Comput. **8**(1), 68–81 (2012)
3. Vaso, M., Knechtle, B., Rüst, C.A., Rosemann, T., Lepers, R.: Age of peak swim speed and sex difference in performance in medley and freestyle swimming. A comparison between 200 m and 400 m in swiss elite. J. Hum. Sport and Exerc. **8**(4), 954–965 (2013)
4. Eichenberger, E., Knechtle, B., Knechtle, P., Röst, C.A., Rosemann, T., Lepers, R.: No gender difference in peak performance in ultra-endurance swimming performance-analysis of the 'zurich 12-h swim' from 1996 to 2010. Chin. J. Physiol. **55**(5), 346–351 (2012)
5. Tanaka, H., Seals, D.R.: Age and gender interactions in physiological functional capacity: insight from swimming performance. J. Appl. Physiol. **82**(3), 846–851 (1997)
6. Joachims, T.: Making large scale svm learning practical. Technical report, Universität Dortmund (1999)
7. Jensen, U., Prade, F., Eskofier, B.M.: Classification of kinematic swimming data with emphasis on resource consumption. In: 2013 IEEE International Conference on Body Sensor Networks (BSN), pp. 1–5. IEEE (2013)
8. Byvatov, E., Fechner, U., Sadowski, J., Schneider, G.: New scheme based on gmm-pca-svm modelling for automatic speaker recognition. Int. J. Speech Technol. **17**(4), 373–381 (2014)
9. Byvatov, E., Fechner, U., Sadowski, J., Schneider, G.: Comparison of support vector machine and artificial neural network systems for drug/nondrug classification. J. Chem. Inf. Comput. Sci. **43**(6), 1882–1889 (2003)
10. Kanellopoulos, I., Varfis, A., Wilkinson, G.G., Megier, J.: Land-cover discrimination in spot hrv imagery using an artificial neural network-a 20-class experiment. Int. J. Remote Sens. **13**(5), 917–924 (1992)
11. Chen, C., Duan, S., Cai, T., Liu, B.: Online 24-h solar power forecasting based on weather type classification using artificial neural network. Solar Energy **85**(11), 2856–2870 (2011)
12. Wikipedia. Usa swimming – wikipedia, the free encyclopedia (2015), 23-August 2015

13. Cai, C.Z., Wang, G.L., Wen, Y.F., Pei, J.F., Zhu, X.J., Zhuang, W.P.: Supercon-
    ducting transition temperature t c estimation for superconductors of the doped
    mgb2 system using topological index via support vector regression. J. Supercond.
    Novel Magn. **23**(5), 745–748 (2010)
14. Hickman, S., Mirzakhani, A.S., Pabon, J., Alba-Flores, R.: A case study on tuning
    artificial neural networks to recognize signal patterns of hand motions. In: South-
    eastCon 2015, pp. 1–4. IEEE (2015)

Predicting Abstract Keywords by Word Vectors

Qing Li[1], Wenhao Zhu[1], and Zhiguo Lu[2(✉)]

[1] School of Computer Engineering and Science,
Shanghai University, Shanghai, China
[2] Shanghai University Library, Shanghai University, Shanghai, China
luzg@staff.shu.edu.cn

Abstract. The continuous development of the information technology leads to the explosive growth of many information domains. Obtaining the required information from a large-scale text in a quick and accurate way has become a great challenge. Keyword extraction is a kind of effective method to solve these problems. It is one of the core technologies in the research area of text mining, and plays a very important role. Currently, the keywords of most text information have not been provided. Some keywords of a text are not contained in the text content. There is not any elegant solution, offered by the existing algorithms, for this problem yet. To solve it, this paper proposes a keyword extraction method based on word vectors. The concept of a text turns into computer understandable space by training word vectors using a word2vec algorithm. This method trains all the words and keywords which appear in the text into vector sets through the word2vec training method, and then the words in the test text will be replaced by word term vectors. The Euclidean distances between every candidate words and every text words are calculated to find out the top-N-closest keywords as the automatic text extraction keywords. The experiment uses computer field papers as a training text. The results show that the method can improve the accuracy of the phrase keyword extraction and find the keywords not appearing in the text.

Keywords: Keyword extraction · Semantic analysis · Word vector · Word2vec

1 Introduction

With the rapid development of the information technology, huge amounts of text information is electronical. How to get useful information from these digital resources quickly and accurately is becoming an important topic. Text data mining, a branch of data mining, is a computer processing technology which aims to extract valuable information and knowledge from a text. The main methods include but are not limited to text classification, clustering, and information extraction. A keyword automatic extraction technology is an important branch in the field of text data mining. It is the most effective way to solve the problem of massive text retrieval. It is also the basic work of document retrieval, document comparison, summarization generation, document classification and clustering. Keywords summarize the theme of the article

© Springer International Publishing Switzerland 2016
J. Xie et al. (Eds.): HPCA 2015, LNCS 9576, pp. 185–195, 2016.
DOI: 10.1007/978-3-319-32557-6_20

information, and help the reader quickly grasp the gist. It has obvious practical significance for its great improvement of the efficiency of information access. However, most text information has not yet provided keywords. The traditional manual method has high accuracy, but its efficiency is low. On the other hand, the computer automatic extracting keywords method can have very high efficiency with low accuracy. At the same time, the existing automatic keyword extraction algorithms are still faced with some problems, such as redundant expression, polysemy, synonyms thesaurus updating dynamically, and interdisciplinary content complexity.

There is another problem in automatic keyword extraction. In the actual research and application, quite a part of keywords includes phrases which are difficult to extract. Phrases have more generalization capability than words and contain more abundant information, so the extraction of keyword phrases is more meaningful. In most of the keywords extraction algorithms, such as in [2, 4] in which consecutive sequences of a few words in the text, as a candidate for a keyword phrase, are highly regarded. But a problem that a sequence of these words are not in accordance with the approved phrase form is not fully considered. In [8], a separation model is described. The method of a separating process for the keywords and phrases and designing different characteristics to improve the accuracy of extraction is also introduced. The promotion effect of keyword phrases is obvious, while the effect of the whole keyword extraction is less than a traditional keyword extraction algorithm.

Most of the preceding automatic keyword extraction algorithms rely on the manual feature selection. The classical features are given in a comprehensive introduction in [7]. However, the process of heuristic feature selection needs prior knowledge, and it is the most time-consuming part of the whole system. Deep Learning, also called Unsupervised Learning, is a new field of machine learning, and the motive [17] is to simulate a human brain mechanism to interpret and analyze data to study a neural network. The distributed data characteristics is found by a combination of the bottom-layer feature and a more abstract high-layer category or feature. The method constructs a machine learning model which has a number of hidden layers and vast amounts of training data to learn more useful features automatically, and then to eliminate manual feature selection process. In the age of big data, all that needed is to put huge amounts of data in an algorithm directly. Let data speak for themselves, and then the system will automatic study from the data. The biggest breakthrough of Deep Learning is in the field of voice and image recognition. In 2013, in Google's open source word2vec tools [9], using the ideas of deep learning through the training, the text processing is simplified to K-dimensional vector operations. The similarity of a vector space is used to represent the text semantic similarity by regarding the words as features. Word2vec can map those features to a K-dimensional vector space and seek deeper-layer features for the text data.

Based on the above methods and encountered difficulties, we believe that the words which contain large amounts of semantic information will be extracted as candidate keywords for the article. Therefore, with the help of the deep learning method, we use word2vec tools to train the term vectors. The smaller the Euclidean distance between two words means the closer semantic meaning. Through vector calculation between test words and a keywords set, we can choose the keywords most of which are representative of the full text semantic information. The method we employ can be a very good solution to the polysemy and synonyms problem. Meanwhile, our experiment adopts the distributed method, and it can achieve good results in a relatively short time. The following sections are arranged as below. The second section discusses the related research to automatic keyword extraction and the word2vec method. The third section introduces our algorithm and experimental method. The fourth section describes the comparison between the method proposed in this paper and other two classic keyword extraction algorithms, and then analyzes the experimental results. Finally, conclusions and prospective discussions are given in Sect. 5.

2 Related Work

Automatic keyword extraction is a process which analyze the article and extract the keywords that can express the main idea of the article according to a certain proportion. The researchers have already obtained a lot of achievements. Literature [18] is the first paper which describes the study of text annotation. Since then, researchers has been working on the automatic keyword extraction technology, which is based on the technology of text annotation for 50 years. And in recent years, there are mainly 3 directions to the study of the area of automatic keyword extraction: 1. statistical methods; 2. Machine learning method 3. Semantic analysis method.

Word2vec [9], whose source code has been released by Google in 2013, is an efficient tool that can convert text words to real value vector. Based on deep learning, Word2vec can analyze the nature language and convert words to vectors. The method can get vector representation terms by building a vocabulary from training text data. These vectors can be used in many natural language processing and machine learning researches. In this way, we can transform text content space to vector space and conduct vector operations [10]. The Euclidean distance between vectors can be calculated easily, which can represent the text semantic similarity.

2.1 Automatic Keyword Extraction Method

As mentioned in the [19], automatic keyword extraction method is mainly divide into the following three categories:

1. Statistics methods, including frequency, TF-IDF and other statistical information. Literature [3] put forward a kind of improved tf-idf extraction method. The method combines high similarity words with paragraph annotation technology and selects the candidate keywords with higher weight by using the word inverse frequency tf-iwf algorithm. The extraction accuracy of the method tends to be low, though it could be more applicable and feasible.
2. Researchers have made some achievements in the area of machine learning. The KEA system, mentioned in Literature [4], is a kind of supervised machine learning methods. Using simple Bayesian technique, the method train and set up a predicting model with candidate phrases and eigenvalue gained before. And it can extract keywords from documents with the model. Other methods like random model and maximum entropy model [5], etc. can also get the same result. However, there are still problems like imbalance between labeled samples in different level, as

well as the limitation of extraction accuracy caused by the over-fitting problem which is existed in the training process of classifier constructing.

3. The study of semantic analysis methods, including speech, grammar and semantic dependency has attracted broadly attention. The methods mentioned in [6], composes the semantic chain according to the semantic similarity, and obtain the keywords with semantic feature analysis. Compared to the former methods, it can mine the potential semantic information in a deeper layer. The quality of keyword extraction is also higher.

2.2 Word Vector

Word vector is used for presenting the digitized terms in the natural language so as to process the natural language.

The original representation method of word vector is one-hot representation. The method suggests that each word can be regard as a length vector. The dimension of the vector is equal to the vocabulary size. Number 1 shows on the corresponding position. But this method cannot capture the similarity between words, and it can easily lead to the curse of dimensionality.

Distributed representation is put forward in Literature [14]. It maps each word to a K-dimensional real vector, and the semantic similarity is can be determined by word distance (cos similarity, Euclidean distance).

There are mainly 3 categories of the word vector generation model:

1. The statistical language model, including context-independent model, n-gram model, decision tree based language model, etc. The neural network language model is described in Literature [11]. The model convert each word to a floating point vector with Distributed representation;
2. Hierarchical language model, including hierarchical probabilistic language model [15] and hierarchical Log-bilinear model [14], is a binary decision-making tree whose leaf node is word.

Word2vec is based on the new Log-Linear Model.

2.3 Word2vec Model

Word2vec proposes two important models: CBOW(continuous bag-of-words model) and skip-gram model.

CBOW [9] is a model to predict the probability of $P(w_t|w_{t-c}, w_{t-(c-1)} \cdots, w_{t-1}, w_{t+1}, w_{t+2} \cdots, w_{t+c})$. Using hierarchical training strategy, every word is represented by c words selected from its context, c is the size of primary window. The structure of the method consists of hidden layer, input layer and output layer. The input layer is used for initializing the term vectors (obtain with one-hot representation method). The sum of vector accumulation is calculated in the hidden layer. And the output layer display the results with Huffman binary tree. The left children represent the probability of the vector of the word is in front of its parent node, and the right child of the parent node represent the probability of this word behind its parent node. All the non-leaf nodes in the output layer is connected with the node in the hidden layer, and the leaf node is the output vector.

Skip-gram model [9] and CBOW model are just at the opposite side. It predict the probability of $p(w_i|w_t)(t-c \leq i \leq t+c, i \neq t)$, c is the size of the context window. The input layer of this method is a single word, which is connected with the Huffman tree. The method has no hidden layer.

The text can be convert to word vector with Word2vec through training. The output vectors can be used for clustering, synonyms, speech analysis and so on. In Literature [11], the authors conduct addition operation using word vector obtained through training. For example, vector('king') − vector('man') + vector('woman') ≈ vector ('queen'), which can reflect the fact that vector space can be used to indicate the similarity of text semantic.

3 Methodology

This section describes the main structure of our algorithm including two parts: First, the procedure of text library; Second, the procedure of testing text. The filter of Punctuation, numbers, stop words and part of speech are included in both of the mentioned parts. The overall process is shown in Fig. 1.

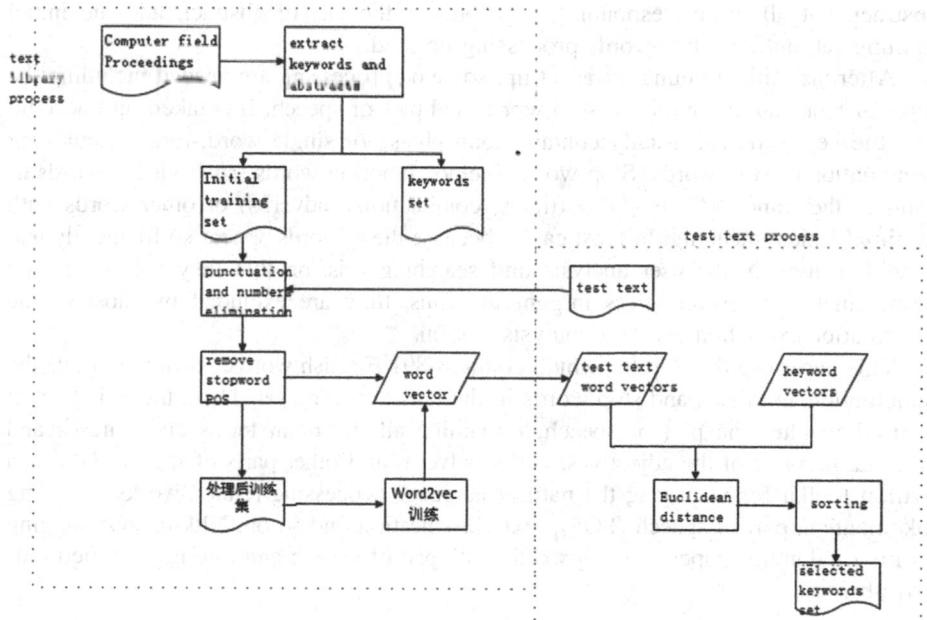

Fig. 1. Overall process

3.1   Text Library Process

3.1.1   Preprocessing of Dataset

The dataset used in the experiment comes from 8064 computer-related English paper records, where each one has five fields including title, paper source, authors, keywords and abstract.

Firstly, we should establish the keyword set: check keywords field, extract all the keywords, then filter out the keywords which appear more than five times in all records (namely, the word is selected by more than five papers as keywords) as keyword set. Meanwhile, in the word2vec training process, each word vector is automatically segmented by a blank. Therefore, regard keyword phrases as a whole, represent the blanks between each word in the phrase with "-" without thinking about the single-word keyword. Then, make the statistics of keyword set, choose the total 4429 keywords, the ratio of keyword phrase and single keyword is 0.679, keyword phrase accounting for about two-thirds. This proportion will be used as the standard to guide the whole process in the latter procedure of testing keyword extraction, it denotes by $\partial = 0.679$.

Secondly, establish the initial training set: for each record, check its keyword field. If the number of keywords which exist in the previously established keyword set is greater than 2, extract the abstract and keyword field of this record. Then, we select out 749 records. Next, we use three cycles: cycle one shows each word in abstract, cycle two represents the appeared keyword phrase, Cycle three means that, for each phrase which appears in the abstract, replace the blank to "-", or for the separate words in the phrase which appears in the abstract, it is automatically extended to the corresponding phrase, remove the middle blank and use "-" instead, Finally, after processing the abstract, put all the corresponding keywords at the last of abstract, add the initial training set, until all the records processing finished.

After the initial training set is set up, some preprocessing are needed including the filter of punctuation, numbers, stop words and part of speech. It is taken into account that the keywords are usually contain noun phrase or single word, rarely containing punctuation or stop words. Stop words include function words (such virtual words as "and", "the", and "of", modal particles, conjunctions, adverbs) or other words with minimal lexical meaning. In most cases, because these words appear so frequently and is widely used in the user analysis and searching mission that they are considered uninformative or meaningless in general. Thus, they are excluded by most of the information extraction and text analysis system.

This paper use the stop list which contains 891 English words. At first, remove the punctuation, numbers, and stop words in the initial training set. Then, the nltk Toolkit is used to filter the part of speech, remaining all the noun terms and phrases and eliminating most of the adjectives, verbs, adverbs and other parts of speech. Nltk is a python toolkit for managing the natural language processing related works including tokenization, part-of-speech (POS), text classification and so on. Nltk of POS tagging tool is used in this paper, tagging words with part of speech and filtering out the terms and phrases.

3.1.2 Generation of Word Vectors

After preprocessing, the post-processing training set trains the documents with the help of word2vec tool. This paper selects the CBOW model and uses the hierarchical training policy, in which the text window is set to 5. Through training, the text is convert into a word vector set of 100-dimensional vector space, and is saved in the file of vectors.bin. The file includes 8,322 words (including the connection phrase), followed by a 100-dimension float vector, which is used as an input to the next process of text testing.

3.2 Test Text Process

For the text to be tested, the first thing to do is preprocessing, whose method is the same as training set, arranging text to a collection of words. According to vectors.bin file and the keywords set, we get the under test word vectors and keywords vectors, calculate the Euclidean distance between each keyword and the word to be tested. Then we sort the keyword, according to ∂ value obtained before and the number of word in the processed text, select the top $T * \partial$ keyword phrases and top $T * (1 - \partial)$. Single keywords as the eventual keywords, according to [16], We select as 1/4 of the totally number of the text.

Since the experiment involves complex calculation of large sample float vectors arithmetic Euclidean distance, stand-alone operation execution speed is so slow that it impacts the experimental efficiency. Therefore this paper is based on the hadoop distributed systems infrastructure, using the distributed file system HDFS and MapReduce programming model, applying 7 computing nodes, which greatly enhances the efficiency of the experiments.

3.3 Analysis of Experimental Result

In this paper, the experimental framework is based on Hadoop. Data input includes four parts including word vector file which obtained from the preprocessing(named "vectors.bin"), keywords set(named "keywords.txt"), testing text(named "testfile.txt"), manual selection keywords of text testing(named "output.txt"). Data Outputs are keywords and their distance which are automatically extracted, in which the distance is selected manually.

This paper uses three evaluation criteria which are commonly used in the field of information retrieval. They are Precision(denoted by P), Recall(denoted by R) and F-measure to analyze the experimental result. Three standard formula are as formula 1, 2, 3 follows:

$$P = \frac{The\ number\ of\ correctly\ extracted\ keywords}{the\ number\ of\ extracted\ keywords} \tag{1}$$

$$R = \frac{The\ number\ of\ correctly\ extracted\ keywords}{the\ number\ of\ manual\ selection\ keywords} \tag{2}$$

$$F - measure = \frac{2 * PR}{P + R} \tag{3}$$

Table 1 lists comparison between the keywords we extracted and the manual assigned keywords in one of the paper record. After preprocessing, it has 24 words, so T = 6, we select the minimum distance of 4 keyword phrases and two single keywords.

From the table above we know that for the phrase keyword, in the automatically extracted four keyword phrases, the correct extracted number is three, P is 75 % while the manual selection number of keyword phrases is five, R equals to 60 %; Based on P and R, the obtained F-measure is 67 %. For the single keywords, in the two automatically extracted words, the correct number is one, so P is 50 % while the manual selection of single keywords is one, the recall rate R is 100 %; Based on P and R, the obtained F-measure also reaches 67 %. For the overall keywords, P, R and F-measure are all 67 %.

4 Experiment

In order to test the performance of the extraction method based on the word2vec, we compare this method with TextRank [1] and RAKE [2]. We randomly take 10 % of the previous 749 papers, 75 papers exactly, as the test set. And then we verify the results of those three methods using P, R and F-measure indexes.

Mihalcea and Tarau (2004) describe a system which applies a series of syntactic filters to identify POS tags for selecting keywords [1]. It is based on PageRank algorithm, and the basic idea of PageRank is: the importance of a web page depends on the quantity of the backlinks and the importance of these pages. PageRank algorithm regards the whole World Wide Web pages as a directed graph, and the node of the graph is a web page. If there is a link from A to B, then there is a directed edge from the A to the B in the directed graph. Hence, the TestRank splits the text into sentences, and the sentences are split into words. Then it sets up the window size, Co-occurrences of the selected words within a fixed-size sliding window are accumulated within a word co-occurrence graph. A graph-based ranking algorithm (TextRank) is applied to rank words based on their associations in the graph, and then top ranking words are taken as the keywords. Keywords which are adjacent in the document are combined to form multi-word keywords.

RAKE algorithm is raised in the paper [2] proposed by Rose S and Engel D in 2010, and it is an unsupervised, domain-independent and language-independent method for extracting keywords from individual documents. The basic idea of this algorithm is: RAKE is based on our observation that keywords frequently contain multiple words but rarely contain standard punctuation or stop word. The input parameters for RAKE comprise a list of stop words (or stop list), a set of phrase delimiters, and a set of word delimiters. The score which is based on the degree and frequency of word vertices in the graph is calculated for each candidate keyword and defined as the sum of its member word scores. Finally the top T scoring candidates are selected as keywords for the document, and it computes T as one-third the numbers of words in the graph.

Table 1. Result of our method

Extracted by word2vec	Manually assigned
Decision-theoretic	Information-retrieval-system
Decision-making	Evaluation
Information-retrieval-system	Information-search-process
Analytic-hierarchy-process	Decision-making
Evaluation	Multi-criteria-model
Retrieval	Analytic-hierarchy-process

Table 2 shows the comparison result using word2vec method, TestRank method and the RAKE method to extract keywords automatically from 75 abstracts.

Table 2. Comparison result

Method keyword pattern	Precision P	Recall R	F-measure
word2vec method keyword phrases	**66 %**	**70 %**	**68 %**
word2vec method single keywords	19 %	31 %	24 %
word2vec method keywords	**51 %**	**61 %**	**51 %**
TestRank keyword phrases	23 %	20 %	21 %
TestRank single keywords	27 %	30 %	28 %
TestRank keywords	24 %	25 %	24 %
RAKE keyword phrases	42 %	18 %	25 %
RAKE single keywords	**41 %**	**38 %**	**39 %**
RAKE keywords	42 %	22 %	29 %

In the table above, the top three evaluation values of keyword phrases, single keyword, and keywords are respectively marked in bold. Obviously, our method can obtain a great enhanced performance in the keyword phrase extraction, and it can get the keywords which don't exist in the abstract but may become a candidate keywords from keywords set via to train a large number of samples. Although our method does not have a very satisfactory performance for the single keywords extraction, due to the practical application, keyword phrases appear to be higher frequency. So the overall performance of the keyword extraction is better than other two ways with a more significant improvement.

5 Conclusion

This paper proposes an automatic keyword extraction method which based on word2vec tools. We obtain the word vectors through training the large-scale samples, the text conceptual space is then convert into computable space. It means that the text information knowledge equals to computer-readable knowledge and facilitate people to perform data extraction or keyword match. By calculating the Euclidean distance between text words and keywords, using the prior knowledge of proportion of single keywords and keyword phrases, we can extract the shortest distance ones respectively. This experiments using the computer field proceedings as the training set and extract the corresponding domain keywords set. The result shows that this method improves the performance of the keyword phrase extraction and find the keywords which are not include in the text at the same time, so that the overall performance of automatic keywords extraction is greatly improved compared to the previous method.

Indeed, our method has some flaws. On one hand, the extraction performance of single keyword doesn't increase significantly compared to the previous methods. However, according to prior obtained domain keywords set, the proportion of single keywords in the overall keywords is not high, the overall performance of the automatic keyword extraction is still enhanced in a large rate because most of the keywords are existed in the form of phrase. On the other hand, the training number of samples is too large, it leads to an increase of the execution time and a decrease of the efficiency. However, the original intention of our method is applied in the large-scale sample problems. For the word2vec tool, the larger the sample size is, the higher accuracy of the semantic meaning of the word vectors would be. And it takes advantages of keyword automatic extraction. Meanwhile most of the previous work of automatic keyword extraction algorithm can only extract the keywords which exist in the text, but our method can extract the rest of other keywords from domain keywords set, those keywords can also summarize the text topic. Hadoop cluster architecture used in this paper can also speed up the overall operating efficiency to increase the integrated performance.

Based on word2vec, we have shown that our automatic keyword extraction technology achieves higher precision in comparison to the existing techniques. However, this method still has some improvements and enhancements in the future work. Firstly, the strong domain dependence. In general, we establish the keywords set in the certain domain according to the training samples, then the test text must be the same domain as the keywords set. So we intend to set up the adaptive model and adjust parameters to select keyword sets in different areas; secondly, the performance of single keywords extraction is relatively low. We can combine our method with the mature automatic keyword extraction algorithm like TF-IDF, etc., to focus on improving the accuracy of single keyword extraction in future work; finally, in order to calculate the distance between two word vectors, in addition to the Euclidean distance, other methods like cosine can also be performed. We will use different methods to calculate vectors distance and compare them to determine the best performance calculation method of keyword extraction.

Acknowledgements. The work of this paper is partially supported by National Natural Science Foundation of China (No. 61303097) and Ph.D. Programs Foundation of Ministry of Education of China (No. 20123108120026).

References

1. Mihalcea, T.P.: TextRank: bringing order into texts. Association for Computational Linguistics (2004)
2. Rose, S., Engel, D., Cramer, N., Cowley, W.: Automatic keyword extraction from individual documents. In: Berry, M.W., Kogan, J. (eds.) Text Mining: Theory and Applications. Wiley, Hoboken (2010)
3. Xiaolin, W., Lin, Y., Dong, W., Lihua, Z.: Improved TF-IDF keyword extraction algorithm. Comput. Sci. Appl. **3**, 64–68 (2013)
4. Witten, I.H., Paynter, G.W., Frank, E., et al.: KEA: practical automatic keyphrase extraction. In: Proceedings of the 4th ACM Conference on Digital Libraries, Berkeley, California, US, pp. 254–256. ACM (1999)
5. SuJian, L., HouFeng, W., ShiWen, Y., ChengSheng, X.: Research on maximum entropy model for keyword indexing. Chin. J. Comput. **27**(9), 1192–1197 (2004)
6. Gonenc, E., Ilyas, C.: Using lexical chains for keyword extraction. Inf. Process. Manage. **43**(6), 1705–1714 (2007)
7. Yih, W., Goodman, J., Carbalho, V.: Finding advertising keywords on web pages. In: International World Wide Web Conference Committee (IW3C2), May 23-26 (2006)
8. Zhunchen, L., Ting, W.: Research on the chinese keyword extraction algorithm based on separate models. J. Chin. Inf. Process. **23**(1), 63–70 (2009)
9. Mikolov, T., Chen, K., Corrado, G., Dean, J.: Efficient estimation of word representation in vector space. Cornell University Library, 7 September 2013 (2013)
10. Mikolov, T., Yih, W., Zweig, G.: Linguistic regularities in continuous space word representations. In: Proceedings of the 2013 Conference of the North American Chapter of the Association for Computational Linguistics. Human Language Technologies (2013)
11. Bengio, Y., Ducharme, R., Vincent, P.: A neural probabilistic language model. Citeseer, October 2001
12. Mikolov, T., Sutskever, I., Chen, K., Corrado, G., Dean, J.: Distributed representations of words and phrases and their compositionality. Cornell Unicersity Library, 16 October 2013 (2013)
13. Morin, F., Bengio, Y.: Hierarchical probabilistic neural network language model. In: AISTATS (2005)
14. Hinton, G.E.: Learning distributed representations of concepts. In: Proceeding of the Eighth Annual Conference of the Cognitive Science Society (1986)
15. Mnih, A., Hinton, G.: There new graphical models for statistical language modeling. In: Proceedings of the 24th International Conference on Machine learning, pp. 641–648 (2007)
16. Hulth, A.: Combining machine learning and natural language processing for automatic keyword extraction. Stockholm University, Faculty of Social Science, Department of Computer and System Science (together with KTH) (2015)
17. Hiton, G.E., Osindero, S., Teh, Y.: A fast learning algorithm for deep belief nets. Neural Comput. **18**, 1527–1554 (2006)
18. Luhn, H.P.: A statistical approach to the mechanized encoding and searching of literary information. IBM J. Res. Dev. **1**(4), 309–317 (1957)
19. Wang, L.: The research of keywords extraction algorithm in text mining. College of Computer Science and Technology, Zhejiang University of Technology, Zhejiang (2013)

Parallel Overlapping Mechanism Between Communication and Computation of the Lattice Boltzmann Method

Zhixiang Liu[1,2], Yong Fang[1], Anping Song[3], Lei Xu[3],
Xiaowei Wang[2,3], Liping Zhou[2,3], and Wu Zhang[2,3(✉)]

[1] School of Communication and Information Engineering,
Shanghai University, Shanghai 200444, China
[2] High Performance Computing Center, Shanghai University,
Shanghai 200444, China
wzhang@shu.edu.cn
[3] School of Computer Engineering and Science, Shanghai University,
Shanghai 200444, China

Abstract. The lattice Boltzmann Method (LBM), different from classical numerical methods of continuum mechanics, is derived from molecular dynamics. The LBM has the following main advantages: including a simple algorithm, the direct solver for pressure, easy treatment of complicated boundary conditions and particularly parallel suitability. The most common models include the Single-Relaxation-Time (SRT) and Multiple-Relaxation-Time (MRT) collision models. In a conventional parallel computing model of LBM, communication and computing are performed individually. When the communication is performed, the computing is waiting in MPI processes. This will waste some waiting time. Therefore, the communication and computing overlapping parallel model was proposed. By the architecture of "Ziqiang 4000" supercomputer at Shanghai University, the hybrid MPI and OpenMP parallel model is proposed. The numerical results show that the presented model has better computational efficiency.

Keywords: Lattice Moltzmann Method · Single-Relaxation-Time · Overlapping communication and computation · Hybrid model · Parallel model

1 Introduction

The lattice Boltzmann method (LBM) is different from classical numerical methods of continuum mechanics and derived from molecular dynamics [1]. The LBM is a truly mesoscopic method. Hydrodynamic variables are computed at nodes as moments of a discrete distribution function. The lattice Boltzmann (LB) method has been developed into a viable numerical tool for computational fluid dynamics and beyond in the past

---

This work was supported by the Major Research Plan of NSFC [No. 91330116].

J. Xie et al. (Eds.): HPCA 2015, LNCS 9576, pp. 196–203, 2016.
DOI: 10.1007/978-3-319-32557-6_21

few years. The LBM has the main advantages, including a simple algorithm, easy treatment of complicated boundary conditions and particularly parallel suitability [2, 3]. The Single-Relaxation-Time (SRT) collision model is the most popular, based on the lattice Bhatngar-Gross-Krook (BGK) equation [4]. The LBM cannot be used to solve the high-Re solutions for incompressible flow. Usually, the LBM with the turbulence modeling [5] or large eddy simulation [6] can be used to high Re-solutions. The multi-grid LBM is also proposed in the uniform grid computation, and the specific identification of the time level for the post-collision state is not important since the completion of an LBM computational step is at the end of the streaming step [7]. The multi-grid method is more complex than the classical LBM and more difficult to parallel computing. But for the numerical simulation of complex objects, the LBM needs large memory requirements and long computation time. So some parallel models are developed in clusters [8–11]. Currently, the clusters are essentially hierarchical architecture, including CPU and GPU. Some researchers have presented CPU-GPU parallel models [12, 13]. In the clusters, the CPU of each compute node is multi-cores and shared memory. For improving parallel efficiency, we need construct a hierarchical parallel model in the hierarchical architecture. In this article, we only consider the parallel model in the CPU part of clusters. The hybrid MPI/OpenMP parallel model is a considerable choice for the hierarchical architecture.

Generally, a parallel model includes two parts: communication and computing. The communication and computing are performed individually. When the communication is performed, the computing is waiting. This will waste some waiting time and affect the computing efficiency. Therefore, the communication and computing overlapping parallel model of LBM will be proposed in the article.

The rest of the paper is organized as follows: In Sect. 2, a brief description of the LBM will be presented. The communication and computing overlapping hybrid MPI/OpenMP parallel model of LBM will be proposed in Sect. 3. Section 4 shows the numerical results and discussion. Finally, Sect. 4 concludes the paper.

2   Lattice Boltzmann Method

The LBM is a simulation technique for solving fluid flow. It treats the fluid as a set of fictitious particles located on a d-dimensional lattice. The lattice BGK model is described by the rate of change of a discrete velocity distribution function [14]:

$$f_i(\mathbf{x} + \mathbf{e}_i \Delta t, t + \Delta t) - f_i(\mathbf{x}, t) = -\frac{1}{\tau}(f_i(\mathbf{x}, t) - f_i^{eq}(\mathbf{x}, t)) \qquad (1)$$

Here f_i is a set of discrete populations representing the particles distribution functions at position at $\mathbf{x}$ time t moving along the direction identified by the discrete speed $\mathbf{e}_i$. Δt is the time interval. τ is the relaxation time which characterizes typical collision process. In two-dimension (2D) case, we consider the D2Q9 velocity model, as shown in Fig. 1,

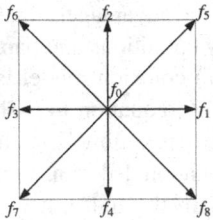

Fig. 1. The D2Q9 velocity model

$$\mathbf{e}_i = \begin{cases} c \cdot (0,0), i = 0 \\ c \cdot (\cos((i-1)\pi/2), \sin((i-1)\pi/2)), \ i = 1,2,3,4 \\ \sqrt{2} \cdot c \cdot (\cos((2i-1)\pi/4), \sin((2i-1)\pi/4)), \ i = 5,6,7,8 \end{cases}, \qquad (2)$$

with the lattice velocity $c = \Delta x/\Delta t$. Distribution functions $f_0 - f_8$ correspond to velocity vectors $\mathbf{e}_0 - \mathbf{e}_8$.

The equilibrium distribution function for the D2Q9 model is in the form of

$$f_i^{(eq)} = \rho \omega_i \left(1 + \frac{\mathbf{e}_i \bullet \mathbf{u}}{c_s^2} + \frac{(\mathbf{e}_i \bullet \mathbf{u})^2}{2c_s^4} - \frac{\mathbf{u}^2}{2c_s^2} \right), \qquad (3)$$

where ω_i is the weighting factor given by

$$\omega_i = \begin{cases} 4/9, & i = 0 \\ 1/9, & i = 1,2,3,4. \\ 1/36, & i = 5,6,7,8 \end{cases} \qquad (4)$$

With the discrete velocity space, the macroscopic density and velocity can be objected as the moments of the distribution function

$$\rho = \sum_{i=0}^{8} f_i, \rho \mathbf{u} = \sum_{i=0}^{8} \mathbf{e}_i f_i. \qquad (5)$$

3 The Communication and Computing Overlapping Hybrid MPI/OpenMP Parallel Algorithm of LBM

In this section, we will present the communication and computing overlapping hybrid MPI/OpenMP parallel algorithm of LBM. According to the descriptions of LBM in Sect. 2, the computing model can be divided into the two parts: collision and stream.

$$\text{Collision}: f_i^+(\mathbf{x}, t) = \left(1 - \frac{1}{\tau}\right) f_i(\mathbf{x}, t) + \frac{1}{\tau} f_i^{eq}(\mathbf{x}, t) \tag{6}$$

$$\text{Stream}: f_i(\mathbf{x} + \mathbf{e}_i \Delta t, t + \Delta t) = f_i^+(\mathbf{x}, t) \tag{7}$$

The computing of collision is only performed on the lattice point. The computing of stream needs the data information on the neighbor lattice points. So, the communications will be only performed for the computing of stream in the parallel model.

Based on the characteristics of LBM, we will present the data partitioning of lattice points in Fig. 2. For convenience of description, the two-dimensional case will be given. In Fig. 2, the entire lattice points are divided into three lattice block, namely, Block_0, Block_1 and Block_2. The gray lattice points in each block need communications with the adjacent lattice block.

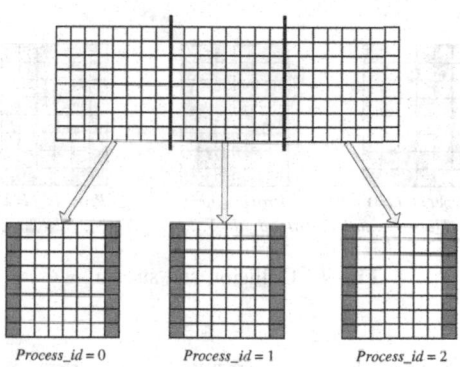

Process_id = 0   Process_id = 1   Process_id = 2

Fig. 2. Data partitioning

After division, the parallel computing model of LBM becomes two parts:

(i) The entire lattice points will be computing by Eqs. (6) – (7).
(ii) The gray lattice points will be communication in the all block.

If we implement this conventional parallel computing model, we will find when the communication is performed, the computing is waiting. This will waste some waiting time and affect the computing efficiency. In order to improve the parallel efficiency, we will modify the parallel model, see in Fig. 3.

In Fig. 3, the each lattice block is divided into two blocks, gray and yellow parts. The yellow block will be computing by Eqs. (6) – (7), see Fig. 4. The gray block not only need be computing by Eqs. (6) – (7), but also need communications with the adjacent lattice block, see Fig. 5. From Figs. 4 and 5, we can get that yellow block has more lattice point than the gray block. The computation time, include collision and stream computing, in yellow block will spend more computing time than gray block without communication time. If total time, include collision, stream and communication, in gray block close to the computing time in yellow time, the communication and computing have been overlapping. It will save the solving time.

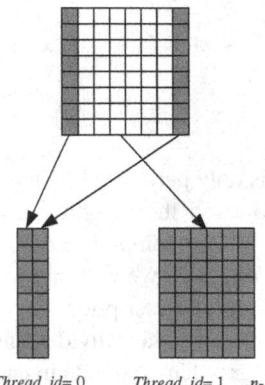

Thread_id= 0   Thread_id= 1,...,n-1

Fig. 3. *n* threads (OpenMP) in a process (MPI) (Color figure online)

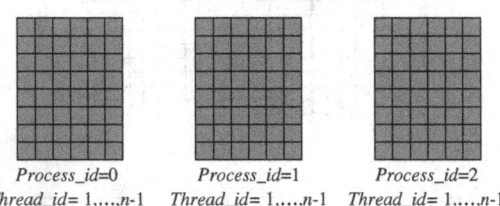

Process_id=0   Process_id=1   Process_id=2
Thread_id= 1,...,n-1   Thread_id= 1,...,n-1   Thread_id= 1,...,n-1

Fig. 4. Collision and stream

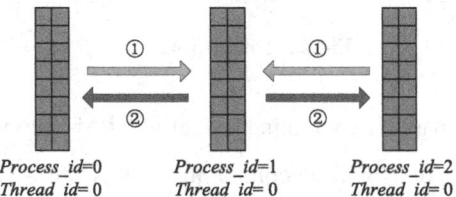

Process_id=0   Process_id=1   Process_id=2
Thread_id= 0   Thread_id= 0   Thread_id= 0

Fig. 5. Collision, stream and data communication

To achieve above the communication and computing overlapping parallel model, we will use hybrid MPI and OpenMP model by the hierarchical architecture of clusters. In Fig. 2, each block is assigned a MPI process (*Process_id* = 0, 1, 2). In each MPI process (*Process_id*), n threads has allocated (*Thread_id* = 0, 1, ..., $n - 1$). The gray block in Fig. 3 will be computed by *Thread_id* = 0 in each MPI process. The communication steps are shown in Fig. 5. The yellow block in Fig. 3 will be computed by *Thread_id* = 1, 2, ..., $n - 1$, see Fig. 4.

4 Numerical Simulations

According to the communication and computing overlapping parallel model in Sect. 3, we will give some results of the numerical simulations. The test cluster is Shanghai University – "Ziqiang 4000". The cluster includes 140 compute nodes. Each node has two CPU (Intel E5-4650, 2.7 GHz/8-core). Compute node is connected by FDR 56 Gb/s InfiniBand network.

Next, the lid-driven cavity flow has been extensively used as a benchmark solution to test the accuracy of a presented parallel model, and compared with Reference [14], see Fig. 6.

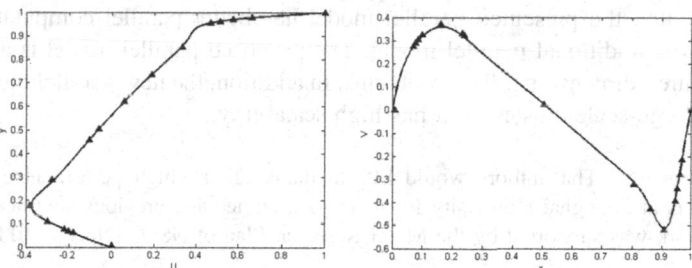

Fig. 6. u,v velocity along the vertical and horizontal line through geometric center at Re = 1000

From Fig. 6, the numerical results agree with the referenced data excellently. And then we will give the parallel performance analysis of the proposed parallel model. The number of grid is 256×256, 512×512, 1024×1024, respectively. The iteration step is 100000. The wall time of our presented parallel model (new) and the traditional parallel model (old) are shown in Fig. 7. In this case, the total computing cores are 32, which includes 4 MPI processes and 8 OpenMP threads.

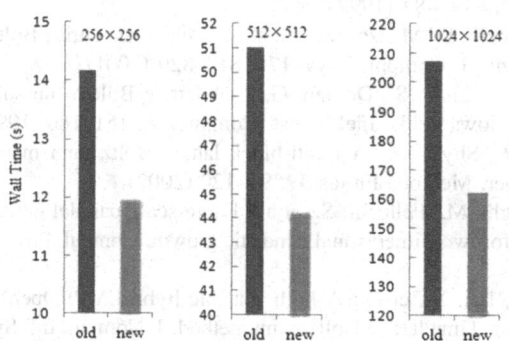

Fig. 7. The Wall Time (Total Cores: 32; 4 MPI processes; 8 OpenMP thread)

Form Fig. 7, the proposed communication and computing overlapping parallel model takes less computing time than the traditional parallel model. For the different grid, the presented method also has better parallel computational efficiency.

5   Conclusions

In conventional parallel computing model of LBM, communications and computing are performed individually. When the communication is performed, the computing is waiting in MPI processes. This will waste some waiting time. So the communication and computing overlapping parallel model was proposed. By the hierarchical architecture of clusters, the hybrid MPI and OpenMP parallel model is used. The numerical results show that the presented parallel model has better parallel computational efficiency than the traditional parallel model. The proposed parallel model is also can be used in the three-dimensional flow problems. In addition, the new parallel model can be used in the large-scale clusters and has high scalability.

Acknowledgements. The authors would like to thank all the high performance computing group members at Shanghai University for their good advice and previous significant research work. This work was supported by the Major Research Plan of NSFC [No.91330116].

References

1. Succi, S.: The lattice Boltzmann equation for fluid dynamics and beyond. Oxford Science Publications, Oxford (2001)
2. Aidun, C.K., Clausen, J.R.: Lattice-Boltzmann method for complex flows. Ann. Rev. Fluid Mech. **42**, 439–472 (2010)
3. Chen, S., Doolen, G.D.: Lattice Boltzmann method for fluid flows. Ann. Rev. Fluid Mech. **30**, 329–364 (1998)
4. Qian, Y., d'Humières, D., Lallemand, P.: Lattice BGK models for Navier-Stokes equation. Europhys. Lett. **17**, 479–484 (1992)
5. Filippovaa, O., Succib, S., Mazzoccoc, F., et al.: Multiscale lattice Boltzmann schemes with turbulence modeling. J. Comput. Phys. **170**, 812–829 (2001)
6. Hou, S., Sterling, J., Chen, S., Doolen, G.D.: A lattice Boltzmann subgrid model for high Reynolds number flows fields. Fields Inst, Commun. **6**, 151–166 (1996)
7. Dazhi, Y., Mei, R., Shyy, W.: A multi-block lattice Boltzmann method for viscous fluid flows. Int. J. Numer. Methods Fluids **39**, 99–120 (2002)
8. Jelinek, B., Eshraghi, M., Felicelli, S., et al.: Large-scale parallel lattice Boltzmann-cellular automaton model for two-dimensional dendritic growth. Comput. Phys. Commun. **185**, 939–947 (2014)
9. Liu, Z., Song, A., Lei, X., et al.: A high scalable hybrid MPI/OpenMP parallel model of Multiple-Relaxation-Time lattice Boltzmann method. J. Comput. Inf. Syst. **23**, 10147–10157 (2014)
10. Vidal, D., Roy, R., Betrand, F.: A parallel workload balanced and memory efficient lattice-Boltzmann algorithm with single unit BGK relaxation time for laminar Newtonian flows. Comput. Fluids **39**, 1411–1423 (2010)

11. Schepke, C., Maillard, N., Philippe, O.A.: Navaux, Parallel lattice Boltzmann method with blocked partitioning. Int. J. Parallel Program. **37**, 593–611 (2009)
12. Ye, Y., Kenli, Y., Wang, Y., Deng, T.: Parallel computation of entropic lattice Boltzmann method on hybrid CPU-GPU accelerated system. Comput. Fluids **110**, 114–121 (2015)
13. Wang, Z., Zhao, Y., Sawchuck, A.P., et al.: GPU acceleration of volumetric lattice Boltzmann method for patient-specific computational hemodynamics. Comput. Fluids **115**, 192–200 (2015)
14. Ghia, U., Ghia, K.N., Shin, C.T.: High-Re solutions for incompressible flow using the Navier-Stokes equations and a multigrid method. J. Comput. Phys. **48**, 387–411 (1982)

A New Equilibrium Distribution Function of the Lattice Boltzmann Method

Wei Xu[1], Zhixiang Liu[2,3], Wenhao Zhu[1], and Wu Zhang[1,3(✉)]

[1] School of Computer Engineering and Science,
Shanghai University, Shanghai 200444, China
`wzhang@shu.edu.cn`
[2] School of Communication and Information Engineering,
Shanghai University, Shanghai 200444, China
[3] High Performance Computing Center,
Shanghai University, Shanghai 200444, China

Abstract. According to the conventional Maxwell distribution function, a new equilibrium distribution function based on a discrete velocity model (D2Q13) is proposed. A parallel lattice Boltzmann algorithm based on this new function is used for simulating the lid-driven cavity flow. The experimental results validate the correctness of the new equilibrium distribution function.

Keywords: Lattice Boltzmann method · D2Q13 · Equilibrium distribution function

1 Introduction

With the traditional numerical methods, the lattice Boltzmann method (LBM) is built on the basis of molecular dynamics methods. It uses a completely discrete mesoscopic model in time and space to simulate fluid motion. The physical basis of LBM derives from the simplification of a microscopic medium and interaction or collision rules between particles. The LBM is mathematically a simplification of the Boltzmann equation by the fully discrete time, space and scattering directions. Although the lattice Boltzmann equation is simple in form, it reflects the macroscopic equations and the laws of physics which still reveal the nature of flow phenomena. The advantages of LBM include a simple algorithm and high precision; pressure can be solved directly; problems with complex boundary conditions can be simulated; it is suitable for parallel computing. Currently, LBM has been successfully applied in many areas of numerical simulation, such as micro/nano-scale flow [1], porous media flow [2,3], and multi-phase flow [4,5].

Qu et al. [6] proposed a new method to construct an equilibrium density distribution function in the simulation of compressible flow at a high Mach number. This new function is distributed to the lattice velocity direction by the Lagrangian interpolation in such a way that all the needed statistical relations

© Springer International Publishing Switzerland 2016
J. Xie et al. (Eds.): HPCA 2015, LNCS 9576, pp. 204–210, 2016.
DOI: 10.1007/978-3-319-32557-6_22

are exactly satisfied. This article will consider the D2Q13 velocity model and propose a new equilibrium distribution function by using a Lagrangian interpolation function to distribute the conventional Maxwellian distribution function to the lattice velocity direction. In addition, we give a parallel LBM algorithm based on the new equilibrium distribution function. The lid-driven flow is simulated to validate the present approach.

The rest of the paper is organized as follows: In Sect. 2, our method of constructing the equilibrium distribution function will be described in detail. Section 3 presents a parallel LBM algorithm. Section 3 shows the numerical results and discussion. Finally, Sect. 4 concludes the paper.

2   Method of Constructing Equilibrium Distribution Function

The gas-kinetic BGK model for the Boltzmann equation [7] is

$$f_\alpha(\boldsymbol{x}+\boldsymbol{e}_\alpha\Delta t,t+\Delta t)-f_\alpha(\boldsymbol{x},t)=-\frac{1}{\tau}(f_\alpha-f_\alpha^{eq}), \tag{1}$$

where the single particle distribution function f_α is a time-dependent function of particle coordinate $\boldsymbol{x}$ and velocity, τ is the relaxation time which characterizes typical collison process, f_α^{eq} is local equilibrium distribution function, $\boldsymbol{e}_\alpha$ is the lattice velocity directions, Δt is a time interval. In two-dimensional(2D) case, we consider the D2Q13 velocity model (See Fig. 1):

$$\boldsymbol{e}_\alpha = \begin{cases} (0,0), & \alpha=0; \\ \left(\cos[(\alpha-1)\frac{\pi}{2}],\sin[(\alpha-1)\frac{\pi}{2}]\right), & \alpha=1,2,3,4; \\ \left(\sqrt{2}\cos[(2\alpha-1)\frac{\pi}{4}],\sin[(2\alpha-1)\frac{\pi}{4}]\right), & \alpha=5,6,7,8; \\ 2\left(\cos[(\alpha-9)\frac{\pi}{2}],\sin[(\alpha-9)\frac{\pi}{2}]\right), & \alpha=9,10,11,12. \end{cases} \tag{2}$$

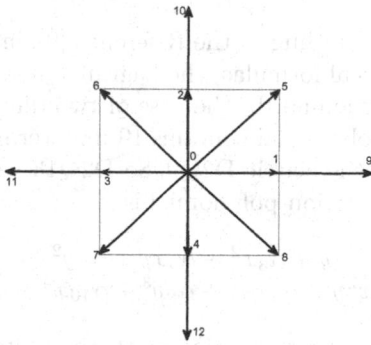

Fig. 1. 13 velocity directions of D2Q13

Figure 1 shows D2Q13 model has 4 velocity directions more than the classic D2Q9 model (9, 10, 11, 12). The Maxwell distribution function is defined as

$$f = \rho(2\pi R_g T)^{-\frac{D}{2}} \exp[-\frac{(\xi - \mu)^2}{2R_g T}], \tag{3}$$

where D denotes space dimension, ξ is the molecular velocity vector, ρ is a density, R_g is a gas constant, T is a temperature. Equation (3) satisfies the statistic relations:

$$\int f d\xi = \rho$$

$$\int f\xi_\alpha d\xi = \rho\mu_\alpha$$

$$\int f\xi_\alpha\xi_\beta d\xi = \rho\mu_\alpha\mu_\beta + p\delta_{\alpha\beta}$$

$$\int f\xi_\alpha\xi_\beta\xi_\varphi d\xi = p(\mu_\alpha\delta_{\beta\varphi} + \mu_\beta\delta_{\varphi\alpha} + \mu_\varphi\delta_{\alpha\beta}) + \rho\mu_\alpha\mu_\beta\mu_\varphi \tag{4}$$

where p is the pressure. α, β, φ are all take the value of $\{1, 2\}$. By Eq. (4), Eq. (1) Restored to the isothermal and incompressible Navier-Stokes Equation [8]:

$$\frac{\partial\rho}{\partial t} + \frac{\partial\rho\mu_\alpha}{\partial x_\alpha} = 0,$$

$$\frac{\partial\rho\mu_\alpha}{\partial t} + \frac{\partial\rho\mu_\alpha\mu_\beta}{\partial x_\alpha} + \frac{\partial p}{\partial x_\alpha} = \frac{\partial}{\partial x_\beta}[\mu(\frac{\partial\mu_\alpha}{\partial x_\beta} + \frac{\partial\mu_\beta}{\partial x_\alpha})],$$

where $\mu = \tau\rho R_g T$.

Next, we consider how to discretize Eq. (3) to the 13 velocity directions of D2Q13. The introduced Lagrange interpolation distribution function $\phi_\alpha(\xi)$ meets:

$$f_\alpha = \int f\phi_\alpha(\xi)d\xi, \tag{5}$$

where $\alpha = 0, 1, \cdots, 12$. According to the Reference [9], in order to ensure Eq. (5) meets the relevant statistical formulas, the Lagrange interpolation polynomial is at least a 3rd-degree polynomial. In the case of two dimensions, the 3rd-degree Lagrange interpolation polynomial contains 10 undetermined parameters which could not determined by the classic D2Q9. So D2Q13 velocity model is chosen, the used Lagrange interpolation polynomial is:

$$\begin{aligned}P(x,y) = {} & \alpha_0 + \alpha_1 x + \alpha_2 y + \alpha_3 x^2 + \alpha_4 xy + \alpha_5 y^2 \\ & + \alpha_6 x^3 + \alpha^7 x^2 y + \alpha_8 xy^2 + \alpha_9 y^3 + \alpha_{10} x^4 + \alpha_{11} x^2 y^2 + \alpha_{12} y^4.\end{aligned} \tag{6}$$

For 13 points, each interpolation function on these points can be represented by Eq. (6)

$$\phi_i(x, y) = \alpha_i \mathbf{b}, \tag{7}$$

where,

$$\alpha_i = [\alpha_{i,1}, \alpha_{i,2}, \cdots, \alpha_{i,13}]$$

$$\mathbf{b} = [1, x, y, x^2, xy, y^2, x^3, x^2y, xy^2, y^3, x^4, x^2y^2, y^4]^T$$

According to the properties of the Lagrange interpolation function, we have

$$\phi_i(x_j, y_j) = \delta_{ij}, i, j = 0, 1, \cdots, 12. \tag{8}$$

Solving Eq. (8) by Maple software, the specific expression of ϕ_i can be obtained. By substitute the expression into Eq. (5), the new equilibrium distribution functions based on D2Q13 velocity model (solving process is relatively complex, here omitted) is as follows:

$$f_0^{eq} = \frac{1}{8}\rho(8 + 2u_1^4 - 10u_1^2 - 10u_2^2 + 8u_1^2u_2^2 + 2u_2^4 - 10c^2 + 10u_1^2c^2 + 10c^2u_2^2 + 5c^4),$$

$$f_1^{eq} = \frac{1}{12}\rho(8u_1 - 2u_1^4 + 8u_1^2 - 2u_1^3 - 6u_1^2u_2^2 - 6u_1u_2^2 - 9u_1^2c^2 - 6c^2u_1 + 4c^2 - 3c^2u_2^2 - 3c^4),$$

$$f_2^{eq} = \frac{1}{12}\rho(8u_2 - 6u_1^2u_2 + 8u_2^2 - 6u_1^2u_2^2 - 2u_2^3 - 2u_2^4 - 9c^2u_2^2 - 6c^2u_2 + 4c^2 - 3u_1^2c^2 - 3c^4),$$

$$f_3^{eq} = \frac{1}{12}\rho(-8u_1 - 2u_1^4 + 8u_1^2 + 2u_1^3 - 6u_1^2u_2^2 + 6u_1u_2^2 - 9u_1^2c^2 + 6c^2u_1 + 4c^2 - 3c^2u_2^2 - 3c^4),$$

$$f_4^{eq} = \frac{1}{12}\rho(-8u_2 + 6u_1^2u_2 + 8u_2^2 - 6u_1^2u_2^2 + 2u_2^3 - 2u_2^4 - 9c^2u_2^2 + 6c^2u_2 + 4c^2 - 3u_1^2c^2 - 3c^4),$$

$$f_5^{eq} = \frac{1}{16}\rho(4u_1^2u_2 + 4u_1u_2 + 4u_1^2u_2^2 + 4u_1u_2^2 + 2u_1^2c^2 + 2c^2u_1 + 2c^2u_2 + 2c^2u_2^2 + c^4),$$

$$f_6^{eq} = \frac{1}{16}\rho(4u_1^2u_2 - 4u_1u_2 + 4u_1^2u_2^2 - 4u_1u_2^2 + 2u_1^2c^2 - 2c^2u_1 + 2c^2u_2 + 2c^2u_2^2 + c^4),$$

$$f_7^{eq} = \frac{1}{16}\rho(4u_1u_2 - 4u_1^2u_2 + 4u_1^2u_2^2 - 4u_1u_2^2 + 2u_1^2c^2 - 2c^2u_1 - 2c^2u_2 + 2c^2u_2^2 + c^4),$$

$$f_8^{eq} = \frac{1}{16}\rho(4u_1u_2 - 4u_1^2u_2 + 4u_1^2u_2^2 + 4u_1u_2^2 + 2u_1^2c^2 + 2c^2u_1 - 2c^2u_2 + 2c^2u_2^2 + c^4),$$

$$f_9^{eq} = \frac{1}{96}\rho(-8u_1 - 4u_1^2 + 8u_1^3 + 4u_1^4 - 2c^2 + 12c^2u_1 + 12u_1^2c^2 + 3c^4),$$

$$f_{10}^{eq} = \frac{1}{96}\rho(-8u_2 - 4u_2^2 + 8u_2^3 + 4u_2^4 - 2c^2 + 12c^2u_2 + 12c^2u_2^2 + 3c^4),$$

$$f_{11}^{eq} = \frac{1}{96}\rho(8u_1 - 4u_1^2 - 8u_1^3 + 4u_1^4 - 2c^2 - 12c^2u_1 + 12u_1^2c^2 + 3c^4),$$

$$f_{12}^{eq} = \frac{1}{96}\rho(8u_2 - 4u_2^2 - 8u_2^3 + 4u_2^4 - 12c^2u_2 + 12c^2u_2^2 - 2c^2 + 3c^4), \tag{9}$$

where, u_1 is the velocity component of x direction, u_2 is the velocity component of y direction and $c^2 = R_gT$. According to Eqs. (9) and (1) developed by Chapman-Enskog can be restored to the isothermal and incompressible Navier-Stokes Equation.

In the article, we only modify the equilibrium distribution functions of LBM. And the others computing parts of LBM is not modified. So, we can use the OpenMP parallel model of classic lattice Boltzmann method in solving the flow problems. In order to verify the correctness of the proposed equilibrium distribution functions, the numerical simulation of lid-driven cavity flow based on the new equilibrium distribution functions is given in the next Section.

3   Numerical Simulation of Lid-Driven Cavity Flow

The lid-driven cavity flow is a classic problem in computational fluid and calculation of heat transfer, commonly used for incompressible flow calculation examples [10]. This examples will be solved by the new equilibrium distribution function of the lattice Boltzmann method proposed in Sect. 2. In lid-driven flow, the upper boundary of a square cavity moves horizontally to the right at a constant speed, while the other three boundaries remain stationary. In this paper, the boundary is treated by non-equilibrium extrapolation scheme.

Here in the simulations, the flow field initial density $\rho_0 = 1$, lid-driven speed U=0.1, the grid is 256×256, the Reynolds number Re is 1000,5000 respectively.

Fig. 2. The streamlines at Re=1000

Figures 2 and 3 show the streamlines of the lid-driven cavity flow at Re = 1000 and Re = 5000, respectively. The streamlines show that the results accords well with the problem itself. To quantify the above results, for Figs. 2 and 3, we tested one- level vortex and the center position of two- level vortex at the bottom left and the bottom right, respectively. Compared with the results of the literature [11–13], Table 1 shows that this simulation results are in good agreement with the results in these literatures.

Fig. 3. The streamlines at Re=5000

Table 1. the vortex position of lid-driven cavity flow (a,b,c represent the literature [11–13], respectively; d is the simulation results)

Re		One vortex		Lower left vortex		Lower right vortex	
		x	y	x	y	x	y
1000	a	0.5438	0.5625	0.0750	0.0813	0.8625	0.1063
	b	0.5313	0.5625	0.0859	0.0781	0.8594	0.1094
	c	0.5333	0.5647	0.0902	0.0784	0.8667	0.1137
	d	0.5406	0.5792	0.0733	0.0615	0.8714	0.1168
5000	a	0.5125	0.5313	0.0625	0.1563	0.8500	0.0813
	b	0.5117	0.5352	0.0703	0.1367	0.8086	0.0742
	c	0.5176	0.5373	0.0784	0.1373	0.8078	0.0745
	d	0.5181	0.5359	0.0765	0.1290	0.8213	0.0805

4   Conclusions

Based on D2Q13 discrete velocity model, a new equilibrium distribution function is proposed by using Lagrangian interpolation polynomial to distribute the conventional Maxwellian distribution function to 13 discrete points. The methods introduced in the paper can restored to the isothermal and incompressible Navier-Stokes equations, and the parallel lattice Boltzmann method with new equilibrium distribution functions is applied to the flow numerical simulation of lid-driven, the results validate the present approach.

Acknowledgments. This work was supported by National Nature Science Foundation of China (No. 91330116).

References

1. Raabe, D.: Overview of the lattice Boltzmann method for nano- and micro-scale fluid dynamics in materials science and engineering. Model. Simul. Mater. Sci. Eng. **12**(6), 13–46 (2004)
2. Tang, G., Tao, W., He, Y.: Gas slippage effect on micriscale porous flow using the lattice Boltzmann method. Phys. Rev. E **72**(5), 056301 (2005)
3. Guo, Z.L., Zhao, T.S.: Lattice Boltzmann model for incompressible flows through porous media. Phys. Rev. E **66**(32B), 036301–036304 (2002)
4. Grunau, D., Chen, S., Eggert, K.: A lattice Boltzmann model for multiphase fluid-flows. Phys. Fluids **5**(10), 2557–2562 (1993)
5. Thömesa, G., Beckera, J., Junkb, M., Vaikuntama, A.K., Kehrwalda, D., Klarc, A., Steinera, K., Wiegmann, A.: A lattice Boltzmann method for immiscible multiphase flow simulations using the level set method. J. Comput. Phys. **228**(4), 1139–1156 (2009)
6. Qu, K., Shu, C., Chew, Y.T.: Alternative method to construct equilibrium distribution functions in lattice-Boltzmann method simulation of inviscid compressible flows at high Mach number. Phys. Rev. E **75**(3), 036706 (2007)
7. Alexander, F.J., Chen, S., Sterling, J.D.: Lattice Boltzmann thermodynamics. Phys. Rev. E **47**(8), 2249–2252 (1993)
8. Kataoka, T., Tsutahara, M.: Lattice Boltzmann method for the compressible Euler equations. Phys. Rev. E **69**(5), 056702 (2004)
9. Cottet, G.-H., Koumoutsakos, P.: Vortex Methods: Theory and Practice. Cambridge University Press, Cambridge, England (2000)
10. He, Y.L., Wang, Y., Li, Q.: Lattice Boltzmann Method: Theory and Applications. Science Press, Beijing (2009)
11. Vanka, S.P.: Block-implicit multi-grid solution of Navier-Stokes equations in primitive variables. J. Comput. Phys. **65**, 138–158 (1986)
12. Ghia, U., Ghia, K.N., Shin, C.T.: High-Re solutions for incompressible flow using the Navier-Stokes equations and a multi-grid method. J. Comput. Phys. **48**(3), 387–410 (1982)
13. Hou, S., Zou, Q., Chen, S.: Simulation of cavity flow by the lattice Boltzmann method. J. Comput. Phys. **118**(2), 329–347 (1995)

A Fast Training Method for Transductive Support Vector Machine in Semi-supervised Learning

Kai Lu, Jiang Xie^(✉), and Junhui Shu

School of Computer Engineering and Science, Shanghai University, Shanghai, 200444, China
{sangocifer,jiangx,sjh1016}@shu.edu.cn

Abstract. Transductive Support Vector Machine (TSVM) is a famous model in solving classification problems in semi-supervised learning (SSL). However, traditional methods of TSVM are always time-consuming, which becomes a bottleneck when there is large scale data. In order to improve the efficiency of a training process for TSVM, we propose a fast training method for classification problems in semi-supervised learning. Different from the traditional algorithms, just few labeled instances are regarded as the initial training dataset at the beginning of our method. In each following iteration, only reliable unlabeled instances are selected and then labels are set by using all instances which are the labels set by the previous iteration. The algorithm finishes until no reliable unlabeled instances can be selected. This core idea makes our proposed method consume less running time than traditional TSVM implementation on SVMlight. In addition, for different degrees of reliable unlabeled instances, different label setting strategies will be applied to keep high accuracy in label setting. Simulations on both artificial data and real-world data have proven that our proposed fast training method can greatly reduce the running time compared to traditional TSVM implementation on SVMlight. Meanwhile, it can reach the same accuracy level in classification.

Keywords: Semi-supervised classification · Fast training · Transductive support vector machine

1 Introduction

In recent years, data is flooding in our daily lives more and more quickly. Every day innumerable data appears. In machine learning, data is segmented into labeled data and unlabeled data. However, labeled data is hard to obtain, because the label setting procedure usually needs high manpower and material resources, such as experienced human annotators, high technological devices and, of course, much time. Meanwhile, there is much unlabeled data which is easy to acquire but hard to make use of. So, in most cases, one dataset contains a small part of labeled data and a large part of unlabeled data. In machine learning, semi-supervised learning (SSL) focuses on this situation.

Semi-supervised learning is halfway between supervised and unsupervised learning. In addition to unlabeled data, the algorithm is provided with some supervision information – but not necessarily in all examples [1]. Semi-supervised classification refers

© Springer International Publishing Switzerland 2016
J. Xie et al. (Eds.): HPCA 2015, LNCS 9576, pp. 211–217, 2016.
DOI: 10.1007/978-3-319-32557-6_23

to the classification problems in semi-supervised learning and it is the direction which our paper focuses on. Obviously, the target of semi-supervised classification is using unlabeled data to assist labeled data to train a better classifier.

Obviously, unlabeled data cannot be used directly because it has no supervision information. Previous work [1] shows semi-supervised classification method can learn information from unlabeled data under some certain model assumptions, such as a smoothness assumption [2, 3], a cluster assumption [4], a low-density assumption [5, 6], and a manifold assumption [7].

It is believed that Transductive SVM [5] (TSVM) is an ideal model in semi-supervised classification. TSVM can be regarded as an extension of SVM. In SVM just labeled data is used in a training process. Based on the idea of Structural Risk Minimization (SRM), SVM uses a loss function to maximize a classification margin, while, in TSVM, not only labeled data but also unlabeled data is considered in finding the max classification margin. So, for TSVM in [8], the hinge loss function has been revised and it is defined as follows:

$$\min \frac{1}{2}|w|^2 + C \sum_{i=1}^{ln} \xi_i + C^* \sum_{j=ln+1}^{ln+un} \xi_j^* \qquad (1)$$

subject to

$$\forall_{i=1}^{ln}: y_i \left[w \cdot x_i + b \right] \geq 1 - \xi_i \qquad (2)$$

$$\forall_{j=ln+1}^{ln+un}: y_j^* \left[w \cdot x_j^* + b \right] \geq 1 - \xi_j^* \qquad (3)$$

where ln is the number of labeled instances and un is the number of unlabeled instances, and w and b are the parameters of a hyperplane. C is a penalty factor and ξ is a slack variable. This loss function leads to a drawback that the loss function is non-convex so that it is very difficult to minimize.

Many efforts have been made on optimizing TSVM. A famous implementation, SVMlight [9], is proposed by introducing a pairwise label switching between the label predictions of unlabeled data to optimize TSVM problem. Chapelle and Zien [6] proposed a method called ∇ SVM which can use a graph kernel on training SVM to train a TSVM with a gradient descent. The graph kernel can be regarded as a special RBF kernel with density information in a dataset. A concave-convex optimization procedure is used to directly optimize the hard non-convex function [10]. A weighted TSVM was proposed for semi-supervised classification on hyperspectral images [11]. Also, TSVM is attempted to apply in multi-class classification problems with hierarchical text classification problems [12].

But most of the existing methods did not consider the time-consuming problem in TSVM. With the increasing of the size of an unlabeled dataset, TSVM methods may need much more time to yield a classifier. In order to improve the computational efficiency of the training process, in this paper we proposed a fast training method for TSVM in semi-supervised classification. Considering an instance relationship based on the smoothness assumption, the training dataset of our proposed method will gradually increase, avoiding the large scale training dataset in traditional TSVM methods, which can significantly reduce the training time consumption. In addition, based on low-density assumption, our proposed method can give high accuracy prediction on unlabeled data so that a high accuracy classifier can be acquired.

The rest of this paper is organized as follows: Sect. 2 introduces the main idea and procedure of our proposed method in detail. Section 3 shows some experiments dataset information and comparisons of our proposed method with a traditional TSVM implementation on SVMlight. Conclusion and future plans of a parallel algorithm of our proposed method are given in Sect. 4.

2 Fast Training Method in Semi-supervised Classification

In traditional TSVM implementation on SVMlight, it is very hard to directly minimize the loss function, which means it is not easy to obtain the global optimal solution. So usually iteration method is used to optimize the TSVM problem. In the famous implementation [9], SVMlight, it firstly trains a prediction label set on all unlabeled data, and then introduces an idea of pairwise of labels switching to optimize the classifier of the SVM training from previous iteration.

It is high time-consuming because in each iteration step, there are SVM training processes and the training dataset is always the whole dataset with the prediction labels from the previous iteration. After this training process, there are a lot of pairwise labels switching to maximum the classification margin and also many parameters should be updated based on the whole dataset.

The purpose of our proposed method is to reduce the time consumption meanwhile to keep the classification accuracy at a high level. The key target is to reduce the size of training dataset in iteration processes. Since there is just a few labeled data that cannot give a good prediction on all unlabeled data, there comes an idea of just using them to give a prediction on reliable unlabeled data.

Our proposed method combines smoothness assumption and low density assumption. Each iteration of main procedure has two parts. The first part is confidence index calculation part to search unlabeled instances of high confidence which means they have specific label tendency. And the second part is label setting process to select reliable labels on those unlabeled instances from previous part.

2.1 Confidence Index Calculation

In this part, the main job is to search the relationships between pairwise of instances so as to find which instances have strong label tendency and helpful on adding into training dataset. This part of work is realized based on smoothness assumption, which indicates that if two instances are close to each other so that their labels are likely to be the same.

In fact, how to evaluate the relationships on pairwise of instances didn't have a specific definition. And how to evaluate the helpful degree base on relationships is also unclear. In our proposed method, considering the assumption of smoothness, firstly we establish the reliability model based on pairwise of instances distance. We call it Label

Consistency Score (LCS). Higher LCS shows two instances are more like to have the same label. And the helpful degree is called confidence index (CI). The meaning of CI will be described later.

In calculation of the instances distance, considering that influence of every dimension on the relationship is unforeseeable, a standardization process is applied on all instances which can be expressed as follow (x_i is the value on i th dimension of instance X)

$$x_i^* = \frac{x_i - m_i}{SD_i} \tag{4}$$

where m_i is mean value on i th dimension of all instances and SD_i is standard deviation on i th dimension of all instances. Then it is easy to derive that the distance Dis_{ij} between instance i and instance j is as follow

$$Dis_{ij} = \sqrt{\left(X_i - X_j\right)^2} = \sqrt{\sum_{k=1}^{n} \left(x_i^* - x_j^*\right)} = \sqrt{\sum_{k=1}^{n} \left(\frac{x_{ik} - x_{jk}}{SD_k}\right)^2} \tag{5}$$

where n is the number of dimensions. Using this distance can reduce the influence of different scale on different dimensions. It can give much more reliability on expressing relationship between instances than traditional Euclidean distance. With this distance, the LCS could be quantified as follow

$$LCS_{ij} = \frac{1}{\exp\left(Dis_{ij}\right)} \tag{6}$$

It can be checked that how likely two instances have same label using LCS. But it is still not clearly how to decide the threshold to distinguish which are helpful and which are not helpful to set label. For every support vector (SV), only the instances with highest LCS is collected. As a double detecting means, SVM is used to give another label prediction to decide which instances are more helpful. Now the CI can be defined as follow

$$CI = \begin{cases} 1 & \textit{highest LCS neighbor and SVM prediction agreed} \\ 0 & \textit{highest LCS neighbor but SVM prediction disagreed} \\ -1 & \textit{not highest LCS neighbor} \end{cases} \tag{7}$$

After we get CI value the label setting process can be applied.

2.2 Label Setting Process

The work of this part is to predict reliable labels on unlabeled instances selected from the previous part. With the CI value, unlabeled data can be divided into 3 subsets. For different subset there is different label setting strategy.

The instances with CI equaling to 1 are regarded as the most reliable on setting label based on prediction. Because these instances have highest LCS on labeled instances and the SVM training has the same label prediction as their nearest neighbors. In our proposed method these instances are set labels by SVM prediction.

The second subset of instances, with CI equaling to 0, is very helpful in approaching the truly classification boundary. These instances which have the highest LCS with their neighbor SVs have a high probability to have the same label with their neighbor SVs. But the SVM training doesn't give the same label prediction. It indicates that those instances are sure between the two classification margins by SVM. This shows that they may have heavy influence on deciding the classification boundary on this iteration. So how to decide which label or no label would be set is with great significance. In our proposed method a double check process is used on these instances. Firstly the LCS of these instances with all labeled instances will be calculated to offer a label tendency based on smoothness assumption. Secondly two different labels are set on them respectively and the better label will be find by checking the hinge loss function. If on training these instances are regarded as outliers, they will be abandoned. Through the previous double check reliable labels can be selected on these instances.

Lastly, there is still a subset of unlabeled data whose CI equals to -1. Those instances are not close enough to SVs, so no operation will be performed on them on this iteration.

After label setting process, a new training dataset is obtained and it is will be used in next iteration. When the training dataset cannot be expanded, our proposed method finishes and the classifier of last iteration is the final classifier.

3 Experiments

This part evaluates our proposed method and compare with above mentioned TSVM method implementation on SVMlight. All experiments are implemented by Matlab code, running on a dell desktop with Intel Core I5 3.10 GHz, 4 GB ram, and the OS is 32-bit Windows 7.

The main target of our proposed method is to improve the method efficiency, and also the classification accuracy shouldn't be sacrificed so it is also an evaluation criterion. In Table 1 the comparison between our proposed method and TSVM of SVMlight on running time and classification accuracy is presented. The running time is the whole method duration time. And the accuracy is the proportion of correct prediction upon the whole dataset including labeled and unlabeled instances.

Simulation experiments are running on both artificial data and real-world data. The artificial dataset (g50c) has 550 instances and each instance has 50 dimensions. It is generated from two standard normal multi-variate Gaussians. And the real-world datasets (hs, isolet, and shuttle) have different sizes and different dimensions (see Tabel 1). They are obtained from [13, 14]. They come from image area, pattern recognition area and machine control area. All datasets have balanced labeled and unlabeled instances and Table 1 provides dataset basic information like the data dimensions, and the sizes of labeled and unlabeled instances in each simulation.

Table 1. Simulations on artificial datasets and real-world datasets.

Dataset	Dim.	Unlabeled	Labeled	Running time		Accuracy	
				Proposed method	TSVM of SVMlight	Proposed method	TSVM of SVMlight
g50c1	50	540	10	**0.9332 s**	7.4849 s	**92.3636 %**	91.6364 %
g50c2	50	540	10	**0.8508 s**	7.0481 s	**88.5455 %**	85.2727 %
g50c3	50	530	20	**0.7270 s**	4.1822 s	89.9091 %	**90.1818 %**
g50c4	50	530	20	**0.7332 s**	5.2376 s	**89.4545 %**	**89.4545 %**
g50c5	50	520	30	**0.7488 s**	5.9732 s	**90.7273 %**	86.3636 %
g50c6	50	520	30	**0.8112 s**	6.3568 s	90 %	**91.0909 %**
hs1	13	260	10	**0.0624 s**	0.5928 s	77.037 %	**78.8889 %**
hs2	13	250	20	**0.0312 s**	0.1560 s	**80.3704 %**	79.6296 %
isolet1	617	580	20	**6.6144 s**	17.1133 s	99.3333 %	**99.5 %**
isolet2	617	580	20	**4.4928 s**	22.7605 s	**99.5 %**	99.3333 %
shuttle	9	18903	400	**10.3897 s**	63.3676 s	99.1377 %	**99.2752 %**

From the records of Table 1 it is clear that our proposed method can improve the efficiency and can also get a good classifier on these datasets.

4   Conclusions and Future Work

In this paper, we proposed a fast training method for TSVM in semi-supervised learning. Our proposed method decreases the size of training dataset in iterations to make several times faster than traditional TSVM implementation in SVMlight. Meanwhile also good classifiers can be obtained to present high accuracy classification predictions.

Attempts have made using matlab parallel system to perform our proposed method on parallel computing. However speedup ratio is not very good because some functions cannot be realized. More effort will be made by using C ++ and MPI programming in future work.

References

1. Chapelle, O., Schölkopf, B., Zien, A.: Semi-supervised Learning. MIT Press, Cambridge (2006)
2. Zhou, X., Li, C.: Semi-supervised classification based on smooth graphs. In: Li Lee, M., Tan, K.-L., Wuwongse, V. (eds.) DASFAA 2006. LNCS, vol. 3882, pp. 757–766. Springer, Heidelberg (2006)
3. Fang, Y., Chang, K.C., Lauw, H.W.: Graph-based semi-supervised learning: realizing pointwise smoothness probabilistically. In: International Conference on Machine Learning (ICML), pp. 406–414 (2014)
4. Chapelle, O., Weston, J., Schölkopf, B.: Cluster kernels for semi-supervised learning. In: Advances in Neural Information Processing Systems, vol. 15, pp. 585–592 (2002)
5. Bennett, K.P., Demiriz, A.: Semi-supervised support vector machines. In: Advances in Neural Information Processing Systems, vol. 9, pp. 368–374 (2001)

6. Chapelle, O., Zien, A.: Semi-supervised classification by low density separation. In: Proceedings of the Tenth International Workshop on Artificial Intelligence and Statistics, vol. 1, pp. 57–64 (2005)

7. Goldberg, A.B., Zhu, X., Singh, A.: Multi-manifold semi-supervised learning. In: International Conference on Artificial Intelligence and Statistics, pp. 169–176 (2009)

8. Zhu, X.: Semi-supervised learning literature survey. Computer Science Technical Report 1530, Department of Computer Sciences, University of Wisconsin at Madison, Madison (2008)

9. Joachims, T.: Transductive inference for text classification using support vector machines. In: International Conference on Machine Learning (ICML), pp. 200–209 (1999)

10. Collobert, R., Sinz, F., et al.: Trading convexity for scalability. In: Proceedings of the 23rd International Conference on Machine Learning, pp. 201–208 (2006)

11. Gao, H.Z., et al.: Semi-supervised classification of hyperspectral image based on spectrally weighted TSVM. Sig. Process. **27**, 122–127 (2011)

12. Selvaraj, S.K., Sellamanickam, S., Shevade, S.: Extension of TSVM to multi-class and hierarchical text classification problems with general losses. In: 24th International Conference on Computational Linguistics, pp. 1091–1100 (2012)

13. http://www.csie.ntu.edu.tw/~cjlin/libsvm/

14. http://archive.ics.uci.edu/ml/index.html

Parameter Identification Inverse Problems of Partial Differential Equations Based on the Improved Gene Expression Programming

Yan Chen[1,2], Kangshun Li[1], and Zhangxin Chen[2](✉)

[1] College of Mathematics and Informatics, South China Agricultural University,
Guangzhou 510642, China
[2] Department of Chemical and Petroleum Engineering, University of Calgary,
Calgary, AB T2N 1N4, Canada
zhachen@ucalgary.ca

Abstract. Traditionally, solving the parameter identification inverse problems of partial differential equations encountered many difficulties and insufficiency. In this paper, we propose an improved GEP (Gene Expression Programming) to identify the parameters in the reverse problems of partial differential equations based on the self-adaption, self-organization and self-learning characters of GEP. This algorithm simulates a parametric function itself of a partial differential equation directly through the observed values by fully taking into account inverse results caused by noises of a measured value. Modeling is unnecessary to add regularization in the modeling process aiming at special problems again. The experiment results show that the algorithm has good noise-immunity. In case there is no noise or noise is very low, the identified parametric function is almost the same as the original accurate value; when noise is very high, good results can still be obtained, which successfully realizes automation of the parameter modeling process for partial differential equations.

Keywords: Improved gene expression · Partial differential equation · Inverse problems · Thomas algorithm

1 Introduction

As the society develops and science and technologies make rapid progress, many problems during their applications can be solved by traditional scientific methods. Scientists need to seek for new solutions instead. For example, changing rules of materials located in untouched place are to be explored; product is designed according to a specific function; a procedure is controlled in accordance with a certain purpose [1–5]; a new kind of material is to be obtained during industrial production. A new sub-discipline derives thereof - an

This work was supported by the Technology Planning Project of Guangdong Province of China with the Grant No. 2015A020209108

J. Xie et al. (Eds.): HPCA 2015, LNCS 9576, pp. 218–227, 2016.
DOI: 10.1007/978-3-319-32557-6_24

Inverse Problem [6–8] study. The inverse problem study which was put forward from actual demands from every sections and subjects is an interdisciplinary and hot study topic.

In the aspect of theory and value calculation of solutions to inverse problems for partial differential equations, scientists have done a large quantity of work. Tsien and Chen proposed PST for studying an inverse problem of one-dimension hydrodynamic speed. The best perturbation method is a kind of numerical iterative method which was put forward based on a perturbation method of operator identification, a linearization technique and an approximation theory of functions. The enhanced Lagrange method mainly identifies unknown parameters during specific equations by improving the Lagrangian algorithm.

Although the solutions to the inverse problems of partial differential equations can be worked out by some traditional methods, they have certain limits.

- It is hard to determine regularization parameters with very harsh requirements on the problems themselves (e.g., sequence and differential);
- Original data may not belong to a data set corresponding to an accurate solution to the problems being discussed (e.g., a range of integral and differential operators), and thus an approximate solution of classical significance may not exist;
- Instability of an approximate solution, i.e., a minor observation error of original data (this is unavoidable in reality) will result in serious deviation between approximation and genuine solutions;
- The ways adaptable to some problems may not be applied in other problems so specific inverse problems must often seek for specific solutions.

Thus, it is a very urgent study subject to breakthrough a traditional way and seek for a new way to solve inverse problems. GEP is a kind of evolutionary algorithm based on genome and phenomena and referred to the gene expression rule in genetics [9]. It intends to combine the advantages of both GP and GA. Unlike GP where an individual is expressed in the form of a tree, an individual in GEP is represented by the isometric linear symbols. GEP has been successfully applied in problem solving, combinatorial optimization, real parameter optimization, evolving and modeling the functional parameters, classification, and event selection in high energy physics [10–13]. But the tradition GEP algorithm needs to be improved because it has some deficiencies.

In this paper, we propose an improved GEP to identify the parameters in reverse problems for partial differential equations. This algorithm simulates a parametric function itself of a partial differential equation directly through the observed values. Modeling is unnecessary to add regularization in a modeling process aiming at special problems again. The test results show that the algorithm has good noise-immunity. In case there is no noise or noise is very low, the identified parametric function is almost the same as the original accurate value; when noise is very high, good results can still be obtained, which successfully realizes automation of a parameter modeling process for partial differential equations.

2 Improved GEP

The genetic code of GEP is the isometric linear symbols (GEP chromosome). Each chromosome can be composed of several genes. GEP gene consists of a head and a tail, where the former may contain both the functional symbols and termination symbols, while the latter only has the terminal symbols. For example, $*+-aQ*+aababbbaab$ is a legal gene, in which * stands for the multiplication operation, Q is the square root operation. The segment without underline belongs to the head, while the underlined segment is the tail. For each problem, the length of the tail t is a function of the length of the head h and the number of arguments of the function with the most arguments n, determined using the following Formula 1

$$t = h(n - 1) + 1 \qquad (1)$$

Obviously, when the mutation, transposition and restructuring operators are just applied into the dominant segment of the gene which can affect the fitness directly, they increase the diversity of the population remarkably. If they are applied into the recessive segment which can not affect the fitness directly, they can only increase the probability for population diversity before performing the mutation operator. For the four standard genetic operators: mutation, IS transposition, single-point restructuring and double-point restructuring, all characters have the equal probability to become the position of the operator. Therefore, the right selection of the position of these characters has a great impact on the validity of the genetic operators.

To verify the above statement, we demonstrate the average valid length of GEP genes used in recent references in Table 1.

Table 1. The average use ratio of gene

Paper	HLG	NNP	NOP	NTP	ELG	ALG	URG
Wenyin Gong 2006	8	2	4	4	7.761	17	45.66 %
	8	5	0	4	3.827	17	22.51 %
	8	4	4	4	5.24	17	30.82 %
Pang Li 2012	10	1	0	4	13.657	21	65.03 %
Xianfeng He 2012	10	5	3	4	4.475	21	22.60 %
Zibing Hu 2012	8	5	4	4	4.478	17	26.34 %
Zhongming Niu 2012	8	6	2	8	6.007	17	35.34 %
Zhengyi Wang 2012	8	6	4	4	3.911	17	23.00 %
Mengwei Liu 2010	8	8	14	4	4.195	17	24.68 %
Xiaoshan Qian 2009	10	14	2	4	1.967	21	9.37 %
	10	15	2	4	1.886	21	8.98 %
	10	16	2	4	1.817	21	8.65 %
Yanchun Wang 2009	19	1	0	4	24.466	39	62.73 %
	19	5	3	4	6.087	39	15.61 %

Where HLG means Head length of gene, NNP means Number of no parameters function, NOP means Number of one parameters function, NTP means Number of two parameters function, ELG means Effective length of gene, ALG means Actual length of gene, URG means Use ratio of gene.

From the utmost right column of Table 1, we can see that the average utilization rate of gene is very low, especially for a function without parameter. The greater proportion of the function without parameter is, the lower the average utilization rate of gene is. In this case, genetic operators with varying positions may take place at the recessive segment of the gene with great probability even though the occurrence probability is satisfied. It will greatly reduce the validity of genetic operators. Therefore, we propose that most of genetic operators can be focused on the dominant segment. It may help maintain population diversity and also increase the convergence rate of GEP. The setting of the occurrence probabilities of the dominant and recessive parts of the gene is determined by the problem. In the paper, the probability is assigned to 0.8, which means 80 % of genetic operation occurs at the dominant part of the gene and the remaining 20 % is kept at the recessive segment.

3 Inverse Problem Algorithm of Parameter Identification for Partial Differential Equation Based on Improved GEP

The inverse problems of partial differential equation are composed of partial differential equation, initial and boundary conditions and an additional condition.

The inverse problems can be classified as follows according to their different math structures: inverse problem of operator identification, inverse problem of source item, inverse problem of inverse time process or initial condition, inverse problem of boundary control, inverse problem of boundary or set.

The article studies the inverse problem of parameter identification for partial differential equation.

3.1 Description of the Problems

The following second order parabolic differential equation is considered:

$$\begin{cases} \dfrac{\partial u}{\partial t} - \nabla(q(x)\nabla u)f(x,t), (x,t) \in \Omega \times (0,T) \\ u(x,0) = u_0(x), x \in \Omega \\ u(x,t) = 0, (x,t) \in \partial\Omega \times (0,T) \\ \text{where } \Omega \text{ is any region with boundary among R} \end{cases} \tag{2}$$

Direct problem of partial differential is a solution to partial differential equation which usually refers to the known $q(x)$ and right-hand item $f(x,t)$, while solution $u(x,t)$, or definite solution problem. The inverse problem of partial differential equation to be studied refers to determine parameter $q(x)$ under the premise that right-hand item $f(x,t)$ and solution $u(x,t)$ are known(are usually observed values of $u(x,t)$), making $q(x)$ satisfying partial differential Eq. 2, which is called as inverse problem of parameter identification for partial differential equation. During actual solution process, we usually look for a $q^*(x)$ to enable solution $u^*(x, t)$ to Eq. 2 composed of $q^*(x)$ is close to $u^*(x, t)$ as possible.

In order to simplify operation, the parameter function mentioned in the Article is continuous function. Furthermore, suppose:

$$\begin{cases} \dfrac{\partial u}{\partial t} - \nabla(q(x)\nabla u)f(x,t), (x,t) \in \Omega \times (0,T) \\ u(x,0) = u_0(x), x \in \Omega \\ u(x,t) = 0, (x,t) \in \partial\Omega \times (0,T) \\ \text{where } \Omega \text{ } is \text{ any region with boundary among R} \end{cases} \qquad (3)$$

Where, function set allowable by $q(x)$ is defined as below:

$$Q = \{q(x) \mid q(x) \in C^0(0,1), 0 < \alpha_l \le q(x) \le \alpha_u\} \qquad (4)$$

In actual application, we just know observed or measured values of $u(x, t)$ at some discrete points rather than all values of $u(x, t)$ within the whole Ω. Therefore, during solving inverse problems process, we usually have infinite solution region limited or discretized. In view of parabolic equation mentioned in the article, we will have solution region between 0 and 1 discretized, and divided into n intervals with equal spacing, in which step is $h = 1/n$ and its node is $x_i = ih(i = 0,1,2,3,...,n)$. Both u_0 and u_n may be obtained based on previous information, and the observed value of $u(x, t)$ can be noted as:

$$\vec{u} = (u_1, u_2, \ldots, u_{n-1}) \qquad (5)$$

Thus, based on the previous hypothesis, our problems can be described how to identify $q(x)$ with the known $f(x, t)$ and $u(x, t)$.

3.2   Algorithm Flow

Step1: $t = 0$ is set, initial group $P(t)$ appears randomly in searching region, the fitness values of all individuals are calculated;

Step2: If shutdown condition is met, or t is larger than the maximum times of evolution given primarily, then jump to Step6;

Setp3: The improved GEP is used to generate a new batch of individuals $newP(t)$;

Step4: According to fitness function, the best individual is chosen from $P(t)$ and $newP(t)$ to consist of a new generation of population $P(t + 1)$;

Step5: $t = t + 1$ jumps to Step2;

Setp6: The best individual q^* now is output.

4 Experiment and Analysis

4.1 Data Set

In order to verify the effectiveness of inverse problem algorithm for parameter identification in partial differential equation based on improved GEP, we conduct modeling
process of the following three groups of partial differential equation which are listed as
below:

$$\begin{cases} \dfrac{\partial u}{\partial t} - \nabla(q(x)\nabla u)f(x,t), (x,t) \in \Omega \times (0,T) \\ u(x,0) = u_0(x), x \in \Omega \\ u(x,t) = 0, (x,t) \in \partial\Omega \times (0,T) \\ \text{where } \Omega \text{ is any region with boundary among R} \end{cases} \tag{6}$$

Where both $q(x)$ and $u(x, t)$ are defined as below, $f(x, t)$ is worked out by $u(x, t)$ and
$q(x)$ through differential equation:

Experiment I: $u(x,t) = e^{\sin(\pi t)}\sin(2\pi x), q(x) = x^2 + x$
Experiment II: $u(x,t) = e^t \sin(\pi x), q(x) = \sin(x) + 1$
Experiment III: $u(x,t) = e^{\sin(\pi t)}\sin(\pi x), q(x) = \sin(x)$

4.2 Parameter Setting

During actual application, limited by measurement ways and objective conditions, the
observed data have some errors. In order to check positive definiteness of construction
algorithm, the effect to the algorithm caused by noise must be considered. Thus, the
experimental data $u(x, t)$ is generated by adding certain noise to $u(x, t)$. In order to verify
effectiveness and robustness of the algorithm, we increase high intensity noise with
intensity up to 20 %, which is never seen in the similar studies. According to the above,
discretization form of the experimental data is represented as follows: $u'_i = (1 + \delta * rand(x_i)) * u(x_i, t), i = 1, 2, \ldots, n - 1$, where $rand(x)$ is consistent distribution random function among $[-1,1]$, δ is noise intensity parameter. The larger the δ is, the higher
the noise in the measured data is, and the larger the error of measured data is.

Other parameters in the experiment are set as below:

Table 2. Parameter setting of GEP

Parameters	Value	Parameters	Value
Set of termination symbols	{0}	Selection algorithm	Roulette
Set of functional symbols	$\{+, \times, /, s, c, q, e, l\}$	Probability of mutation	0.044

(Continued)

Table 2. (*Continued*)

Parameters	Value	Parameters	Value
Size of Populations	50	Probability of IS transposition	0.1
Number of experiments	100	Length of IS transposition	5
Number of iterations	10000	Probability of RIS	0.1
Fitness	1	Length of RIS transposition	5
Number of gene	1	Probability of double-point restructuring	0.3
Head length of gene	8	Probability of single-point restructuring	0.3

In the Table 2, *0* in the terminal symbol set denotes *h, s, c, q, e* and *l* in function symbol set denote *sin, cos, sqrt, exp* and *ln* in separate.

4.3   Experimental Results

In order to verify the effectiveness of the proposed algorithm, inverse problem algorithm of parameter identification of partial differential equation based on improved GEP is used to carry out $q(x)$ modeling to Formula 13 without noise. The individuals of $q(x)$ worked out after 10000 generations is: *+0c0***000000000 of experiment I, and its corresponding formula is $(cos(x^4) + x)x$; +cs*s**0000000000 of experiment II, and its corresponding formula is $cos(x^4) + sin(x)$); *0c*/**0000000000 of experiment III, and its corresponding formula is $xcos(x^3)$ (Fig. 1).

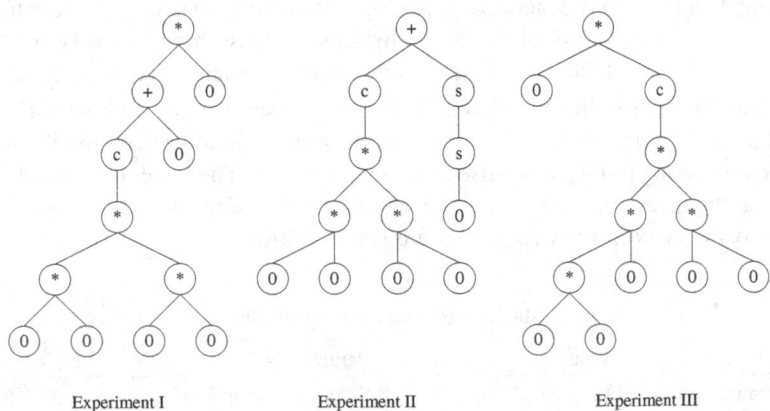

Experiment I   Experiment II   Experiment III

Fig. 1. Expression tree

In order to compare the effect to the algorithm caused by number of interval n for interval Ω of u_i and noise intensity, we conduct cross test to the algorithm at $n = 10$, 20, 40 and $\delta = 0$, 1 %, 5 %, 10 %, 20 %, and use standard deviation

$$\sqrt{\sum_{i=1}^{n}(q_i^*(x) - q_i(x))^2}$$ of $q^*(x)$ value after modeling and original $q(x)$ value as error

value to analyze the algorithm, the result is shown as below table:

Table 3. Comparison of $q(x)$ of experiment I

n	δ				
	0 %	1 %	5 %	10 %	20 %
10	0.00320758	0.003360028	0.00320758	0.003330037	0.003444834
20	0.001339974	0.001262695	0.00136832	0.00136832	0.002043285
40	0.000300552	0.000373398	0.000300552	0.000373398	0.000399655

Table 4. Comparison of $q(x)$ of experiment II

n	δ				
	0 %	1 %	5 %	10 %	20 %
10	0.002311815	0.002311815	0.002311815	0.002878937	0.002852782
20	0.003550171	0.003359276	0.003359276	0.003550171	0.004419626
40	0.001022876	0.00100906	0.001025013	0.001660657	0.001022876

Table 5. Comparison of $q(x)$ of experiment III

n	δ				
	0 %	1 %	5 %	10 %	20 %
10	0.00729483	0.007539142	0.00729483	0.00729483	0.007539142
20	0.001497322	0.001608236	0.001608236	0.001802701	0.001608236
40	0.000274258	0.000274258	0.000274258	0.000453881	0.000274258

As shown in Tables 3, 4 and 5, when the noise intensity δ is increasing gradually, the error value of $q(x)$ is becoming larger and larger, which shows that the wrong observed data will cause certain influence to the rightness of the model and the regularization process is usually necessary. However, for the algorithm, even if the noise intensity increases to 20 %, the error of $q(x)$ still remain within a small scope, and the algorithm does not join in regularization item, this shows its robustness is very good. It can prohibit the influence to the modeling that the observed value error has through the algorithm itself.

5 Conclusion

In the article, the improved GEP is applied in the inverse problem of parameter identification of partial differential equation. The structure of its algorithm is realized and three groups of experiments are designed to verify the effectiveness of the algorithm. Different noise intensities and intervals are chosen to conduct comparison experiments through three groups of experiments as shown in Tables 3, 4 and 5. When the noise intensities is becoming stronger, the error values are becoming larger and larger, which shows wrong observed data will cause certain influence to the rightness of the modeling. However, for the algorithm, even if the noise intensity increases to 20 %, the error of $q(x)$ still remain within a small scope. The reason is that the function itself is directly modeled by observed value for the inverse problem of parameter identification of partial differential equation, the function formula may be stable within a certain form, which is not like the other algorithms. Traditionally, the discrete prediction value is obtained after the observed value, then the modeling process will be affected very easily by noise and regularization process must be added in view of special problem. Therefore, it can be seen that the algorithm does not need standard type designated in advance according to special problems and special regularization process. It can be applied widely by aiming at inverse problem of parameter identification of common partial differential equation. Furthermore, according to these three groups of experiments, the algorithm has strong stability. In view of common problems, optimal solution may be tendency after finite iteration. In addition, the algorithm has strong robustness. Even if the noise intensities increase to 20 %, the algorithm is still able to finish the right identification process of parameter equation without being affected by the noise.

References

1. Audouze, C., De Vuyst, F., Nair, P.B.: Nonintrusive reduced-order modeling of parametrized time-dependent partial differential equations. Numer. Methods Partial Differ. Equ. **29**(5), 1587–1628 (2013)
2. Wang, Q., Wen, J.: Analytical and numerical stability of partial differential equations with piecewise constant arguments. Numer. Methods Partial Differ. Equ. **30**(1), 1–16 (2014)
3. Bao, W., Song, Y.: Multiquadric quasi-interpolation methods for solving partial differential algebraic equations. Numer. Methods Partial Differ. Equ. **30**(1), 95–119 (2014)
4. Hsiao, C.-H.: Numerical inversion of laplace transform via wavelet in partial differential equations. Numer. Methods Partial Differ. Equ. **30**(2), 536–549 (2014)
5. Herrera, I., de la Cruz, L.M., Rosas-Medina, A.: Nonoverlapping discretization methods for partial differential equations. Numer. Methods Partial Differ. Equ. **30**(5), 1427–1454 (2014)
6. Romanov, V.G.: Inverse Problems of Mathematical Physics. Brill, Leiden (1987)
7. Groetsch, C.W., Groetsch, C.W.: Inverse Problems in the Mathematical Sciences. Springer, Wiesbaden (1993)
8. Isakov, V.: Inverse Problems for Partial Differential Equations. Springer, New York (2006)
9. Ferreira, C.: Gene expression programming: a new adaptive algorithm for solving problems. Complex Syst. **13**(2), 87–129 (2001)

10. Li, K., Li, Y., Chen, Z., Wu, Z.: A new dynamic evolutionary algorithm based on particle transportation theory. In: Proceedings of the International Conference on High Performance Computing and Applications (HPCA 2004). Lecture Notes in Computational Science and Engineering, pp. 81–92. Springer, Heidelberg (2005). ISBN:103540257853 (ISTP)
11. Li, K., Chen, Z., Li, Y., Zhou, A.: An application of genetic programming to economic forecasting. In: Proceedings of the International Conference on High Performance Computing and Applications (HPCA 2004). Lecture Notes in Computational Science and Engineering, pp. 71–80. Springer, Heidelberg, (2005). ISBN:103540257853 (ISTP)
12. Wazwaz, A.: A new method for solving singular initial value problems in the second-order ordinary differential equations. Appl. Math. Comput. **128**(1), 45–57 (2012)
13. Nieto, J.J.: Periodic boundary value problems for first-order impulsive ordinary differential equations. Nonlinear Anal. Theor. Methods Appl. **51**(7), 1223–1232 (2012)

Author Index

Printed in the United States
By Bookmasters